The 1916 Battle
of the Somme
Reconsidered

The 1916 Battle
of the Somme
Reconsidered

Peter Liddle

Pen & Sword
MILITARY

First published in Great Britain in 2016 by
Pen & Sword Military
an imprint of
Pen & Sword Books Ltd
47 Church Street
Barnsley
South Yorkshire
S70 2AS

ISBN 978 1 78340 051 5

Typeset in Ehrhardt by
Mac Style Ltd, Bridlington, East Yorkshire
Printed and bound in the UK by CPI Group (UK) Ltd,
Croydon, CR0 4YY

Pen & Sword Books Ltd incorporates the imprints of Pen & Sword
Archaeology, Atlas, Aviation, Battleground, Discovery, Family
History, History, Maritime, Military, Naval, Politics, Railways, Select,
Transport, True Crime, and Fiction, Frontline Books, Leo Cooper,
Praetorian Press, Seaforth Publishing and Wharncliffe.

For a complete list of Pen & Sword titles please contact
PEN & SWORD BOOKS LIMITED
47 Church Street, Barnsley, South Yorkshire, S70 2AS, England
E-mail: enquiries@pen-and-sword.co.uk
Website: www.pen-and-sword.co.uk

Contents

List of Plates

Source of plates, Liddle Collection unless otherwise stated.

The chapter-head drawings are from the letters of Adrian Hill written during the Battle of the Somme. The letters are held in the Liddle Collection, Brotherton Library, the University of Leeds.

1. A platoon of Liverpool Pals in barracks in 1914.
2. The 1st City Battalion, The King's (Liverpool) Regiment.
3. Killed in action at Gommecourt, 1 July, aged twenty-three.
4. Wakefield and district learn the scale of local losses.
5. The recently widowed Thomas Jackson, 8th East Lancs, was killed on 15 July, leaving his four-year-old son, an orphan.
6. Ready if not ferocious: a 'Leicester Tiger'.
7. Scorn for men who did not volunteer or who tried to evade the Military Service Acts.
8. A square in Albert before and during the Battle of the Somme.
9. The Virgin and Child of Notre Dame de Brebières, Albert.
10. General Sir Douglas Haig, Commander-in-Chief BEF and other senior British officers. (National Army Museum 73957)
11. General Sir Henry Rawlinson. (IWM 4031)
12. Necessary training but circumstantially different from reality.
13. A packet of cigarettes for every man, provided by the officers of the 17th Battalion, The King's (Liverpool) Regiment.
14. First graves: men killed in the last days of June.
15. It was necessary to ensure that messages transmitted by earthed Morse buzzer were not offering 'information of value to the enemy'.
16. British prisoners being escorted to the rear through Fremicourt in July. (*An Der Somme*, Munich 1917)
17. Official panoramic photo showing John Copse and Serre.
18. A German photograph of Gommecourt Wood in July. (*An Der Somme*, Munich 1917)
19. A German photograph of the ruins of Gommecourt, July. (*An Der Somme*, Munich 1917)
20. La Boisselle: the entrances to a captured German dug-out, July.
21. The Deccan Horse await their move into action, 14 July.
22. An RFC Observer's log-book.
23. Lanoe Hawker RFC, at the time of his VC investiture, 1915.

Maps

Acknowledgements

My first acknowledgement must be to all the men and their families who over the years have entrusted their 1916 soldiering or air service memorabilia to my care. This is the material – original letters, diaries, photographs, sketches, maps, official documents and recollections – which has been both the book's main source and its inspiration. I had long wanted to write it, and felt a responsibility so to do as I read and reflected upon so much original personal experience documentation, and reconsidered some of the generalisations made and uncritically accepted upon aspects of the First World War. My thanks to so many are offered with the anxious hope that the book would have rung true to the men who experienced the Somme and who, decades later, contributed to the archives I was building up. I am particularly touched that Reg Glenn, at John Copse, Serre, on 1 July 1916, should have honoured this book when first published by contributing a foreword.

The conditions for writing this book in its original form nearly twenty-five years ago were facilitated by my 1914–18 archive work becoming the Liddle Collection within the Library of the University of Leeds in 1988. To all those who worked to achieve this end I am indebted to an unfathomable degree. Some names are engraved indelibly on my conscience – David Dilks, Alan Roberts and Reg Carr from the University, then Kenneth Rose, Paul Stobart and Brian Perry, among many more, known and unknown.

I remain sincerely appreciative of all those who helped in the production of the 1992 book *The 1916 Battle of the Somme: a Re-Appraisal* but specifically with regard to this new edition I must first acknowledge my debt to the recently-published research judgements of the historians Gary Sheffield, whose focus has been on the High Command, and William Philpott, whose attention has been directed towards the Battle of the Somme as a three-nation struggle, while my concentration had been on junior officers and men in the ranks.

From my publishers, Pen and Sword, through commissioning editor, Rupert Harding, I had the challenge of tackling this re-consideration, and I have welcomed the opportunity, confident that copy-editing, the illustrations and a new presentation of the book were in good hands. Once again, the hard-pressed staff and volunteers of regimental museums have been generous in their support and I thank in particular Ian Martin at the Museum of the King's Own Scottish Borderers in Berwick and Sarah Stevenson and Philip Mather at the Fusiliers Museum in Bury, Lancashire.

At the Brotherton Library in the University of Leeds it was very special to be able to re-examine the letters of Philip Hirsh VC which I was privileged to accept from the donors but which came in after the publication of this book in 1992. This led me to look again through the material deposited by Philip's brother, Frank, and whether or not it were to have been available for my use long ago, my goodness it fully deserved inclusion here.

The generosity of David Millichope in making available to me before the publication of his book on Halifax in the Great War, his text and research material on the Duke of Wellington's West Riding Regiment, may be characteristic of a man leading such inspired research as is being undertaken by the Halifax Great War Society but it was still a wonderful gesture for which I remain particularly grateful.

Dealing with countless computer problems and issues of presentation, my beloved wife, Louise, has come to my rescue on occasion after occasion. In this respect my happily recognised debt goes far beyond academic matters.

In conclusion, this book is re-dedicated to those who were there, on the Somme, in 1916, and it is so dedicated, with profound respect.

Peter Liddle
Mickley, North Yorkshire, 2016

Foreword

How much I have enjoyed reading this comprehensive, illuminating history of the battles on the Somme in 1916. My perspective was that of the ordinary soldier, one of the Sheffield 'Pals' in the 12th Battalion York and Lancaster Regiment. I knew little or nothing, of course, of the whole and greater organising of the battles but looking back today on my experience in 1916, I find the detail and spirit of this book truly convincing.

What memories it has stirred! The blowing of the mine, the sudden silence when the guns stopped and then the song of the skylark overhead.

I believe this book should be widely read, especially by new generations to whom the events must seem like distant history, for in reading this account it would be difficult for anyone to forget the men who made that distant history.

Reg Glenn of Oughtibridge, Sheffield, 1991, in 1916, Corporal Glenn, 12th (Service) Battalion (Sheffield), The York and Lancaster Regiment

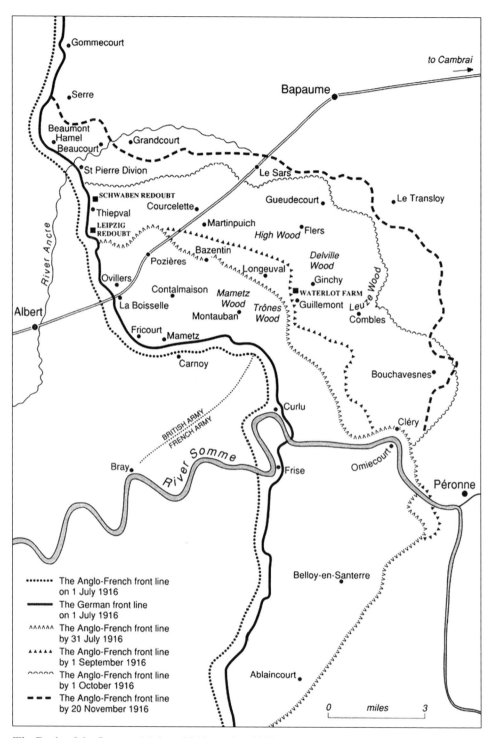

The Battle of the Somme, 1 July to 20 November 1916.

Introduction: The Somme, Our Heritage

Saturday afternoon.
Oct. 21st. 16.

With a hundred years having passed since the 1916 Battle of the Somme, its mention still gives rise to deeply-felt emotion which swirls within all who have a sense of our recent history, that is the history which continues to resonate through experience within our own families, our villages, towns, cities and regions and because we recognise that the Great War had such a shaping effect on our world today.

History is no exact fixed science. Nor of course is memory – memory as personally experienced or as received down the generations. Judgements, whether expressed by those remunerated for their study of the past, or held passionately from a range of influences by those outside the profession, or simply the opinions shaped by the 'education' of received wisdom, will be subject to change. Furthermore, even in times of what appears conclusive approbation or condemnation, there will always be another point of view. There may be a swift readiness to dismiss such a point of view as not acceptable in 'these enlightened times', but it would, in all likelihood, have been more shrewd to be aware that with the passage of time, those discordant voices may herald the new wisdom. Whether one were to choose Henry VIII and the Dissolution of the Monasteries, the Civil War and the execution of King Charles I, the Peterloo Massacre, the iniquity or achievements of the

British Empire, or indeed the 1916 Battle of the Somme, this has been the case and will continue to be the case. Today's verdict may be 'old hat' if not tomorrow, then before too long. From the point of weighing matters up for oneself, the actual period of change in the balance of a debate, has much to commend it.

In the shaping of opinion and the damaging of a reputation, seldom can three books have been more influential than the publication, first in 1923 of Winston Churchill's third volume of his history of the Great War, *The World Crisis*, dealing with his interpretation of how the 1916 Battle of the Somme was conducted, then of David Lloyd George's self-serving memoirs in 1935, and finally Basil Liddell Hart's condemnation of military leadership in the Great War, *The Real War*, published in 1930. Even today, in the centenary year of the Somme, these volumes, First World War history 'Bibles' of the past, unread as they are likely to be by new generations, condition the way many reflect upon the First World War – 'costly futility' – and upon the Commander-in-Chief of the British Expeditionary Force from the end of 1915, Sir Douglas Haig – an unimaginative, unfeeling man, exercising command from a position of remote comfort.

What irony there lies in such judgements having no prevision in Churchill's case, nor remembered conscience for Lloyd George and Liddell Hart, of the colossal numbers of veterans who made the pilgrimage of respect to attend Haig's funeral only a few years after the publication of Churchill's volume. Were the ex-servicemen there simply because patently he had served them after the war in his tireless work for the Royal British Legion or were they there also because they had served under his command in France and remained proud of this?

Though a second world war was to intervene and temporarily to still the flood of criticism which precluded balanced consideration of the Somme and of Haig, the new war was perceived as more justifiable and having been waged far more economically in terms of its military manpower and wisely in its strategic deployment of resources – casualties in Bomber Command and those in Normandy in 1944, and successive deployment of troops and naval resources to Greece and to islands of the Aegean make this comfortable assumption somewhat less than conclusive! – but after the war, and in particular in the 1960s and 1970s, in books, lectures, film, theatre, in BBC

Radio and Television programmes and in school classrooms, the Somme and 'Passchendaele' were represented as the needless slaughter of Britain's best by the tactics of elderly, unimaginative, unintelligent, unfeeling, Generals – all 'schooled' as cavalrymen of course – living safely in comfort and privilege in well-appointed chateaux far from the squalid danger of the line.

There was an exception, BBC TV's 1964 multi-episode Great War series, devised, written and presented by John Terraine. Terraine's 1963 biography of Haig, *Douglas Haig, the Educated Soldier*, and then the TV series, were to make some inroads into the public perception outlined above, but perhaps more significantly in the thinking of some military historians restless against the 'needless slaughter' verdict and that of bovine leadership.

It may appear curious to attribute some credit for these re-evaluations to German historians but it seems to this author that in convincing so many of Germany's culpability for the war, Fritz Fischer and Imanuel Geiss had also demonstrated that the war could not, from a British point of view, be considered unnecessary; her losses, therefore, not a wanton waste.

With regard to the way the Somme and later battles had been fought, what Terraine had sought to make clear was the framework within which Haig had to operate, a framework from which escape was impossible. To many, the argument failed to convince. The passage of time and changed values provided the starting and the finishing point within which they operated: the war had been but dubiously justified; its length, terrible toll, colossal national effort for insignificant gain of ground during the war and its empty victory at the end – what had it all been for, except to demonstrate ruinous incompetence?

Terraine had stressed the constraints of coalition warfare, with Britain militarily for so long the junior partner, the inexorable commitment to attack when the state of weapons development gave all advantage to the defence, there being quite simply no flank to turn by deception – the trench system complete from North Sea to Switzerland – and there being no means of maintaining control of a battle once joined. Above all he emphasised that Britain and France were facing the colossal strength of their main enemy exactly where that enemy chose to place his main military resources.

Terraine's defence of the High Command on the Western Front and hence how we might reasonably consider the Somme in British history, has been taken up, further considered, developed, substantiated, amended and also, of course, predictably derided. Haig's achievements have been registered and errors acknowledged by a succession of non-doctrinaire historians of whom the most recent are William Philpott and Gary Sheffield. They stand in what this author judges an honourable group of contemporary historians which must include the names of Brian Bond, Peter Simkins, Nigel Cave, John Bourne and Stephen Badsey.

There are those who take a different standpoint, perhaps most notable the Australians, Trevor Wilson and Robin Prior, and the Canadian, Tim Travers. Who is stuck in his trench and defending it, and who, dangerously by definition, has his head above the parapet to get perspective? This book, while focusing on what it was like to serve on the Somme, certainly leans towards the 'Philpott/Sheffield School' but will seek to pay due reference to the arguments of those who judge differently.

For those living through the years of the war there had been nothing hitherto which had come near to making so ineffaceable an impact as the Somme. The East Coast raids, the Zeppelin bombing, losses without discernible gain in France, seemingly scandalous and costly defeat at the Dardanelles and in Mesopotamia, the disappointment of Jutland, the beginnings of commodity shortages, the spreading rash of auxiliary hospitals, the overwhelming concentration upon war industries, and then, less depressingly, the raising of the New Armies and widening opportunities for women, all these events or developments had certainly made some impression and had educated the nation away from any vestige of suspended exhilaration at the anticipation of glorious victories to be won in defending the Nation's honour. It was going to be a long war.

By June 1916, this was fully recognised. At the same time, a tremendous endeavour was about to be launched in France, the 'Big Push'. Everyone at home knew that the young citizen-soldiers were now ready in huge numbers. They had had, it seemed, lengthy, thorough training and colossal industrial effort had supplied them, again, it seemed, with every need in guns and ammunition. An uplifting victory would surely be won now and this might open up the way towards ultimate victory.

In the event, the first week of July was devastatingly to shatter such anticipation. Instead, it brought to the great population centres of the

United Kingdom a shocked communal sense of grief. The telegraph boy with his small enveloped sentence of death, the postman with black-edged letters of condolence, the closing of the blinds in house after house and street after street, the wearing of black armbands; these were the signs of cities suddenly shrouded in mourning. Within a few days town newspapers were printing photograph obituaries of local men reported killed, wounded or missing and, as the battle continued, one local weekly, the *Halifax Courier*, was sometimes picturing up to forty-five such cases, never less than twenty. In some communities the scale of loss was worse. There was disbelief, loss of hope, resentment, a freezing of the emotions manifest in either inaction or in mechanical pursuit of routine stripped of any real purpose. There was also, it must be said, a kind of solace in the near-universality of the suffering. Not to have received a telegram meant continued anxiety – was one on its way?

Touchingly, a tide of concern for others was released, its most moving evidence today to be read in the letters received by those newly-bereaved, and still more heart-rending, in their attempt to make response. For many of those in grief, there was some refuge in the concept of sacrifice for others. There was a need of something upon which to hold in this time of trial. Any conclusion that the death had been futile, cruelly drew the sufferers towards despair. There remained a glimmer of hope and hence of comfort in fixing upon the idea of duty having been done – King, country, community and family had been honourably served, even unto the very end. A head bowed in sorrow could be raised a little by pride in duty performed.

And so the Somme scorched its way through the daily thoughts of all who had sons, husbands, fathers, sweethearts, brothers and friends there. To this imprint may be added the ineradicable memories of those who were in France and who came back. From now on, nothing was ever to be quite the same. It is small wonder that our vision even today of the First World War is framed by the trenches, scarred landscape and broken bodies of the Somme, reinforced by images of the Ypres Salient and its battles approximately a year later. Mentally, without need of conscious decision, eyes move along the serried uniform ranks of white stones in quiet green cemeteries and the picture is transposed to that of silent respectful November crowds at city cenotaphs or village memorials and music almost unbearably sad – these are the visions which bind us to our past in the villages, fields and woods of Picardy.

Our perceptions are entirely reasonable but likely to be limited. They may fail to see the worldwide scale of the war in its four and a half years. We are likely to be disregarding or ignorant of the technological dynamism of the war which inexorably imposed its logic so cruelly upon those brought by fate to fight at this time. Nevertheless, in its kinship with the personal impact of the Somme in 1916, our being appalled at the brutal unanticipated shock of the cost without benefit of the heralded offensive, even in its legitimacy, needs some qualification.

Two further points may be made about the sociological legacy of a battle fought so long ago. The first relates to the values of a society which, at all levels, was subjected to the Somme. It must be appreciated that the ideals, opinions and prejudices of 1916 are not those widely held today. There may be similarities, but there are wide dissimilarities. Attitudes are subject to the influence of experience, reflection and later times – they change. It is a fascinating exercise examining letters or diaries from the past in an attempt to make soundly-based conclusions on the general response to the circumstances of the war made by people of similar occupation or socio-economic group. A natural development of such an enquiry is to look for the influences which shaped such a standpoint. What is not so reasonable is the wearing of a mantle of moral superiority in so doing. Such an approach from our privileged latter-day position lays summary scorn upon the 'misguided' beliefs of our forebears and then, on finding evidence of a viewpoint which conforms to our currently fashionable perception – no matter that it was held in 1916 by a minuscule minority – that viewpoint is extolled as a beacon of light in a world of deluded darkness.

On 9 July 1916, Lance-Corporal Elmer wrote of his battalion, which had suffered heavy losses on 1 July in front of Mametz, 'The 9th Devons have been in the thick of it again and I am proud to say have come out with great honours.' We should not doubt his pride in what he calls the tackling of a difficult task. All his officers had been hit. He lists his friends who have been killed, among them Corporal Collier who 'died leading No 5's bombing section on. The bombers did great work this time.' He names those remaining unscathed and then explains in this letter to his former officer, now recovering from wounds received at the Battle of Loos: 'We are now back having a spell and reorganising and shall soon be ready for them again if needed.'[1]

Second-Lieutenant Goodwin of the 8th Battalion York and Lancaster Regiment, wrote on the eve of the infantry assault on the Somme: 'If I do go out [i.e. am killed] it's a fine thing to have given one's life for one's country.' Are we to question the sincerity of his statement in what was in fact to be his last letter?[2] Another subaltern to fall had written, 'Our cause is a good one and I believe I am doing right in fighting.'[3] A father, losing his second son to the war, accepted in a letter to the Commanding Officer from whom he had received notification: 'These losses are very terrible but I can assure you make us here all the more determined that they shall not be in vain. I would sooner see all my boys go and myself too than that the German military power should not be crushed.'[4]

In the fourth month of the Somme, with mud and rain memorably adding to the trials to be faced, Private Shewing, in a Trench Mortar Battery, wrote to his Gloucestershire rector that such miseries as they were enduring had to be accepted 'to save our proud Empire'.[5]

Now the weight of personal experience evidence supporting such sentiments as have been laid out here is conclusive, and it remains something of a mystery as to why a strange mixture of patronising disdain and sheer ignorance of this fact should have been successful in obscuring that which was readily verifiable. Certainly to present striking exceptions to a general consensus is interesting and subjectively informative, but it is no more than that. Herein lies the second sociological point which might be made about the Somme and the somewhat less than magic mirror distortion of changed attitudes as they have been reflected in the post-Second World War literary legacy of the Somme.

On the subject of books about the war and as long ago as 1930, Douglas Jerrold in his *The Lie about the War*, denounced the then literary fashion which peddled 'the illusion that the war was avoidable and futile' and that 'it was recognised as futile by those who fought in it'. Jerrold's judgement is directed against those writers who repetitively, brutally and exclusively presented all the suffering, horror and desolation of war 'as without meaning so far as the declared purposes of the struggle are conceived, because these declared purposes are, to the writers and critics of the moment, either so many impudent and deadly frauds or so many irrelevancies, to the achievement of which the blunders and crimes of the military were only so many obstacles'.[6] One shudders to think what this angry commentator would have made of Paul Fussell's 1975 selective use of evidence and the conclusions he reached, as evinced by his magisterial judgement that 'Another reason the image of crucifixion came naturally to soldiers was that behind the lines almost daily they could see some Other Ranks undergoing Field Punishment Number One for minor infractions. This consisted of being strapped or tied spreadeagled to some immobile object.'[7] It is perhaps as well that Jerrold was spared the widely-seen stage, film and television screen distortions of factors associated with the 1915–17 Western Front experience, *Days of Hope*, *Oh! What a Lovely War* and *The Monocled Mutineer*.

The purpose behind such presentations was of course plain enough, and historically they have been deservedly discredited, but even John Keegan, with more scholarly intent, wrote in his *The Face of Battle* that 'the silent majority of the war generation probably perceived [in the protest verse of Sassoon, Graves and Blunden] a truthfulness to which they could assent' – a striking, unverified hypothesis making no allowance for the wealth of quite contrasting evidence of that generation's actual response at the time.[8]

While the battle was being waged, an official film of the Somme went some way towards bridging the gap between the civilian's perception of the battlefield and participatory reality. Some poets certainly went much further. Robert Graves in *Big Words* (1916) had his young soldier on the firestep waiting to go into action, cursing, praying, sweating and wishing that he had not uttered all the proud words previously declaimed. The message was clear: there was no place for such concepts as nobility in service and sacrifice, and the message was to be endorsed. Siegfried Sassoon's poem *Does it Matter?* (1917) vented a mordant contempt for what he saw as the shallowness of society's expression of sympathy for its war-damaged men:

Does it matter? – losing your legs? …
For people will always be kind,
And you need not show that you mind
When others come in after hunting
To gobble their muffins and eggs.

Sassoon's next unfortunate, the blinded soldier, appears more classless than the man deprived of his hunting!

> Does it matter? – losing your sight? …
> There's such splendid work for the blind;
> And people will always be kind,
> As you sit on the terrace remembering
> And turning your face to the light.

Of course the sighted lack a comprehension of blindness and the mobile lack an understanding of an incapacity in freedom of movement, but is the emotional effectiveness of Sassoon's verse conclusively true of all such victim's sense of the utter wastefulness of his loss and of the superficiality of the concern of those around him? Did all families, the staff of all institutions, did society itself, never show any depth of awareness in the cruel consequence to so many of their service in the war?

> … For they'll know you've fought for your country
> And no one will worry a bit.
>
> (From J. Silkin (ed.), *The Penguin Book of
> First World War Poetry*, pp. 126–7)

It is not a true parallel for comparison, but contrasting evidence to Sassoon's theme has resulted from some interviews the author carried out separately with eight men who had lived into their late eighties or nineties with grievous disabilities from war wounds. All the men had lost limbs in the Great War. Towards the end of his interview, each man was clearly offered an extended opportunity to speak of any deep-rooted resentment at the personal cost of his service in the war and also at any sense of a subsequent rejection by society. The men were from different social backgrounds and had varied pre-war employment and interests. The seemingly cruel but necessary stimuli of sport, girlfriends, dancing, employment, self-awareness or esteem, were all introduced in the interview, and yet not in a single case, other than a long-waged conflict over the percentage disability of a pension award, was a response given along the lines which might have been anticipated. Should evidence along these lines but nearer to 1916 be required, then the documentation of the death in prolonged agony of W. G. K. Boswell, mortally wounded on the Somme, dispels the falsehood that men never held on to their ideals to the end, suffering in the extreme a terrible penalty inflicted by war.[9] Poor Boswell's predominant concern, expressed to his father, was that in giving vent to the torment of his pain he had 'let down his school'.

In a book entitled *A War Imagined: The First World War and English Culture*, the American, Samuel Hynes, accorded heroic stature to the men of letters who denied those concepts encapsulated in 'the old Lie' *Dulce et decorum est pro patria mori*. He cited with something approaching veneration those poets, novelists and indeed artists who excoriated the validity of such ideals. His heroes challenge the myths bovinely accepted by an unthinking majority. With some puzzlement he accepted that for long after the war the delusive message of Rupert Brooke and Ernest Raymond had claimed far more adherents than those who railed against such empty nonsense. The legitimacy of Hynes's presumptions about English culture remains as a major question against his thesis, but additionally it seems as if his argument were to be far more in tune with the liberal academic chorus of the late 1960s and 1970s than with an understanding of the 1914–18 period. The plain man's contemporary song clearly has an unacceptable dissonance for his ear. Conformity and continuity are the last things Hynes wants to find in a war where, as he revealingly put forward, the young went off with 'their heads full of high abstractions like Honour, Glory, and England …' and 'were slaughtered in stupid battles by stupid generals'.[10] Accordingly there is not much room for surprise at the American's disregard of the abundant evidence pointing in a different direction from his central argument.

By definition anything published other than privately has to be seen in a context which includes commercial among other considerations. The early literature of the Somme could scarcely be immune from this universal factor of publishing activity. A work could be of such literary excellence that the publisher believed that it would succeed on that alone or, poem, play, novel or memoir, it would have to be in such accord with the prevailing spirit of the time that it would be attractive to the potential customer. A third possibility, that of the work being written by a well-known person, should be mentioned, and this again is not least a commercial factor.

In reflecting upon the differences in the prevailing spirit of wartime and that of the early post-war years and then a decade later, it is clear that the literary legacy of the Somme is influenced to a considerable extent by its evolving market. Post-war ex-soldier unemployment and unsatisfactory conditions of housing, pensions and welfare provision, offered fertile ground for the fast-growing seed of doubt as to whether the war were to have led to any improvement in the lives of the men who had fought and won it. Indeed could not its very length and cost in lives and in suffering be laid in variable measure on politicians and generals alike? In this respect, the politicians were rather better at defending themselves, but Hugh Cecil makes clear in an essay in *Home Fires and Foreign Fields* that a literary expression of anger at the folly and humbug of war animated the work of numerous novelists, like for example Gristwood's *The Somme*, in which the very first paragraph sets the tone: 'Before the world grew mad, the Somme was a placid stream of Picardy, flowing gently through a broad winding valley northwards to the English Channel and then came 1914 and the pestilence.'[11] Some eschewed such an approach as anachronistic in the sense that opinion and sentiment from one period of time were inappropriately being implanted in an earlier. At best the net result of this would be distortion, at worst a wholly false picture. For such critics only writings rooted in contemporary evidence properly revealed the detail and emotion of happenings or feelings from the past. In a perceptive article on James Churchill Dunn, the Regimental Medical Officer of the 2nd Royal Welsh Fusiliers, and subsequently author of *The War the Infantry Knew 1914-19* (anonymously edited for publication by Dunn in 1938), Keith Simpson made it quite clear that Dr Dunn was one of those men who, having experienced the war, was convinced that the 'majority of war books were written in an emotional reaction in the aftermath of the war or to make money and gain publicity through sensationalism, and therefore did not accurately reflect what had actually happened'.[12]

If it were to be thought a jaundiced view that takes exception to a novel based on the war because it seems tailored to its market, then perhaps more acceptable would be the cautionary word offered in relation to its retrospective nature. A novel or a poem is crafted. It has to meet literary disciplines of construction and in a poem, single words, never mind phrases, have to be carefully selected, matching in metre and rhyme as the poet seeks his imagery and skirts the danger of contrivance. And yet in the last analysis a poem certainly is contrived. Furthermore, it may be rooted in the past experience of the poet; it may have all the intensity of a word-gifted man baring his soul in its revulsion against the ugliness of war, but is it to be heard as a universal response to front-line experience? However heroically some may have performed their military duties, a more appropriate veneration of this verse would be as from certain poets either inspired by or captured by their war, not as the 'Soldier Poets' who expressed universal truths from which the true nature of Everyman's experience can be discerned. What distinguishes these poets and marks them off from their fellows is not just their talent but their unusually developed sensibility. It should be more widely recognised and entirely reasonable that they speak for themselves and for kindred spirits. When John Lehmann used the poets as illustrative that from the Battle of the Somme 'despairing hope [was] almost buried beneath the huge weight of disillusionment' and that there was a belief that it was increasingly not merely stupid but almost criminal not to negotiate an end to the slaughter, he is leaving reality well behind.[13] As far as contemporary evidence from the front-line soldier is concerned, Lehmann's verdict is so wide of the mark that he has missed the board, but he does reintroduce the established point that a poet such as Sassoon, who had served on the Somme, was to be so affronted by Home Front ignorance of Western Front experience that, in Sassoon's own words, he had 'deliberately written to disturb complacency'.[14] But there was little need for Sassoon's verse in the disturbance of any remaining complacency – published casualty lists were seeing to that. What is also worth stating is that Sassoon's very intent was ill-conceived. It was scarcely going to be helpful for those on the Home Front to have too clear a perception of the Somme during the battle. The war could have been lost in the United Kingdom just as easily as on the seas or in France, and all the factors which could have combined to produce such a dire result link to the question of morale. When the wartime poet bridged the gulf between the fighting front and the Home Front, we should be aware that he was crossing a chasm which was necessarily there. It was essential to the soldier as well as to the civilian, even when it silenced multitudes of men on leave, puzzled and affronted some, and convinced many on returning to France that their's was the true reality, shorn of all artificiality and pretence.

On the Somme there was a basic, simple though demanding framework within which to fulfill one's obligations. It was made acceptable not just by a sense of duty or of there being no alternative, but by the fairly-shared burden for all within sight and the considerable compensation of comradeship.

Where then can we go for the authentic voice of soldier experience of the Somme? Here we are in a continuing debate, one which dates at least as far back as 1929 with Jean Norton Cru's devotion to the theme in his book, *Temoins*, published in Paris. In 1985, J. M. Winter, looking at soldier writing about the war, contended that no matter the theme, tone or construction, the unifying element in all such work is that it springs from 'the old trench mind'.[15] This may be so, but in retrospective and published literature the changed circumstances, the new influences and the fact of publication should act as efficient brakes on the vehicle of easy generalisation. The soundest material from which to make generalisation about soldier experience of the Somme must surely be in any large body of unpublished letters and diaries of men who were serving in the line there in 1916. Documentation of this nature, like all forms of evidence, requires critical scrutiny. The purposes of a particular letter, the circumstances under which it was written, the man who wrote it, the person to whom it was written, an awareness of the influence of the external censor or the man sensitively censoring his own letter for the recipient's sake; these are some of the subjective factors relevant in assessing such evidence. There is an undeniable individuality in a letter or a diary which shines like an intellectual traffic-light stuck on red with regard to the drawing of more general conclusions than those limited to observations upon that soldier. Nevertheless, an abundance of evidence pointing in the same direction offers safer ground for an academic advance. Among archival collections like those held in the Imperial War Museum or in the Library of the University of Leeds, there is a huge body of such material. The one in Leeds is on-line catalogued and digitally cross-referenced in such a way as to allow for the making of cautious generalisation and thus come nearer to an understanding of the Somme experience.

Kindred with regard to being introduced to an individual's experience of the Western Front, though not allowing for wider conclusions, are some published letter collections of acknowledged merit like the excellent Cecil Slack's *Grandfather's Adventures in the Great War*, or, of a different nature

– a very good memoir and much more recently published (2011) – *Joffrey's War, A Sherwood Forester in the Great War*.[16] Christopher Stone's letters in *From Vimy Ridge to the Rhine* have the special merit of showing us humour and controlled compassion while serving on the Somme, as well as what might be expected in this instance, a gift for the telling phrase. On 18 October 1916, Stone wrote from the Somme to his wife: 'I shall get very fat if I live long as adjutant. Soon they will have to build special dug-outs for me and I shall have to leave the trenches over the top after dark because I shan't be able to get along inside them. The tanks will use me to hide behind in an attack …' Then, five days later, we have an account of a burial: 'One of them was a private called Russell Davies and when they emptied his pockets before burying him they found his will; and it appears that he was curator of the Brighton Museum and was leaving his collection of iron work to the South Kensington Museum. He had enlisted in this battalion and was what is called the company sanitary man. [Men such as R-D] are the real heroes of the war, and it's only we who know them who can honour them properly.'[17]

Orders are Orders, the story of a Manchester Pal, Albert William Andrews, was privately published in 1987 in a more modest format than the Stone letters. It is an account of experiences up to and including the Somme, drawn from a diary and put together while Andrews convalesced from both shell-shock and a shoulder wound. There is not a great deal directly from the diary but the narrative and the pride in his unit ring true.[18]

Different terms of reference governed two books by the South African, Ian Uys. For the first he chose a precise location on the Somme, *Delville Wood*.[19] Here the South African Brigade had fought steadfastly under such appalling and prolonged circumstances that in the grim litany of the Somme's savagery of sustained attack and counter-attack, Delville Wood stands unenviably pre-eminent. What the author did was to research everything which had been written by those who were there and then to track down and interview survivors. The result is a valuable book in which the biographical notes on contributors is a fully justifiable element. The telling of this story from unpublished official sources, personal letters and diaries, reminiscences and material from published accounts should certainly earn this book a place among the best books of its kind on the Somme. Uys followed up this book with the excellent idea, successfully carried through, of writing about the Germans struggling to hold Longueval Wood.[20]

More recently still, the determination to reveal collective experience through the testimony of many individuals has been exercised in the United Kingdom in a succession of books on the locally recruited battalions which received their first major testing at the start of the 'Big Push'. The Barnsley and the Accrington Pals were well served by Jon Cooksey and William Turner respectively, the Sheffield Pals similarly by Ralph Gibson and Paul Oldfield, and the Liverpool Pals by Graham Maddocks.[21] Most recently, the record of three Service battalions of the Northumberland Fusiliers, *Tyneside Scottish*, has been admirably brought together by Graham Stewart and John Sheen.[22]

These splendid books make good use of both 1916 and modern cartography as well as private photographs, official orders and local newspaper material. Understandably the concentration is heavily upon 1 July and all that led up to this day, but the books provide essential published documentation of a fundamentally important sociological factor about the British troops on the Somme. This factor is of course the numbers of battalions recruited from the northern, urban, industrial communities. The men had worked together before the war and had enlisted together in units which identified them in common currency as battalions named after their locality – Salford Pals, Leeds Pals, and so many more. Recent research has led to a clearer understanding of distinctive differences between battalions previously held to be of a standard pattern – the Leeds Pals certainly did not fit a common pattern, earning themselves in their city a 'snooty' reputation by reason of their somewhat exclusive occupational basis of recruitment. However, in the main, the Pals trained together, went overseas together, some briefly to Egypt, before their battalions were assembled in France to prepare for the Somme – and here in France, the men who had known each other in school or workplace before they had put on khaki, were in such number to die together in front of Serre or some other location on the Somme 'earning' its tragic association on that first day of the great endeavour.

Quite some time has now passed since the nation lost the last of its veterans of the Great War but every aspect of the 1916 Battle of the Somme continues to be probed, dissected, examined and judged. Debate and dispute: it is tempting to liken it to bombardment and counter-bombardment, but of course only theories and reputations are at stake, not lives. What seems certain is that there will be no ultimate betrayal of the men who fought on to the Somme – they will not be forgotten. In his magisterial book on the Somme, *Bloody Victory* (2009), William Philpott indicts the 'wanton waste brigade': 'It is wrong and morally reprehensible to dismiss this human phenomenon on the grandest scale as a futile engagement in a futile conflict, as so many do.'[23] Certainly one of the foremost contributions Philpott has made to a balanced understanding of the Somme is to draw attention to the skilled German defence of their positions, not just in their secure subterranean strength, not just in the scientific siting of machine-gun strongpoints but in defensive tactical doctrine and the professional skill and tenacity of their troops. Somehow these factors have been lost in the easier or more familiar focus on the deficiency of British High Command.

The aim of *The 1916 Battle of the Somme Reconsidered* is to make a contribution to the debate on the Somme, but above all to present evidence from letters, diaries and recollections of British and Commonwealth soldiers who were there. The author has appreciated the deepening of our understanding as a result of such books as *Bloody Victory*, and anticipates with keen interest the vision of Matthew Richardson in his book which will examine French and German personal experience source materials. When Richardson's book is published, these two historians, with the works of Sheffield too, will have made a major contribution to an understanding of the 1916 Battle of the Somme from every perspective, above all one which leaves us with an awareness of the colossal scale of this epic three-nation trial of battle.

The volume presented here will focus on the wide range of required contributions in the performance of military duties and tasks in addition to that which is so grimly familiar, the role of the infantryman in 1916. It will emphasise that there were four-and-a-half months of battle to be endured and a consideration on any shorter timescale is completely to misunderstand the Somme experience and the battle's true significance, a tragically costly but essential contribution to the winning of the war. By means of illustrating the range of tasks to be performed by the British and Commonwealth soldiers during the battle, the book's purpose is to make clear, often uncomfortably so, what it was like to be there in 1916.

Chapter 1

The Battle of the Somme:
Concept, Planning and Preparation

In almost all respects the position of the Allies at the end of 1915 was disappointing. Outright failure at the Dardanelles was matched by defeats on the Eastern Front and for the Serbian army in the Balkans. Costly endeavours in France had met with little success. A dangerous situation was developing in Mesopotamia. In Egypt a need had arisen for a Western Desert Force as well as to secure the Suez Canal against the Turkish threat. An attempted British landing on the coast of Tanganyika had been a fiasco and the military consequences further disadvantaged the forces engaged in the difficult East African campaign. Over-optimistic views of what might be achieved from Macedonia had led to an expeditionary force being sent there, but to date it had not rescued the Serbs from their defeat and it was now somewhat shamefacedly hedged-in defensively by its own barbed wire. The new ally, Italy, was heavily engaged in battle with Austria but a dividend from this did not seem to be held by Italian, or indeed by Russian, hands. Finally in setting this depressing scene for Allied strategic consideration, the Royal Navy had not exercised the sort of demonstrable command of the seas which would have given heart to politicians and generals only too aware that Russia was hard-pressed, and there seemed small reason for confidence that the

Germans could be expelled from the defensive positions they had taken up securing their gains in economically valuable and cherished acres of France and Belgium. In a general picture of gloom, the approaching readiness of Britain to play a fuller military part on the Western Front shone some rays of sunshine as the Allies considered their options for a co-ordinated offensive in the New Year.

From June 1915, co-ordinated effort had been under consideration and from November with an increased sense of urgency through meetings, conferences and the circulation of memoranda. That no fanciful ideas were being entertained of the achievement of a swift, cheap victory was clearly attested on 27 March 1916 by General Joffre, the French Commander-in-Chief, at a conference where the British and the French Prime Ministers were present: 'We have to destroy the morale of the German Army and nation.'[1] This was in fact precisely what the German Army was endeavouring to achieve against the French at Verdun with their offensive on that sector now nearly five weeks in operation. The German blow here and an Austro-Hungarian attack on their Italian Front imposed serious constraint upon the Allied plans. In the event, the main burden of carrying out co-terminous offensives fell upon Britain and Russia. The idea, as conceived by Joffre and presented at the end of December 1915 to Sir Douglas Haig, the new British Commander-in-Chief, had been for a huge, 60-mile-frontage, Franco-British offensive on either side of the Somme. Aspects of a developing plan had been discussed and solutions reached when the Germans struck at Verdun in late February, destroying in a blow the scale of the Allied intention. The compromise reached may be categorised as the retention of the French idea but in larger measure to be fulfilled by the British.

Clearly there was a need for Britain to play an increased role in operations on the Western Front. In Britain's New Armies there was an uncommitted resource and France, where manpower resources were fully stretched already, was now being subjected to a massive new onslaught. By no statistical comparison had Britain's military effort in Flanders and France been on a scale to earn equality of voice in Anglo-French military deliberations. France now expected the evident imbalance of commitment to be redressed. This, and anxiety over Verdun, drew all French thinking concerning the appropriate location for the belated British contribution, aouth to the

Somme. Here the British Expeditionary Force would be harnessed into a responsibility which could not be shrugged off – a reality, as made clear by Terraine, which this particular military coalition demanded from Britain in 1916.[2]

Sir John French, Commander-in-Chief of the BEF when the French offensive in Artois was planned in 1915, had been reluctant to accept the Gallic choice for a related British offensive at Loos that September. Haig had more than shared his reservations and there had been little, if any, profit from that battle. Now, in the early months of the following year, Haig would have chosen attack from Flanders rather than Picardy to free the Belgian coastal ports from U-Boat use, but again the British were unavoidably required to dance to the French tune.

Tim Travers has argued that the hierarchical structure of the British army, the limitations of intellect and the socio-educational experience of the senior officers, the very way in which the Army went about its business – appointments, promotions, dismissals and Haig's own deviousness in this respect – precluded the possibility of fresh thinking in tackling problems of the nature of the Western Front in 1916. In his book *The Killing Ground*, he set out to prove that, for the Somme, Haig's predominant concern was how to apply 'traditional principles to what was seen as a new and puzzling form of warfare' – he was, in other words, considers Travers, out of his depth.[3]

Travers lays out his case with conviction but it remains unproven in at least two linked respects – the way in which the war might have been more efficiently prosecuted is not tackled (perhaps this is the unattainable evidence which the prosecutor needs for conviction) and in Travers's book there is no examination of Haig's undeniable achievement in 1918 which is now lauded on all sides and is seen by many as one solidly grounded in the great battle on the Somme two years earlier.

Was it then the imperative of coalition warfare which led Haig first to accept his responsibility in Picardy and then to plan according to principles the carrying-out of which would inexorably drain the German ability to wage the war in the West, or was it something else? Was it Haig's inflexible cast of mind, his incapacity to break out of received patterns of problem-solving into imaginative thinking, which led to the way the Somme was fought? It seems to this author that the balance of the case rests with Haig's professional assessment of the nature of the war and the soundness of his acceptance that this dictated the only means by which it could be waged on land. However, there is a matter which will require further discussion and that is the issue of Haig's retention of some hope of a breakthrough – proof either of a properly-held provision for the achievement of a highly-desirable situation, as is argued by Gary Sheffield, or confirmation of a one-track mind as held by Haig's detractors. Just occasionally the case for the latter is declaimed with such baleful venom, as in Denis Winter's *Haig's Command*,[4] that, paradoxically, the uncommitted probably fly to the other camp.

The lack of a strategically-significant objective behind the German battlefront on the Somme is in stark contrast to that behind Nieuport and Messines. Haig had indeed encouraged the development of offensive planning early in 1916 for Flanders but it was Verdun which was to neutralise all such thought. On 14 February, a week before the Germans struck at Verdun, Haig formally accepted that he would launch the required major offensive on the Somme. An Army, the Fourth, newly formed on 1 March, would take over a 20-mile front which stretched from the River Somme itself northwards as far as Fonquevillers. On the shoulders of this Army would rest the main responsibility for the battle.

The front selected for the assault had the German salient at Gommecourt as its northern extremity, then to the south the villages of Serre and Beaumont Hamel just behind the German first line. As the opposing trench systems south of Beaumont Hamel inclined more to the east, they were severed by the course of the River Ancre. To the south of this river the village strongpoints in or behind the German forward positions were Thiepval, Ovillers, La Boisselle and Fricourt, before, quite strikingly, the front took up an eastward alignment in front of Mametz and Montauban to the north. Here the Fourth Army boundary met that of the French Sixth Army which held the line up to the River Somme.

There was a clearly perceptible ridge behind the German positions on both sides of the Ancre, which had an obvious tactical significance. If it were not to be captured, the same operational disadvantage which had occurred on three fronts at the Dardanelles, the enemy continuing to hold the higher ground, would obtain in the new huge undertaking. This link with the events of the previous year can quite reasonably be made even allowing for the dramatically different configuration of the ridges in Picardy and those behind Anzac Cove, or far less strikingly behind the village of Krithia on the Gallipoli Peninsula.

Adjacent to the villages between the meadow and marsh-bordered Ancre and Somme rivers or breaking the open landscape of gently sloping fields scoured by the occasional valley, were woods which were named but had not yet the evil renown with which they would soon be associated – High Wood, Delville Wood, Trones Wood, Bazentin-le-Petit Wood and Bernafay Wood. Transversely across the battlefront from south-west to north-east, the road from Albert, which was about one-and-a-half miles behind the British front line, cut a straight course to Bapaume, nine miles behind the German front line.

At no point were the opposing front lines widely separated and in addition to fortified localities behind their line at Montauban, Mametz Wood, Contalmaison, Pozières and Serre, the Germans had a completed second-line position on their commanding ridge and a third line in preparation. A key feature, known to some extent by British High Command but the significance of which was not fully appreciated, was that the German positions had been deeply dug as a concrete warren of security against Allied artillery bombardment.

The developing tactical appraisal made by Fourth Army Headquarters had to have a resolution of interrelated problems. Was the Fourth Army to attack along the whole extent of its positions and would success be achieved more completely by prolonged bombardment or by surprise? General Sir Henry Rawlinson, in command of the Fourth Army, concluded that a prolonged bombardment would in several respects make things easier for the assault troops. The Commander-in-Chief considered Rawlinson's proposals lacked the element of surprise and that he had set tactical objectives which were too modest in width and depth. As debate was joined on these differing approaches, Haig was counselled by his artillery adviser, Major-General Birch, that the plan was asking too much of the artillery resources. The divergence between Haig and Rawlinson in aim and method was tactical but also philosophical. At this stage Haig had faith in a breakthrough such as had not yet been achieved on the Western Front; Rawlinson considered that adequate artillery preparation and an assault in set stages would secure limited but valuable gains of the higher ground which overlooked the British positions.

Travers has maintained that: 'Haig's hope for the breakthrough was so strong that he had not clearly thought through alternatives in case of failure.'[5] He had reserves of cavalry in place to exploit such a breakthrough but as the plans developed and Rawlinson's reservations were seen to be as significant as was his loyalty in following his Chief's directives, Travers judgement was that Haig became confused over the nature of the battle being prepared, thus a twofold indictment can be put forward. First, there should have been no confusion in Haig's mind when he was about to commit human and material resources on an unprecedented scale, and second, it was hypocritical of Haig subsequently to claim that the battle had been to serve the French and Allied cause by so hammering the German Army in a prolonged offensive, *une bataille d'usure*, that it would be permanently damaged.

William Philpott, in *Bloody Victory*, and Gary Sheffield, in *The Chief*, interpret matters quite differently. Broadly they follow Terraine who maintained that the conclusion drawn by Haig from the overall Allied picture, and more crucially the scene in France in mid–March, was that the British effort must be made 'with maximum strength, aiming at the maximum result – the defeat of the German Army in the field'.[6] Hence the German Army was to be beaten, by initial breakthrough or breakthrough at some stage if possible, or, if it had to be, by being worn down to a shred. Planning for either embraced the other.

On the specific issue of breakthrough, Sheffield considers that 'the evidence strongly suggests Haig's plans to seize the German Second Position on the first day of the battle was achievable, at least on the southern sector'.[7] Sheffield maintains his balanced case by stating that there are mistakes made in planning and preparation but the charge of confusion of aim in Haig's mind cannot be sustained. In this chapter we shall be looking at the issue of blameworthiness on the part of the Commander-in-Chief in regard to any mistakes in planning and preparation and what also must be addressed is the issue of Rawlinson's differing view from that of his Chief in what was achievable from the Big Push.

Until quite recently it has been received wisdom that, all along the line of the attack on 1 July, the infantry assault was made by measured advance of uniform, linear, intervalled waves of heavily-burdened troops in extended order, this being based both on an appraisal of the anticipated effectiveness of an unprecedentedly prolonged heavy preliminary bombardment, and then on the perceived limited capacity of New Army troops to advance by anything other than such procedure – there is official documentation to that effect in a GHQ memorandum of 8 May. It stated: 'Officers and men generally do not now possess that military knowledge arising from a long and high state of training, which enable them to act promptly on sound lines in unexpected situations. They have become accustomed to deliberate action based on precise and detailed orders.'[8] Certainly, in training, this method of advance would give an impression of the required irresistible forward movement. However, Trevor Wilson and Robin Prior, no friends of High Command, and then William Philpott, have shown that there were different approaches taken by local command in some sectors, and a more flexible procedure must be conceded in the endeavour to maintain the momentum of the attack in a deep battle. Philpott makes the point that: 'It is overly simplistic to judge that the British army was too rigid or conservative in its tactics and command. It was keen to learn, engaging with its task thoughtfully and professionally: but to date its commanders, officers and men had relatively little experience of large-scale offensive operations.'[9]

A related point is made by the same historian with regard to the readiness of the New Army infantry battalions for their battle initiation: yes, they were under-prepared for what they would face – not undertrained in terms of fitness or morale, but without the weapons training in assault to turn confidence into competence – but there were variations in the degree of readiness because some New Army units had received appropriate training. It was not just French artillery support that accounts for some striking British infantry success at the southern end of the line but the performance of the well-trained troops in that sector.

Beneath the overwhelming determinants of ill-fortune on 1 July, that is British artillery failing to neutralise defence from the opposing positions and then the remarkable resilience of the German troops occupying the shelled trenches and strongpoints, more than the degree of readiness of the assaulting troops would be influential factors on the day. The issue of communication control or rather absence of control of the battle once joined was of material importance. Signallers laying telephone lines were as vulnerable to shelling as the means of communications they laid. Runners might or might not get through, their reports might or might not then be out of date, carrier pigeons and message-carrying dogs might indeed get to their destination, flares might be correctly interpreted, but any possibility of effective adjustment of original orders as a result of receipt of intelligence by these means was virtually out of the question.

Concerning the issue of definite knowledge of the concreted depth of defence of the German positions and that these positions had not been neutralised by the preliminary bombardment, it is simply not established that there was sufficient intelligence conclusively to that effect – yet another hoary myth of condemnatory hindsight. However, the reality of the strength of the German positions made more serious still the several areas of inadequacy in the Fourth Army's artillery resources and errors in their deployment. There was an insufficiency of heavy guns, of howitzers and of high explosive shells. There was a serious deficiency in the quality of the shells and so extensive was the frontage of the attack that a far greater number of heavy artillery pieces would have had to be available to make decisively effective the evenly spread deployment arranged. Guns and howitzers were not concentrated on particular sectors judged to be critically important. Of course, the artillery statistics seem awe inspiring – 1,537 guns and howitzers, approximately one field gun for every 21 yards and one heavy artillery piece for every 57 yards. In the eight days commencing 24 June, 1,732,873 shells were fired by the Fourth Army. There was relatively a still heavier concentration of artillery support on the French sector on the right of the British battlefront.

However, it has been clearly established that the actual tonnage of British high explosive material falling upon the German front line was less impressive than superficial computation would suggest in that it produced fountains of earth and much surface damage but caused 'quite trifling' concussion downwards to the hiding places of the German trench garrisons.[10] To which point might be added the disappointing percentage of shells which failed to explode.

What needs additionally to be grasped is the great length of the line being attacked, 25,000 yards, the remarkable strength and sophistication of the concrete positions beneath the German trenches, the quality of the troops sheltered by those positions and the availability to the Germans of adequate reserves. On 1 July, there were thirty-four German battalions in readiness; in five days another fifty-four were brought in. The numbers and quality of the German troops throughout the Battle of the Somme, in defence and in counter-attack, demanded proper estimation in 1916 and no less should this be the case today. Historians like Philpott have addressed this too frequently neglected perpective, though Terraine, with regard to German counter-attack response, stressed this as a factor which never received adequate attention from those who simply saw the British engaged in costly attack. Ian Uys, many years ago too, deserved credit for his focus on German counter-attacks in the Longueval area but a far wider scope has now been tackled with an essential French dimension too.

The preliminary and unprecedentedly heavy bombardment opened on 24 June, continuing for seven days, but for all the reasons previously listed, the German wire remained a major barrier on many sectors, those troops reaching it bunching before possible breaches making themselves easy targets for the enemy machine-gunners. The trenches had been pulverised but not neutralised in terms of what remained secure below ground, and its exits to the surface unblocked. Of further disadvantage was the inadequately developed capacity to identify and swiftly to knock out of action German gunnery interfering with all stages of the infantry move forward and the machine-gun posts uncleared and, in an outflanking position, enfilading advance on a narrow sector.

A very different series of problems was to be encountered from Rawlinson's particular preoccupation with the consolidation of the first objectives on their being captured; it was the crossing of No Man's Land, getting through the wire and into the trenches to be taken before the enemy surfaced from subterranean protection and wrought havoc upon the lines of men making that attempt.

Deception and surprise are fundamental precepts of military success. In 1991 they were outstandingly achieved in the Gulf. In 1982 at the Falklands, when logistical factors were still more disadvantageous, they played a notable part in undermining an opposition force in possession of the objective to be assaulted. Against an opponent of a vastly different character, they achieved a remarkable initial advantage in Normandy in June 1944 but if one were to go back still further to the First World War and Allied endeavour on the Western Front, nothing similar could be secured. When attention is fixed upon a common element of success in 1944, 1982 and 1991 – superiority in the air – temptation arises to see this as the vital factor missing in 1916, but this will not do. In fact, the Royal Flying Corps (RFC), only four years after its foundation, went far towards winning its own Battle of the Somme. All the tasks set before it were carried out effectively and within the technological limits of the air war in the middle of the First World War, demonstrably the RFC achieved superiority before the battle commenced and then maintained it during the first months. It may be questionable to sever the flying arm from the Army of which it was simply a Corps, but the point is made to show that we must look elsewhere to explain the absence of surprise gaining decisive advantage. The answer lies in the constant close proximity of the huge forces of modern industrialised states facing each other with the full deployment of their military manpower and material resources in positions fixed now by many months of conflict. The trench positions were continuous from Switzerland to the North Sea. There was simply no flank to turn; how was surprise to be achieved?

There were inexorable determinants to land warfare in France and Flanders during the central years of the Great War – the current stage of weapon technology, the absence of any means of securing protection for infantry advancing across No Man's Land against an entrenched enemy and the lack of any means swiftly to make and take advantage of a breakthrough. As yet there was no mechanised, armed and armoured vehicle, sufficiently fast, reliable and capable of coping with the terrain, swiftly to cross a cratered No Man's Land, then crush its way through the wire and get over a trench system before breaking through into open country. We should remember the denial of all road and rail facility to any force which threatened such a breakthrough and the absence of Senior Command eye and voice control over a developing situation in the noise and smoke of battle. The defender who remained secure in his position of concealment, maintained his morale and, with good weaponry, an adequacy of ammunition and sound leadership, stood firm, held overwhelming advantage. These were the factors which rivetted conformity and constraint upon all Western Front initiative. To them may be added the requirement to attack by the principal land power of the Western Entente: France. A failure constantly to bear in mind the daily reality to the Frenchman of his loss, is to cloud any understanding of the Allied military position in France. Rich agricultural and industrial patrimony had been lost together with the North Eastern railway network. All this held in the thrall of an enemy who had, in the memories of some and in the minds of all, defeated and robbed her in 1870–1. There was too the devastating, continuing loss of French lives. The land and its people had to be cleansed of the accumulated outrage of German despoliation.

Of diminishing significance in June, 1916, because of refined French infantry tactics in the assault, were the vestiges of the discredited *attaque a l'outrance*, which had animated pre-war French military thinking. Despite the fearful losses of the August 1914 Battle of the Frontiers and then the cost without profit of successive offensives in the following year by the French on a large scale, and the British on a smaller, the requirement of sweeping the Germans out of France conferred some continued influence on discredited theory. There is ready material here in contemporary official papers, French and British, for the historian to scorn concerning the unrealistic assessment of the potential in attack of cavalry and of infantry, imbued with high morale. Sir Douglas Haig, the cavalryman, has left a number of such documented or anecdotal hostages to fortune and they have served as ready tools to undermine his reputation.

While Haig, by military education, personal inclination and more significantly the nature of the Allied position in France, was certainly in accord with the inter-Allied agreement for co-ordinated offensives, it is important to remember the instructions he had received from his political master, Lord Kitchener, Secretary of State for War, on 28 December 1915. 'The special task laid upon you is to assist the French and Belgian Governments in driving the German armies from French and Belgian territory.'[11] Given the strength of the German positions on the Western Front, this could only have been attempted, never mind achieved, by a major and prolonged offensive. Haig was locked into a circumstance which had no kinship with the war which had inspired the French doctrine of the offensive, the 1870 Franco-Prussian debacle, but was one which would have been recognised immediately by General Ulysses S. Grant, the victorious Commander-in-Chief of the Union Forces in the American Civil War.

Grant's grand strategy of destroying the capacity of the South to continue her prosecution of the war and his stranglehold on Robert E. Lee's army in a series of engagements in Virginia in May 1864 designed to damage that army beyond repair, was quite simply, a decisive success. In the Virginian Wilderness and in the advance upon Richmond, he had attacked relentlessly when all advantage lay with a provenly skilled defender. Heavy Union losses were incurred. In particular, Grant's reputation was to be lastingly damaged by fruitless attacks at Cold Harbor in June 1864, but by such methods the South was battered into submission.

When one considers the significance of her coastline in this American Civil War, of her railways and rivers, of the vast spacial context of the war, it is surely noteworthy that the war was won by a strategy of attrition which included the application of that concept by military tactics as well as by economic deprivation. The geographical scale of the 1915–17 Western Front was far more confined and the possibility of outflanking manoeuvre non-existent. We should not be surprised at the winning of this war by attritional methods – be saddened and repelled by it, yes, but not surprised at it – it lay in the nature of the war. The transformation of Haig, the disappointed disciple of French theory, into the practitioner of an updated version of Grant's philosophy, was completed by the Battle of the Somme. It is evident that he retained his vision of breakthrough beyond the launching of the attack on 1 July, right into mid-September and arguably still later. In a letter to Joffre on 28 June he stressed that having broken the enemy's line between the Somme and Serre, secured the positions about Bapaume and thence to Ginchy, he would seek to 'enlarge the breach by gaining possession of the area between Bapaume and Arras' and with further success achieved he would 'move forward to the line Cambrai-Douai' and beyond, in accordance with whatever move the enemy made to frustrate 'our advance Eastwards'.[12] To read his December 1916 despatch on the battle where he lists the original objectives as:

[i]   to relieve the pressure on Verdun;
[ii] to assist our Allies in the other theatres of war by stopping any further transfer of German troops from the Western Front;
[iii] to wear down the strength of the forces opposed to us.

but makes no reference to his hope of a breakthrough, may be taken as evidence of his limitation as a man[13] but is it a reasonable expectation to look in such a document for a confession to that effect and that he had learned that, as yet, the Germans remained too strong for a breakthrough to be achieved but that the cost to them of holding their positions rendered them vulnerable if the pressure were maintained?

Such a disclosure would have been damaging to national morale and have given ammunition to critics whose chorus would rock the essential stability of those directing the Army's endeavour. However, we may still be left with a feeling that Haig lacked that combination of confidence and humility which would have allowed him to echo Grant, who wrote of Cold Harbor, admittedly in memoirs and not in the furnace of war, that he had 'always regretted that the last assault at Cold Harbor was ever made ... no advantage whatever was gained to compensate for the heavy loss we sustained'.[14]

Before looking at Haig's men on the ground who, on 1 July, would be in the forefront of the great design, proper reference must be paid to the tasks being carried out by the RFC. As early as 25 April, aerial reconnaissance had reported the construction of formidable new defences behind the Somme front. As a consequence, intensive efforts were made systematically to photograph from the air the whole line in front of the Fourth Army. The machines engaged in this work had to be protected and, both by escort and by fighters engaged in offensive patrolling which included attacks on enemy kite balloons, British photographic and other reconnaissance, short and longer range, were maintained and German endeavours forestalled. There was much to hide in the way of movements and concentration behind the Fourth Army, much to photograph, observe, bomb and harass behind the German lines in addition to the continuous duty of artillery observation. A special consideration was to be the need to hinder the movement of German reinforcements from the moment the infantry attack was launched. From fourteen squadrons, at least 185 British aircraft, eighty-one of which were single-seat scouts, were available for use on the whole front from Gommecourt southwards on 1 July. They were opposed by an enemy total in the region of 129.

There is a need to be mindful of the British Kite Balloon sections. Their vital work of observation was dramatically arrested by a violent storm on

23 June when several balloons were struck by lightning and destroyed. The balloon of No 5 Section in the Northern, Third Army, area, was wrenched from its winch and whisked away towards the trenches rising rapidly. 'The two observers hurriedly tore up and scattered their notes, maps and photographs. At 13,000 the balloon was swirling in a snowstorm accompanied by vivid lightning and thunder.' A series of exceptional emergencies then ensued and only quick thinking by one of the observers averted disaster. The remarkable aerial adventure, fully described in the *Official History of the War in the Air*, left one officer severely frostbitten and both badly shaken.[15] It is a useful reminder that natural or technical calamity was potentially attendant upon the work of the men of the Kite Balloon sections as well as their vulnerability to enemy aerial attack. On the subject of kite balloons and the work of the RFC in the last days of June, a note of new technical development was struck by the successful use by British aeroplanes of Le Prieur rockets and phosphorus bombs in destroying eight German kite balloons.

From airfields at Fienvillers, Vert Galand, Les Alencons, Bertangles, Lahoussoye, Baizieux, Allonville, Marieux, Bellevue and others, the varied work of the RFC over the Somme was conducted. Maintaining supremacy in the air was costly and as the Germans redressed the imbalance of machines in the area and introduced superior aircraft in the form of Halberstadt and Albatros fighters in September, the struggle became still more stern. It was consistently fought as the British had required it to be fought, over the German lines, so that vital aerial support for the forces on the ground continued without interruption except by decree of the weather. In this lay the RFC's victory in the skies over the Somme.[16]

During June, there were High Command debates over the date of the initial infantry attack, the hour and the length of the preliminary bombardment. On 16 June, Haig made clear in a General Staff letter that if there were to be a break in the enemy resistance, 'the advance was to be pressed Eastwards far enough to enable our cavalry to push through into the open country beyond the enemy's prepared lines of defence'.[17]

Communications and facilities for billeting, feeding and watering the huge host of men and animals which concentrated upon the scattered villages north and south of the Ancre, were woefully inadequate. The road and rail system was nowhere near sufficient for the guns, ammunition, stores and supplies being assembled in the area and then deployed. It was estimated that the Fourth Army needed thirty-one trains daily to cater for its needs, up to seventy trains during an offensive, so new lines were built, new railheads and sidings established and the number of such major engineering undertakings was augmented by those concerned with improving water supply by boring and the installation of pumping equipment and by roadwork engineering.

The good weather eased the problem of the shortage of accommodation in houses and barns as field bivouacs sufficed reasonably where hutments had not been erected. Feeding the guns and keeping them satisfied involved the creation of huge ammunition dumps which had of course to be camouflaged. Feeding the men and the horses was another problem on a vast scale, and, fully stretched as they would be in the event, the provision of sixteen mainly tented casualty clearing stations, and three advanced operating theatres were readied to take men from the nineteen main dressing stations organised by the Divisional Field Ambulances. Thirty-nine Advanced Dressing Stations and nine Collecting Stations for walking wounded completed the medical provision behind the work of the Regimental Medical Officer, orderlies and stretcher bearers. So much for what might be called 'defensive preparedness' – while all this was being put into effect, miners were engaged in completing the preparations for underground explosions to destroy German positions. Mametz, Fricourt, La Boisselle and Beaumont Hamel were the chosen locations.

We must now deal with the infantry, men trained in the main from the Fourth Army Tactical Notes to advance in extended order with intervals of two to three paces between each man. A hundred or so paces behind such a line would come the next of successive waves of men likewise in extended order. Protected by the overwhelming effect of the bombardment which at timed intervals lifted for their progress, some men would carry into the advance an abundance of heavy, awkwardly-shaped equipment. The assaulting waves were not meant to hurry and, burdened as all were, they could not hurry, but there was to be, after all, no need for them to hurry! As has been made clear not all the assaulting battalions would follow this procedure.

The military character of the infantry battalions in the line for 1 July was diverse, a point which perhaps needs re-emphasis in view of the widely-held perception that the men were all from New Army units. In the northernmost sector facing Gommecourt were two Territorial divisions of General Sir Edmund Allenby's Third Army, the 46th North Midland and the 56th London. Among the units in these divisions there was a fair amount of active-service experience. The most northerly Fourth Army division was another Territorial unit, the 48th South Midland. No 1 July assault was planned for them but to their south was the 31st Division. These New Army men facing Serre had been locally recruited. They were authentic Pals: Hull Commercials, Hull Tradesmen, Hull Sportsmen and 't'others' in the 92nd Brigade; Leeds Pals, Bradford Pals (two battalions) and Durham Pals in the 93rd, and in the 94th Brigade, the Accrington Pals, Halifax Pals, two battalions of Barnsley Pals and the Sheffield City Battalion.

North of Beaumont Hamel was the Regular Army 4th Division with two Territorial Battalions attached to it, then the Gallipoli-famed 29th Division also of course Regular Army. Beaumont Hamel was on the 29th's left front and this Division with several of its battalions having added to their renown on the Peninsula, perhaps most notably, despite heavy losses, the Lancashire Fusiliers and Dublin Fusiliers, had the unusual feature of a Canadian unit in its 88th Brigade. This was the Newfoundland Regiment which had been attached to the division in the later stages of the Gallipoli Campaign and had remained with it for service in France.

The 36th Ulster Division had a special character by reason of its military trained and Protestant background as Ulster Volunteers. They had the task of advancing on both sides of the River Ancre. South of them, opposite Thiepval, was the 32nd Division, one of composite nature with two Regular battalions and New Army units of Pals drawn together by region, like the Lonsdales, by city, like the three Salford Pals Battalions, and by regional occupation, like the Newcastle Railways and Newcastle Commercials, and the three battalions of Glaswegians, the Commercials, the Tramways and the Boy's Brigade.

Opposite Ovillers was the 8th Division, two-thirds Regular and one-third New Army. South again to face La Boisselle, was the 34th New Army Division, entirely recruited locally – Edinburgh, Grimsby, Cambridge and two full Infantry Brigades of the Northumberland Fusiliers (Tyneside Scottish, Tyneside Irish). The 21st Division was mixed in character, Regular and New Army, but with the New Army battalions from Newcastle,

Richmond, Pontefract, Lincoln and Taunton. They were to attack north of Fricourt. To their south was the 50th Brigade from the 17th Division, all New Army, with three battalions to suffer disastrously in front of Fricourt, the 10th West Yorks, 7th East Yorks and 7th Green Howards.

The 7th Division had seven Regular battalions and six New Army, the latter including three battalions of Manchester Pals and one from Oldham. Mametz lay in front of them and to their right was the 18th Eastern Division, entirely New Army. This division was to attack on the left of Montauban which was to be assaulted by the 30th Division. This, the most southerly stationed British division, had its right flank boundary with the French Sixth Army. The 30th Division had four battalions of Liverpool Pals, four of Manchester Pals, a St Helens-recruited Pioneer battalion and four Regular battalions.

Units had undergone intensive training in tactical procedures of the offensive on ground taped out to represent the objectives for which they would strive. The men were fit, well-fed and tanned by the sun. They had enjoyed recreational opportunities for bathing, cricket, football and athletic sports. Morale was high, though of course tension increased as the hour approached. The team sports and sing-songs were a reflection of and a sustenant of the self-confident identity men felt in their units. The hard work in training is not to be minimised. A contemporary account by Rifleman C. M. Woods of the 1st Bn London Regiment has details of field days, lecture after lecture on machine-guns, the digging of a new forward trench, a stretcher-bearing and first aid course and several rehearsals for the attack. On 21 June his battalion moved out of the line at Hebuterne for baths at Halloy, pay and 'every possible privilege as this was to be our last rest before we attacked'.[18]

Tommy Easton, a Northumberland miner, wrote of the training with the 34th Division. 'Week after week we walked behind live barrages of shells from trench mortar batteries. When they increased their range we moved forward, always keeping at a safe distance and learned by these methods to follow a creeping barrage.'[19] When Easton's battalion, the 21st Northumberland Fusiliers, moved into the trenches opposite La Boisselle, a German trench raid proved an unnerving experience, some Fusiliers being captured. Easton recorded that it was generally recognised that by such means the enemy would be well-informed of the imminence of an attack and his battalion was temporarily moved out of the line.

Robin Money, who had served in France in 1914–15 with the Cameronians, was in 1916 attached as second-in-command of the 15th (Service) Battalion Durham Light Infantry. In a Field Message book diary, he wrote of the coming offensive: 'It appears that in about a week's time we shall be required to prance into the Hun trenches – well cheeroh and I hope the Huns will like it.' This Regular Army Officer had been away from the Front for some months and expressed concern as to whether his nerves were to be in as good order as was his general state of fitness. He was impressed by his new men, less by their officers, and as for the preparatory organisation for Z Day, a day which, in the event, was postponed, he thought that 'nothing seems to have been spared to make this show a success – nothing seems to have been overlooked'. Although he continued to express concern about his own readiness for battle and was puzzled by the low attendance at Communion after a good address by the Divisional Commander who 'in a manly straightforward way touched on the religious aspects of the war', he found the atmosphere at dinner in the Officers' Mess excellent with everyone very confident. He added: 'Not quite so confident as the CO's brother-in-law, Irwin in the Royals, who says that the cavalry's objective of the night of 1 July is Cambrai.'[20]

For the 4th Battalion Worcesters, a Regular unit, the training exercises had not always been successfully conducted. Though trenches had been marked out by furrows and flags, an attack had still lost direction when 'the Essex on our right cut right across and into us. It was our fault I may mention.' The training, noted this diarist, William Strang, was across acres and acres of cultivated land and 'we are doing very great damage to intensive cultivation'.[21] There is an interesting parallel of realism or apprehension between the men in Strang's Company, Strang himself and indeed Robin Money. It stands in some contrast to the sense of elation expressed in the letters and diaries of men with less front-line experience. Reference has been made to the keenness of the men of the London Rifle Brigade and H. G. R. Williams wrote that: 'All the preparations for the attack struck us as being very thorough. Everyone knew exactly where to go and what to do.'[22]

Together with the thoroughness of the planning, an important component of the confidence felt by many was in the seemingly irresistibly destructive weight of the bombardment. The way in which it communicated its power to the infantry is nicely captured by George Norrie, a subaltern newly-attached to the 6th Queen's Royal West Kent Regiment. On 29 June he wrote to his mother: 'Very hot stuff here and I am enjoying myself. Talk about "shell-out" this show beats it – I think I was made for it.'[23]

The bombardment was originally planned for a five-day period. Wire-cutting and registration of targets was to be followed by the systematic destruction of trenches and all fortified emplacements. Billets, communications, enemy artillery batteries – plans were meticulously drawn up not merely to neutralise all positions but for deception too. The bombardment was timed to accustom the Germans to a schedule during which they could be expected to remain under cover and then on the day of the attack, instead of the regular 80 minutes intensive bombardment with which each day commenced, there would be but 65 minutes before the barrage would lift from the German front line. The author of a recent history of the Royal Artillery considered Major General Birch's plan a 'masterpiece' but whatever may be the case about the plan and the inadequacy or defectiveness of the instrument to deliver it, the plan itself was to be variably interpreted by the Fourth Army Corps Commanders.[24]

Bad weather, which seriously interfered with the work of the RFC, resulted in a 48-hour postponement of Z Day which brought it to 1 July. The difficulties of aerial reporting were made clear in the log of RFC observer, Lieutenant T. L. W. Stallibrass, whose work was conducted from a Morane Saulnier. '27 June. Clouds at 800 ft. Tried to work our artillery for special trench bombardment, but it was impossible.' Since the 24th he had taken photographs and brought back information of much railway activity by Bapaume, new trenches and wire and a new enemy battery in action. He also recorded on one occasion that his wireless was 'dud', graphically described on the 26th, 'Gas attack going on. Gas going too high. S of Fricourt the gas was blowing over our own trenches' and also acknowledged a failure to observe shells from the 78th Siege Battery RGA, on the intended target.[25]

From the ground, too, observation by trench periscope from camouflaged vantage points was frequently made difficult by weather conditions and the smoke and dust of explosions. On occasion however, seemingly conclusive evidence was obtained. I. R. H. Probert, whose battery was firing upon targets in the vicinity of Mametz and who had been sufficiently critical to record 'some prematures and several short', nevertheless considered of Mametz village on 30 June 'there was not much left to bombard'.[26]

The 'Left Group Artillery Plan' in support of the 34th Division made clear the specific tasks to be undertaken.

The bombardment will be for five days known as U, V, W, X and Y. Assault to be delivered on Z Day. During the bombardment the Left Group's Task will be as follows:

1. Wire cutting in accordance with orders issued.
2. Preventing repairs at night to wire cut and to hostile defences and strong points broken down by Heavy Artillery during the day.
3. Searching Trenches and Approaches.
4. Intensive bombardment according to Corps Scheme to be issued later.

There are four pages of detail and yet these were only 'General Instructions'. In an additional Field Message Book instruction, marked 'secret' and found among the papers of Lieutenant A. Laporte Paine in the Field Artillery, anticipation or at least proper procedure, is made clear: 'At zero hour on Z Day horses will be harnessed up and wagons packed ready to move.' There were special instructions for each day and special instructions for each type of work. An examination of the sheaf of papers kept by this one young artillery officer of one artillery brigade, the 175th, would indicate the complex detail of the paperwork before a shell was fired but one small document will have to suffice here. 'Secret OC 175 Bde RFA. Herewith copies of: BM/SP/44 of 23 June 1916. Appendix V. Amendments No 1 to 34 Div Arty Time Table for Z Day. Amendments No 2 to 34 Div Arty Operation, Operation Order 10, First Phase 34 Div Arty Time Table. Please peruse and amend accordingly. 26 June 1916. Signed by the Lieutenant and Adjutant 175 Bde RFA.'[27]

By patrols in No Man's Land or small-scale raiding, some Intelligence was gained about the conditions of the German wire and about the strength in which the enemy front line was held but it was too varied even to the same sector as to give a conclusive picture. Where such a picture could be given about the wire in front of Gommecourt and Thiepval it was far from encouraging and Haig himself, on the night of 30 June, expressed serious concern that VIII Corps, which included the 29th Division, had not carried out a single successful raid into the positions they would be attacking at Beaumont Hamel. Strang of the 4th Worcesters had written interesting diary entries relating to this. On Thursday evening 22 June, he had led a wire-cutting patrol in No Man's Land. It 'went well, no hitch, and the men worked well'. On Tuesday 27 June, the Divisional Commander addressed the 4th Worcesters in their training area, praised them and said he was proud to have them in his division, the 29th. On that evening the Newfoundland Regiment had raided and 'found the trenches full of Huns. They slew a lot but lost heavily themselves. They raided the night before and turned tail … The Essex raid tomorrow night. They have a party out on the bombing ground now putting up wire for the raiding party to cut in practice tonight.' The Company Commander was there in charge and he seemed 'a very keen and well-informed officer'. On Thursday 29th, the night of the Essex raid, the diary relates that 'the Dublins raided last night. News of an HLI raid bringing in 46 prisoners. A record surely.'[28] As it happens, the HLI battalion to which reference was made was not in the 29th Division but perhaps we may here legitimately use hindsight concerning the strength of the German positions at Beaumont Hamel. These front-line positions were not captured until the last days of the battle, four and a half months later, so it seems reasonable to suggest that the poor record of VIII Corps in raiding was not, as Haig had stated, due to the fact that the staff 'had had no experience of the fighting in France'.[29] The VIII Corps Intelligence Summary No 95 for the period 25/26 June is unequivocal on raids. 'Raids attempted all along the Corps Front were unsuccessful, in some sectors owing to failure to cut the wire, and in others owing to intense machine gun and rifle fire.'[30] For those weighing up the chances for the infantry on Z Day more calmly than was encouraged by the exhilaration induced by the bombardment, such a report did not bode well.

Chapter 2

The First of July

The task set before the infantry of the Fourth Army was the capture of the Montauban, Pozières, Serre higher ground and then to secure positions linking Ginchy to Bapaume. While the Fourth Army went for the Montauban to Serre ridge, the Third Army was to attack Gommecourt and maintain an active posture on its more northerly front. Success in these objectives would enable a collaborative attack upon Bapaume and the Arras area. It was this stage which was to see General Gough's force, including his cavalry, driving northwards to exploit the breach which had been opened for him by the Fourth and Third Armies. Of course the timing of this stage was completely dependent on the successful achievement of the preliminary objectives.

For the Fourth Army, the detail held within the orders issued at every level is impressive. The Operation Order for the 23rd Battalion Northumberland Fusiliers provided paragraphs on Information, Objectives, Intention, Bombardment, Gas, Smoke, forming-up positions, alignment in the crossing of No Man's Land, Company Objectives, Procedure during the advance – 'The extreme importance of a resolute advance must be clearly impressed on all ranks and the advance must continue regardless of whether other units on our flanks are held up or delayed'. In the orders, there is a sub-heading on the wearing of a distinguishing mark in cloth and further sub-headings on iron rations, on water, on bombs, wire breakers, stretcher bearers and wounded – 'All ranks must be clearly warned that men are on no account to assist wounded'. There is a complete appendix on Signalling and Communications and further sub-headings on Advanced Brigade Headquarters, Sanitary – 'Latrines are to be constructed as soon as possible on reaching objective' – Prisoners, Brigade Dumps, Liaison Officers and Miscellaneous – 'Hand grenades are difficult to replenish; they must not be thrown indiscriminately'. It is to be noted that this being the 4th Battalion, Tyneside Scottish, 'Pipers will accompany their companies' but particular interest, in retrospect, is held by the information on 'Dress and Equipment'. In addition to his rifle and equipment, less pack, every man was to carry two extra bandoliers of small-arms ammunition, three Mills grenades, one iron ration and rations for the day of the assault. He would have his haversack and waterproof cape, four empty sandbags, two gas helmets and a pair of Spicer goggles against tear gas. Unless he were a bomber or a signaller, he would carry a pick or a shovel and then a full water bottle and a mess tin in his haversack. Some men would carry bombs in a special bucket or in a waistcoat carrier or they would have wire cutters.[1]

A soldier's 'fighting order' equipment would include his steel helmet and entrenching tool, a rolled ground sheet and water bottle. Apart from items to be kept in his haversack, like spare socks and a shaving kit, he would also have a field dressing. Allowing for variations, each infantryman was to carry about *66lbs* of equipment. The Official Historian recognised that such a weight made it 'difficult to get out of a trench, impossible to move much quicker than a slow walk, or to rise and lie down quickly'.[2] In the event, many thousands of men offering so bulky and slow-moving a target would crumple to the ground quickly enough and would not rise at all.

As the last hours of waiting were endured, there is evidence of a range of emotional preparation for what lay ahead. For many there was confidence and the sort of shared pent-up excitement that is felt by members of a good team facing an important sporting context, but within the heightened sense of fellowship, private apprehension swirled turbulently. For some it was a time for silent contemplation, for others, hollow jocularity. If opportunity were to allow, there was drink, an issue of rum; there was also prayer. Many wrote letters, a proportion of them being letters only to be sent in the event of death. It is sobering today to think of the self-control required to disguise apprehension before one's fellows, though each unit would have had its lugubrious prophets of doom upon whom there may have been divested in jest and in scorn, the anxieties of all and sundry. From countless letters and from other evidence, what sustained men was

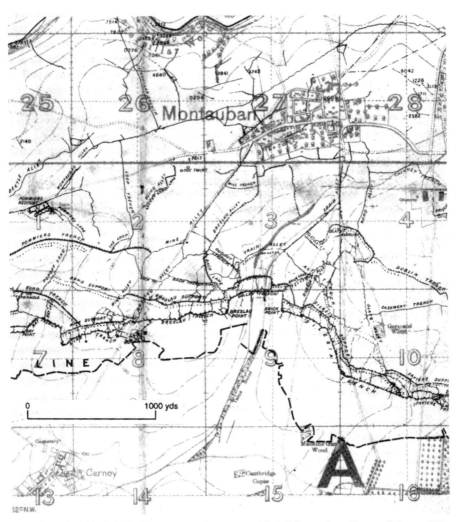

Map 2: MONTAUBAN: From a trench map entitled 'Montauban Parts of sheets 57D SE 57C SW 62D NE 62C NW Trenches Corrected to 2.6.16'. Scale 1:20,000 (50mm = 1,000m). From the map used by Lt E. W. Willmer 17th Bn The King's (Liverpool Regiment). (*E. W. Willmer, Liddle Collection*)

unit pride, close comradeship, belief in their cause and the necessity of avoiding the fate of being found wanting in the eyes of others. Expressions of love and gratitude to parents in these letters are touching and, among so many examples, the words of a subaltern in the 4th Battalion of the Gloucester Regiment seem selflessly noble. Having affirmed that the country's cause was a good one, deserving of his loyalty, and apportioning his wordly goods to his family with money for a children's hospital, he wrote: 'To you – Mother and Father – I owe all. The thought of you two and of my brothers will inspire me to the end.'[3] Fate decreed that this young officer's letter was soon to be posted for him.

On the extreme right of the British line, battalions of the 18th and 30th Divisions faced the enemy positions in front of Montauban. In heavy artillery the Germans were strikingly outmatched here, so much so that artillery opposition to the infantry advance was virtually snuffed out. Additionally the British had raised ground for observation of the enemy positions which greatly assisted the accuracy of artillery registration. The dividend for this lay in the most efficient wire-clearance shelling along the whole of the British battle front and the two divisions, though they each suffered more than 3,000 casualties, took all their objectives on the ridge and Montauban village itself. This remarkable achievement was paralleled by the French on their right. With ingenuity and the digging or carrying capacity of many men, two large flamethrowers had been installed below ground to assist the assault on the 18th Divisional front. The oil would be forced by high-pressure gas along pipes laid in mine galleries which lacked only the breaking of the surface crust before emerging into No Man's Land only 60 yards from the enemy front line. The pressure and a steel cutter would break the crust. On several occasions before 1 July one or both tunnels had been blown in by the shelling of No Man's Land but they had been repaired and at Zero Hour the two nozzles appeared, rising to a height of about two to three feet. 'The automatic lighters functioned perfectly and with a roar the streams of oil became ignited and shot forward towards the enemy, being traversed slowly from side to side, while dense clouds of black smoke, flecked with flame, rose a hundred feet into the air. No living thing could possibly survive under this visitation.'[4] The flanks of the attack of the 8th Battalion Norfolks, (18th Division) made uneven progress and the battalion lost eleven of its twenty-two officers and 292 other ranks as casualties. Nevertheless an unscathed officer, Eric Miall-Smith, wrote home on 4 July of 'a glorious victory'. Visibility had been obscured by the smoke of the explosions but:

> The first thing I remember was seeing six Germans in a mine crater, about 15 yards across, firing their rifles like mad at us. I approached with some of my platoon by heaps of blown-up earth and threw two bombs into the crater. One German escaped further back and was killed by some others, my bombs killed three and the rest of the men dealt with the others. My company got to their objective, but were held up by a German strongpoint, where we fought for about three and a half hours before we took it, and collared over 100 prisoners in it … I know I accounted for four Germans, so I have done my bit. I am glad it is over, and I am quite sound. I am not shaken and my nerves are all right so long as we are given a rest.

In the same letter, the writer offered a glimpse of the heat of battle as experienced in his vicinity.

> I saw parties of Germans during the attack fire on our fellows until they were within a few yards of them; then, as soon as they found out that there was no hope for them they threw down their arms and rushed forward to shake our men by the hands. Most of them got their desserts and were not taken prisoners. Some of the wounded Germans were shooting men in the back after they had been dressed by them. They are swine – take it from me – I saw these things happen with my own eyes.[5]

D. J. Capper was to record many years after the event a less searing image of prisoners taken at Montauban. He remembered those he saw as thoroughly demoralised, one beseeching that he should be spared as he clutched at Capper's knees fluttering a photograph of wife and children before him. 'I remember feeling inward amusement at adopting a "tough guy" approach towards so comparatively harmless and frightened an individual when I was myself having to make a great effort at disguising my own "windiness".'[6]

As has been stated, there were special reasons helping to account for infantry success on the 30th Divisional front, but nevertheless the achievement at Montauban of the 89th Brigade, in which there were three battalions of Liverpool Pals, the Kings (Liverpool) Regiment, was uplifting on a day of desperate, costly, disappointment. The story of the Liverpool Pals on this day is a special feature of a book on the Pals by Graham Maddocks. It is a story worth telling. The 17th Battalion, for example, lost fewer than twenty soldiers in the gaining and consolidation of its objective, an uniquely economic success for 1 July. How the experience of this battalion contrasts with others is made clear in 'matter of fact' recollections by one of the officers, E. W. Willmer.

> On the first day I was in the support line and so got a marvellous view of all that happened. It was a lovely sunny morning and promptly at 7.30 our barrage lifted from the German front line to their support line and waves of British troops left the trenches and walked out into No Man's Land with bayonets fixed and rifles at the carry. There was no hurry and very little resistance. Our casualties were small and we gained our objectives without trouble and dug in at our new position.[7]

There was sterner resistance in the vicinity. Men of the 2nd Battalion Royal Scots Fusiliers were in the second wave and moved off at 8.30 a.m. Their Medical Officer, Captain G. D. Fairley, was certainly busy before he himself was wounded. All this is recorded in his remarkable diary. He had treated wounded in British trenches, had intercepted more to record their cases as he crossed between support and forward positions and then as he moved on from the British front line there was heavy shelling close by.

> A number of dead and wounded were lying around, some in the barbed wire entanglements. Up the slope the German fire trench lay less than a hundred yards away. I decided to get in the wounded before further advance. While waiting in the open for the stretcher squad a shell burst six feet away and wounded me in the right arm as well as Private Alcock one of the stretcher bearers who was near me. The time was 10 a.m. I got back to a dug-out in the Fleche [a point where the British front

line jutted out] fainted twice and recovered gradually. My wound was dressed.

Fairley resumed his duties, treating a stream of wounded filtering back to the Fleche dug-outs. German wounded were treated as well. 'They muttered Kamerad and something else frequently.' Later he went back to a Collecting Post where two captured German medical officers were in assistance. He returned to the British front line area, collected and treated more wounded while they were all under heavy shelling, and then in the evening, with stretcher bearers, crossed over into the captured German trench system. Though he saw many unexploded shells, the trenches were still almost 'flattened' and with the awful litter of dead and dying. He found the Royal Scots' new HQ about 100 yards short of Montauban village. Having located it he returned down Valley Trench and established an Aid Post under Lance Corporal Miles, a Medical Orderly. There was more heavy shelling and Fairley passed new craters 'smoking with lyddite. We came upon a case of "shell-shock". An emotionally distraught soldier was going back, cowering, cringing and gabbering with fright at the shell fire.' A main Aid Post was established before he re-crossed No Man's Land and learned that his relief, Lieutenant Potter, had gone up. He walked back alone south-westwards through Billon Wood to Billon Farm where there was an Advanced Dressing Station and from here at 1.30 a.m. on 2 July he was taken by motor ambulance back to a dressing station off the Bray-Corbie Road.[8] The diary helpfully records this wounded Medical Officer's progress 'down the line': Corbie by the afternoon of 2 July – Amiens in the evening (South Midland Casualty Clearing Station). 6 July by motor ambulance to an Ambulance Train bound for Camiers (No 20 General Hospital). 9 July Motor ambulance to Etaples. Ambulance train thence via Abbeville and Rouen. 10 July Le Havre and Hospital Ship (*Asturias*). 11 July Southampton. Train to London (Waterloo) motor car convoy to No 1 General Hospital (Camberwell). Fairley's experience at Montauban is set here to provide a proper balance against that recalled by Willmer but in general terms the further north the battlefront is described, the more striking the contrast with the relatively 'economic' success of the 30th Division.

Fricourt and Mametz lay behind the positions attacked by the 21st and 7th Divisions respectively and there were military and topographical factors which made the enemy front-line positions particularly hard nuts to crack. Here the two villages had been turned into fortresses, with the intervening trenches developed in depth in every sense. The communication trenches which led through intermediate lines to the front line were far too numerous all to be destroyed in the bombardment and though the shelling did much to diminish artillery opposition it had not destroyed the well-sited machine-gun nests. The estimated strength of Fricourt village itself led to its removal as an initial objective and an attempt to outflank it until such time as it was judged safe to assault it frontally. The explosion of mines at several points, especially under the Tambour Salient in front of Fricourt village, was part of the scheme to deceive the Germans about plans here. The explosions under the Tambour Salient were also designed to throw up mounds of earth which would block enfilade fire being directed from this strongpoint onto the attack on its southern flank. The artillery support for the two infantry divisions concerned was designed quite specifically to place a covering curtain of destruction in front of the troops as they advanced – the 18-pounder field guns having to increase their range at the rate of 50 yards a minute. It was certainly a window on the future for the 'creeping barrage' but it was at this stage asking a great deal of men, guns and ammunition. In some respects too, inventiveness was hampered by misunderstanding at senior level. It seems that some Divisional Commanders, in their dislike of having gas stored in cylinders in their forward positions, wanted it released and rid of at an earlier stage than when it was likely to be most effective, that is, immediately before the attack.

During the planning of the 9th Battalion the Devonshire Regiment's part in the 7th Division attack upon Mametz village, 'Captain D. L. Martin, who commanded A Company and was an artist by profession, had made a most wonderful and accurate plasticine model to assist in showing his men what lay before them.'[9] The danger spot upon which Martin's model focused attention was Mansel Copse. A German machine-gun, 800 yards from the copse, caught Martin and his company there with devastating results. Another company in the battalion (D Company) was also badly hit in following up to support the remnants from the initial attack. With so high a percentage of officer casualties, leadership devolved upon NCOs and, as the Regimental History makes clear, they were not found wanting.

The Division was to take its first objective of Mametz village but had had to overcome stern opposition. The advance of the 9th Devons had been completely covered by enemy enfilade fire and some idea of the psychological impact on survivors or those who had missed the attack for one reason or another can be gathered from the diary of an officer, J. D. Upcott, who returned to his battalion on 10 July after attendance at an Army Instruction School at Flexicourt. The lorry in which he was travelling drew up at Ribecourt.

> I saw the Padre and jumped out. His news was ghastly – everyone I care for gone: all four officers of my company killed: dear Harold died most splendidly before the German lines. He was shot through the stomach and Lawrence killed behind him by the same shot. Iscariot was shot through the heart below Mansel Copse and all his staff killed round him; Smiler killed about the same place, getting his bombs up. No single officer got through untouched. The men did grandly – going on without officers and reaching all objectives. They got Mametz about four o'clock. They were beyond all praise … I think everybody is looking forward tremendously to the time when we shall have another go at them.[10]

It is worth remarking that Lance Corporal Elmer of this battalion who actually experienced the attack, had indeed expressed a steely readiness to face battle again 'if needed'.[11]

Responsibility for the advance north of Fricourt and for a readiness to attack Fricourt itself when the moment was judged right, fell to the 21st Division. The 50th Infantry Brigade from the 17th Northern Division was attached to the 21st Division for the purpose of this attack and three of the battalions, all New Army, the 10th West Yorks recruited from York, the 7th East Yorks from Beverley and the 7th Green Howards from Richmond were to participate in a wholly disastrous unfolding of tragedy upon tragedy in this sector.

The third and fourth waves of West Yorks crossing No Man's Land to establish a defensive flank upon Fricourt were almost completely destroyed by the machine-gunners who had emerged safely from both the mine and

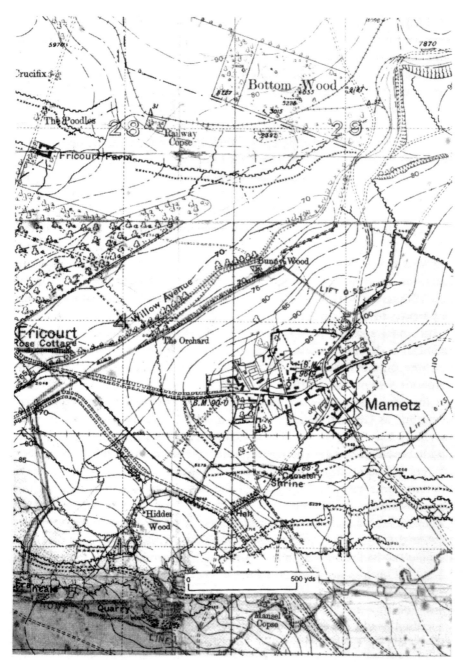

Map 3: MAMETZ: From the trench map entitled 'France sheet 57D SE 4'. Scale 1:10,000 (approximately 6in to a mile). Ordnance Survey 1916. Trenches corrected to 27.4.16, minor corrections to detail made 5.5.16. From the map used by 2nd Lt K. S. Mason (MGC). (*K. S. Mason, Liddle Collection*)

the shelling at the Tambour Salient. Later in the morning, the leading companies which had got into their first objective but were now unsupported were cut off and overcome as German defence was co-ordinated against them. There were survivors, like Philip Howe, whose extraordinary account appears in Martin Middlebrook's *The First Day on the Somme*,[12] but with a total of twenty-two officers and 688 other rank casualties, the battalion had ceased to exist. The 7th East Yorks with the 7th Green Howards, less one of its companies which had mistakenly been led into attack at 7.45 a.m. by the Company Commander, Major R. E. D. Kent, and been destroyed, were called upon to restore the calamitous state of affairs in front of Fricourt at 2.30 p.m. 50th Brigade HQ had represented to Divisional Command that this frontal attack would be useless until the 10th West Yorks' flank defence objective had been secured but the orders to attack were received. The Green Howards were first to enter No Man's Land opposite what the Official Historian has described as the 'strongest part of the Fricourt defences between Wing Corner and the German Tambour, still occupied in force'. The wire had few gaps and they were narrow. 'Whole lines fell in the first fifty yards and within three minutes the battalion lost fifteen officers and three hundred and thirty-six other ranks.'[13]

The East Yorks' War Diary records complete costly failure. Written orders were received at 1.45 p.m. and at 2.33 p.m.; 'C and D Companies advanced over the parapet to attack towards Red Cottage but owing to heavy casualties from machine-gun fire it was found impossible to reach enemy front line and B Company did not advance beyond our front line.' At 3.15 p.m. the following was wired to Brigade HQ: 'Have had probably 150 casualties out of first six platoons going over. West Yorks appear all to have come back. Think you can safely shell German front trench … one cause of failure was the short notice. Major King had only just time to get to front line by Zero and I had not then reached the Reserve Company. There was only a ladder here and there so men started out in file. The whole German trench opposite us appeared to be occupied by the enemy.'[14]

A similarly sad fate attended the efforts of the 63rd Brigade on the left of the 50th. Still further to the left, the advance of the 9th and 10th Kings Own Yorkshire Light Infantry was supported by the 15th Battalion Durham Light Infantry. R. C. Money, Second-in-Command of the DLI, recorded the awkward narrowness of the trenches for movement:

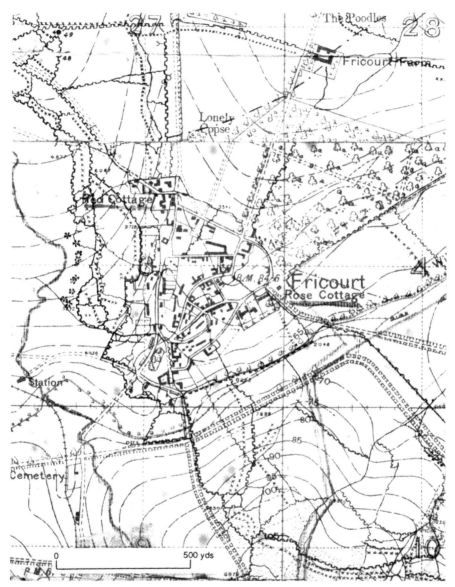

Map 4: FRICOURT: From the trench map entitled 'France Sheet 57D SE 4'. Scale 1:10,000 (approximately 6in to a mile). Ordnance Survey 1916. Trenches corrected to 27.4.16, minor corrections to detail made 5.5.16. On the morning of 1 July, this map was used by 2nd Lt K. S. Mason (MGC) in command of a machine-gun section of four guns. At 7.30 a.m. the guns opened fire on the German front line in the Fricourt sector where there was intended to be no frontal attack. Thirty minutes later, the range was to be lifted to interfere with the movement of German reinforcements coming up between Red Cottage and Rose Cottage. Evidently this fire did not materially minimise the fate of the three Yorkshire battalions attacking Fricourt. (*K. S. Mason, Liddle Collection*)

Yet the men got out somehow, and all things considered into very decent order – and on we went – the Regiment very well – there were a lot of shells going about, a lot of bullets too – it was slightly uphill and we arrived at the German trench, perhaps 300 yards away, absolutely done to the world. It is a marvel how the men got all the stuff they were expected to carry along with them. It was not much use trying to go over the top. Huns had got together in twos and threes with machine guns and had to be bombed out. Our casualties were heavy as the Germans fought to the last despite the fact that their trenches had turned into a mere succession of mine and shell craters. Doubtless they had sheltered in their dug-outs and turned out as soon as the barrage had lifted. The Colonel, Bleadon and myself had soon lost touch with the Regiment and worked our way down Lozenge Alley, hoping to get to the remains of the battalion at Sunken Road. As we were going along a shell apparently from a Stokes Gun exploded near us and put a piece into my left wrist which was rather painful and cut the Colonel's face. However, Bleadon tied me up and we went on. From one or two dug-outs shots were fired at us but a No 5 Mills grenade, put down with the occupants, put a stop to that sort of thing. Then we came to a place where a machine gun was making it very lively by getting everyone who went from one shell hole to another. We loosed off rifle grenades at him and got by but he was not put out of action and was making one end of Sunken Road pretty bad when we got there. Here we found a lot of men of different battalions but very few officers – these men seemed content to sit down and rest and the NCOs were not enterprising which contrasts unfavourably with the Huns' practice.[15]

In summary and allowing for attempts later made to consolidate or improve earlier gains, progress had been made on both flanks of the Fricourt-Mametz frontage attacked, particularly on the right with the taking of Mametz village and its environs but in the centre there had been no real gain whatsoever and the endeavour had been fearfully costly.

To the north were the tasks of the 34th Division – first a wider No Man's Land, then the trough and slopes of Sausage Valley and finally as the distance between the intervening lines narrowed, the village of La Boisselle before

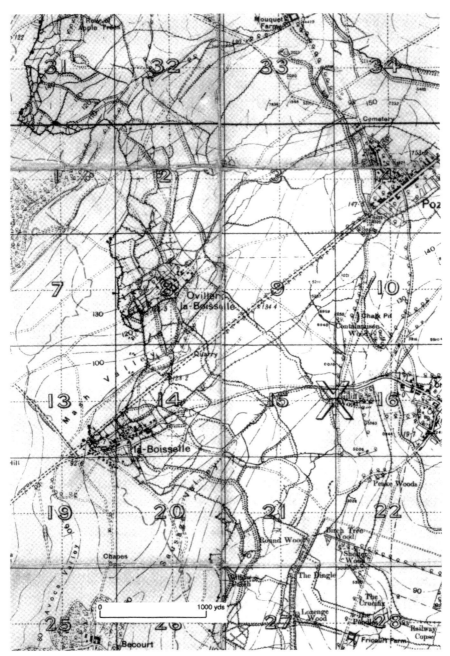

Map 5: OVILLERS LA BOISSELLE (AND POZIERES): 'France sheet 57D SE Edition 2B'. Scale 1:20,000 (approximately 3½in to 2,000 yds). Ordnance Survey 1916. Trenches corrected to 28.4.16. (*C. L. Paul, Liddle Collection*)

No Man's Land widened again at Mash Valley. North of Mash Valley was the village of Ovillers La Boisselle, an objective for the 8th Division. Menacingly dominating and outflanking any British forward movement were spurs from the main ridge behind the German positions. These spurs shouldered their way into the enemy lines offering the Germans elevations from which to command Sausage and Mash Valleys. However, the Germans had more than just a topographical advantage: they had constructed exceptional strongpoints of which La Boisselle village was but one and there were six lines of trenches to take, over a depth of approximately two miles.

Two great mines were to destroy the frontal shoulders of the La Boisselle village fortress but its forward face was to be bypassed in the first assault. It was anticipated that it would be so flattened in the main bombardment and by supplementary trench mortaring, that small parties of bombers, supported by Lewis and Stokes teams moving into the flanks of the village, would deal with any survivors with fight left in them. Such was not to be the case. The bombardment was ineffectual against the deep dug-outs. Furthermore the Germans were ready, having picked up a telephoned British order indicating an imminent attack.

As the first and succeeding lines of infantry moved out from their positions in front of Ovillers La Boisselle, front line or in support, they were, in the words of an artillery liaison officer attached to the 23rd Infantry Brigade (8th Division), knocked down 'like lines of tin soldiers swept over with a stick'.[16] All this was observed from the air by T. L. W. Stallibrass, whose log stated that:

As we neared the lines an immense cloud of smoke and dust was hanging over La Boisselle – this being the result of the large mine exploded by British which partly destroyed Hun front line and formed an enormous crater … At 7.30 a.m. the artillery ceased firing on the Hun front line and our infantry got out of the trenches on a front from Montauban to La Boisselle on the XV Corps front and from La Boisselle to Thiepval on III Corps front. They could be plainly seen crossing 'Nomansland' and falling down under heavy machine-gun fire. The noise even from the air was intense.[17]

Pipers of each company of the battalions of the Tyneside Scottish to make for La Boisselle itself, just to the south of its sister village, clambered up the ladders, or by whatever other means, over the parapet to lead the men into the exposure of infantry attack. The book, *Tyneside Scottish*, provides unforgettable, inspiring but horrifying images of the courageous leadership of these men as viewed by others and in one case by the contemporary letter of a Piper who survived. Three of the accounts are selected here:

- I saw the Piper jump out of the trench and march straight over No Man's Land towards the German lines. The tremendous rattle of machine gun and rifle fire, which the enemy at once opened on us and completely drowned the sound of his pipes. But it was obvious he was playing as though he would burst the bag and just faintly through the din we heard the mighty shout his comrades gave as they swarmed after him. How he escaped death I can't understand for the ground was literally ploughed up by the hail of bullets. But he seemed to bear a charmed life and the last glimpse I had of him, as we too dashed out, showed him still marching erect, playing furiously, and quite regardless of the flying bullets and the men dropping all around him.
- I never heard the pipes but I did see poor 'Aggie' Fife [Lance Corporal Piper, Garnet Wolsley Fyfe]. He was riddled with bullets, writhing and screaming.
- The only thing the matter with me is I have a finger blown off. The only thing disabled is the pipes. I got them blown away when I was playing the charge.[18]

A pathetic vestige of evidence of what had happened to one man symbolic of many, lies in the letter of a Corporal Booth of A Company, 8th York and Lancasters. He was playing his part in giving evidence to establish the fate of a newly-arrived officer.

I saw Lieutenant Goodwin go over the top near La Boisselle on the morning of 1 July – exact time 28 minutes past 7. He advanced towards the German lines – was shot and fell on the barbed wire. He was a signalling officer. He had not been with us very long. He came to us as a

> Draft Officer: he seemed quite fearless in the attack. I went over the top at the same time, was slightly wounded and lay in the open for about 12 hours. Lieutenant Goodwin was still on the wire when I got away.[19]

The 8th Battalion York and Lancasters had in fact been involved north of La Boisselle as part of the 8th Division's endeavour which had led to some penetration on either side of the village of Ovillers La Boisselle but no consolidated gains at all on that day. The 34th Division took and held some ground to the south of La Boisselle and to the south of Sausage Valley but again at a heavy price. Tyneside Irish and Tyneside Scottish battalions of the Northumberland Fusiliers with a Northumberland Fusiliers Pioneer battalion formed two of the brigades of the 34th Division. Tommy Easton of the 21st Northumberland Fusiliers recalled being reassured in the battalion's assembly positions by the calm demeanour of his officers during the last minutes of the bombardment, talking quite casually with the artillery forward observation officer, who was in fact describing the nature of the shells by the colour of the smoke. The earth under their feet had shaken with the explosion of the mine, then the whistles had blown and they clambered out.

> Keeping in line and extended order men began to fall one by one. Our officer said we were alright, all the machine guns were firing over our heads. This was so until we passed our own front line and started to cross No Man's Land, then the machine guns began the slaughter. Men fell on every side screaming with the severity of their wounds. Those who were unwounded dare not attend to them, we must press on regardless. Hundreds lay on the German barbed wire which was not all destroyed and their bodies formed a bridge for others to pass over and into the German front line.

The few Germans remaining in this position were bombed out of action and the Fusiliers then attempted to prepare some form of parapet to the rear of the trench. Easton describes the means by which supplies and a telephone cable were brought up through a small sap-head which had been blown not many yards from the German front line. He was a signaller and they soon fixed up a telephone link to Brigade HQ from the bottom of the stairs of a dug-out. The dug-out was also serving as a collection point for severely wounded men who had, by one means or another, been brought into cover there. Here too were the stretcher bearers, all, according to Easton, wounded themselves: 'All patiently awaiting the help that never came, for many of them just died, for nothing much could be done for them until darkness set in.'[20]

The responsibility and the price of regimental officer leadership in battle could hardly be better illustrated than in Private Easton's own brigade, the 102nd. The four Commanding Officers were killed, two of the four second-in-command officers were killed, the others wounded, two of the four adjutants killed, the others wounded. In the 103rd Brigade, fifteen of the sixteen company commanders were casualties. For their inconsiderable gains on the flanks, the 8th and 34th Divisions had suffered over 11,000 casualties. Wilfred Owen's poetic analogy of cattle being driven to slaughter may have cruel substance in terms of shuffling steps towards death but the men were led, not driven, and leaders and led shared the same fate.

North of Ovillers, the fortified village of Thiepval was the main strongpoint as an obstacle to the 32nd Division. On higher ground, sloping down to the Ancre which here ran north/south behind the British lines, Thiepval was flanked to the north by the Schwaben Redoubt and then on the river at St Pierre Divion and to the south, by the major defence construction of the Leipzig Salient. Enfilade fire upon any approach was assured by the siting of the German line and there was more than adequate strength in depth. Thiepval was a key dominant location.

The attack on the right was delivered by the 32nd Division across the Ancre; to the north it was to be by the 36th Division. From the text of the War Diary of the 16th Northumberland Fusiliers (32nd Division) awful images emerge. 'The enemy stood upon their parapet and waved to our men to come on and picked them off with rifle fire.' Subsequent waves of men were cut down too and the official account continues 'The men of the attacking companies moved forward like one man … Not a man wavered and after nightfall we found, in several places, straight lines of ten or twelve dead or badly wounded as if the Platoons had just been dressed for parade.'[21]

On the right of the Northumberland Fusiliers, the 17th Highland Light Infantry had stolen some initiative from the defenders of the Leipzig Salient

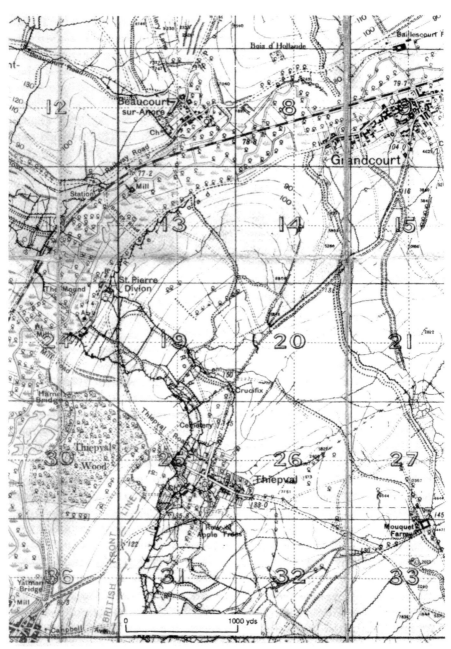

Map 6: THIEPVAL: From the trench map entitled 'France sheet 57D SE Edition 2B'. Scale 1:20,000 (approximately 3½in to 2,000 yds). Ordnance Survey 1916. Trenches corrected to 28.4.16. (*C. I. Paul, Liddle Collection*)

by moving out of their trenches and working their way forward seven minutes before the barrage lifted. The front of the redoubt was taken but all further prospect of progress was nullified by enfilade fire from the 'Wonder Work' strongpoint. The 36th Ulster Division had penetrated a good deal further on a narrow frontage and had captured the Schwaben Redoubt. Here too, the leading companies had left their trenches early and crept towards the German positions which were still being pounded by Stokes Mortars as was the wire by 2in mortars and a huge 9in mortar. Assisted by this, their training, discipline and fervour, the Ulstermen took three lines of trenches but on their flank the fortified position at St Pierre Divion could not be taken and from here machine-guns began to take their toll.

Lance Corporal Quinn of the 10th Royal Irish Rifles was in the first wave, in charge of a bombing section. Six of them, held up actually within the German barbed wire, took refuge in a shell hole. They were returning enfilade fire when five of them were hit and one showed that his nerves had gone. Quinn was hit twice in the wrist; three of the men were killed. The three survivors cowered in the shell hole till night fell and then attempted to crawl back to their jumping-off trench. Memories of intense pain in the crawl with a broken arm ironically include those of the nettles encountered.[22] E. J. Brownlee also had graphic recall of his experience held up at St Pierre Divion. 'I got to the German wire when I got hit in the jaw, breaking it at the joint passing through my tongue and coming out at the left of the Adam's apple. I also had one through my left arm above the elbow. I lay from 7.30 to noon with terrible loss of blood and bothered by flies.'[23]

Where the advance was successful, it could not be controlled. It ran into the British bombardment, had to wait, and in so doing, gave the German defenders of this, the second objective, time to man their parapet. Despite this, some groups of men succeeded in bursting into their objective. Here, of course unsupported, disconnected from even their several points of success, they were critically vulnerable. It is possible that the situation could have been saved and the Ulster success consolidated if the Corps Commander were to have accepted the offer of the Commander of the 49th Division in reserve to bring his men through to support the breach but the Corps Commander judged that the situation was more needful of aid on his right and the opportunity was gone.

It is in the nature of things that a unit in reserve may have its sub-units deployed separately as occasion warranted but the calls upon brigades and battalions of the 49th Division during 1 July seem to have resulted in no effective support anywhere. This, and the continued concentration of frontal assault on Thiepval village while leaving the Ulster Division unsupported, were surely errors at Corps command level. Due allowance for the problems of the gathering and transmission of accurate information to Headquarters may be made but the lack of any good result from all that the Ulstermen had grasped and momentarily held, is more than a sad story.

From the 49th Division, a senior officer in the 4th Battalion York and Lancaster, Douglas Branson, wrote:

> We spent the first day till 2.30 p.m. in assembly trenches in a wood receiving all sorts of news and hoping for the best. In the evening we were told to hold a section of the old front line and were assured (quite erroneously) that the British were holding a line a mile and a half in front. We did not know the position, it was very dark and there was considerable shelling and the Companies found it very difficult to find their way to a position which could only be pointed out to them on the map. Meanwhile the Division supposed to be well in front was rapidly running back chiefly through lack of support from behind.[24]

The Schwaben Redoubt was conceded in the late evening when the Ulstermen were attacked yet again, this time from three sides. An organised withdrawal was carried out and an epic endeavour had ended in failure. For all that had been essayed by the two divisions, 36th and 32nd, there remained but the gain of the Leipzig Salient and a stretch of about 1,000 yards of the German front line on the left of Thiepval.

North of the Ancre, a series of ridges and valleys, the commanding positions of which were all held by the Germans, faced the 29th, 4th and 31st Divisions. In the southern sector, the fortified village of Beaumont Hamel was fronted by a well-sited trench system where No Man's Land was about 500 yards in width. The intervening distance narrowed northwards, through the 4th Division front until another fortified village set further back from the front line, Serre, which was the objective of the 31st Division.

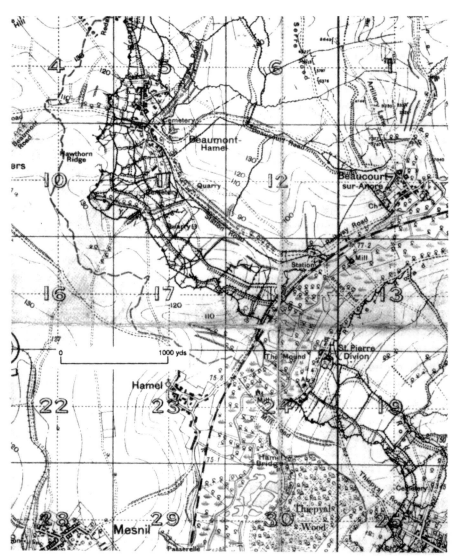

Map 7: BEAUMONT HAMEL (AND BEAUCOURT): From the trench map entitled 'France sheet 57D SE Edition 2B\'. Scale 1:20,000 (approximately 3½in to 2,000 yds). Ordnance Survey 1916. Trenches corrected to 28.4.16. (*C. L. Paul, Liddle Collection*)

The valley across which the 29th Division would have to approach Beaumont Hamel was completely exposed to this objective and indeed to the ridge to the rear. It was an unenviable task. There was not the sheer flatness of ground to cross as at Suvla Bay, Gallipoli, for the IX Corps in

August 1915 but, as in the Aegean instance when speed was essential and was not achieved, here again speed of crossing No Man's Land in this amphitheatre was not a factor in the planning – the key would lie in the bombardment doing its work conclusively. The key may not have been the wrong one but it did not turn the tumblers effectively and there were bars to the door too.

On the whole VIII Corps' front, planning required the infantry to advance at a rate of 50 yards a minute behind a creeping artillery barrage. On the 29th Division front, tunnels forward were dug to be opened out as advanced Stokes Mortar emplacements and a huge mine had been prepared under the German strongpoint known to the British as Hawthorn Redoubt. There had been much Senior Command debate on the optimum time for the firing of this mine. The surprise factor together with the time it would take British troops to reach and occupy the forward lip of the crater clearly had a relationship to the timing of the lifting of the bombardment from the redoubt. The problem was not satisfactorily answered. The firing of the mine at 7.20 a.m. and a brief hurricane bombardment of the German front line simply alerted the defenders to the imminence of an attack which from numerous indicators was expected. There were dire results from the readiness of the Germans who immediately shelled and machine-gunned the British front and support positions when the 29th Division was moving into place for Zero Hour. Of course the German machine-gunners were freed from the Allied bombardment which had lifted for the occupation of the crater and additional batteries, unregistered by the British, brought down fearfully effective shelling on the 29th assembly areas. Furthermore, the nature of the ground hid the German wire from observation. From a feature which became infamous, Y Ravine, enfilade machine-gun fire could be directed unhindered upon the flank of the battalions as they made their burdened way under shelling and across No Man's Land. Many men had not even got through the narrow gaps in their own wire. They were caught as they naturally bunched at the points of emergence and made unmissable targets.

The concatenation of all these circumstances was visited most terribly upon the 1st Battalion Newfoundland Regiment. A total of 710 casualties was suffered in the advance from support positions over the top towards the British front line, those men still unscathed getting through the wire there and a small number actually reaching the German front line before they too disappeared into history. One who did survive, Frank Moakler, got no further than a wall of bodies in the gap in the British wire ahead of the most forward trench. He had been wounded but did not realise it until he felt the sticky wetness of his tunic. In the fever of excitement and intense noise of machine-gun and shelling, he had simply put his head down to 'avoid' the bullets and trusted in his steel helmet.[25]

The special preparations indicative of a huge undertaking, together with the heavy German shelling, had combined to make men of the 1st Border Regiment, Regular soldiers though they were, and with Gallipoli experience, 'excited and nervous', A. T. Fraser recalled. He himself had survived the torpedoing of the troopship *Royal Edward* in the Mediterranean in August 1915 and with his own 19th birthday just reached in June 1916 he was unusual in having the three stripes of a sergeant. 'In Acheux wood we were kitted out with new clothing, uniform and boots and fed on beef and chicken and puddings and beer so we knew this must be the prelude to the battle.' In the early hours of 1 July his platoon had had 'ample rum' and a dixie of tea. As they actually waited to go over the top, each platoon was brought a wooden step-ladder. Quite specifically they had been ordered to walk, not run. 'The officer and I agreed on the place where our step-ladder should be, and I remember thinking that he had to go up first and face whatever was coming and then I had to see the platoon up the ladder and then go up myself. I think I prayed for him.'

The mine exploded, the whistles blew, the officer led his men off into machine-gun fire. Seven of the twenty-seven-strong platoon were hit getting out of the trench. 'I just had to lay them on the fire-step clearing the ladder for the next man to go up.' Out in No Man's Land, so fierce was the fire that an order was heard to lie down. During this brief pause, perhaps a minute, 'our 2nd-in-command Major Meiklejohn never lay down, he walked to and fro in front of us fretting at the delay and slapping his breeches with his cane.' Fraser's officer had already been hit and the Sergeant himself would be hit when they moved.[26]

A similarly sad story of heavy losses occurred on the 4th Division front but sectors of the enemy front line were penetrated. The lack of success on the flanks of this penetration, the efficient German tactical response and the difficulty of bringing up troops to support and consolidate the incursions, resulted in the gains having to be conceded.

Men of the 1st Battalion Royal Irish Fusiliers were among those troops to be used in support of the initial assault. From their assembly trenches alongside a sunken road, they were shielded from enemy observation. The first indication to them of what was happening ahead was encouraging: it was a file of prisoners being escorted back by a sergeant. The keen-eyed adjutant of the Royal Irish, Captain Carden Roe, noticed that the sergeant was wearing the ribbon of the Victoria Cross. As officers and men waited tensely for further evidence of progress, three white lights shot into the sky on their right, then more, then several sets. It seemed to be the success indicator the officers knew would mark the capture of the first objectives.

As their excitement rose, Carden Roe was called to a field telephone in a dug-out and hopes were dashed by the voice of the 10th Brigade Major urgently halting any forward movement because the signals were single rockets all along the line indicating that the assault battalions were held up. As the two leading companies had already set off in diamond formation for the British front line it was too late to halt them. The rest of the battalion awaited further orders. At about 4 p.m., D Company was sent forward to support the stand of a party of officers and men, principally Seaforth Highlanders, lodged in the German defence work known as the Quadrilateral. The remaining companies chafed at their hours of inactivity though Carden Roe pointed out in his account 'few of us desire unnecessarily to thrust our heads into the jaws of danger'. He himself was given no choice in this matter. He was ordered to Brigade Headquarters and here the Brigadier instructed him to make his way up to the Quadrilateral to cancel messages already despatched by runner to the effect that the officer in command there, Lieutenant-Colonel Hopkinson, was to be supported in his increasingly besieged position.

Instead, Hopkinson was ordered by Divisional Command to withdraw after nightfall. Carden Roe reached the sunken road and from here 'no other course being open to me, I ran down it towards the Quadrilateral'. At first it seemed as if the German position was empty but he met two khaki-clad figures carrying grenades and they led him to Hopkinson's command post. Despite a maelstrom of explosions of shells, trench mortars, grenades and machine-gun fire, the beleaguered officers and men seemed in high spirits, full of what they had achieved and of the souvenirs acquired. Withdrawal seemed a matter to be viewed with some regret. Carden Roe got lost on his return journey, familiar trenches destroyed as recognisable landmarks and yet full of men, many wounded, representing not just different regiments but different brigades and even divisions. In all the confusion he was impressed by what he saw – 'unwounded men cleaning their rifles and quite evidently preparing themselves for the morrow'.[27]

The responsibility of the men of the New Army 31st Division was to guard the flank of the 4th Division attack. The fortified village of Serre, set at an angle behind the enemy front line, stood in their way. Here, again, the British bombardment had not neutralised the German defences. The first men over the top before Zero Hour, finding their way through the lanes of the British wire, then to lie down in the last minutes before the whistles blew, were caught by shelling and machine-gun fire before they moved forward in their extended order waves. When allowance is made for bombardment which had not done its work, the composure, initiative and efficiency of the German defenders have to be respected. Some of them even carried machine-guns into the shell holes in advance of their positions the better to destroy the attackers. Interest was certainly earned here on the capital asset of being on the defensive in 1916 warfare.

Four battalions of Pals from Hull, two from Bradford and two from Barnsley, a battalion from Leeds, from Accrington, one from Sheffield, from County Durham and a pioneer battalion of Yorkshire miners: some had been on active service for six months, had been briefly in Egypt, but all were now going into a major action for the first time. It was to be under the most disadvantageous circumstances possible. Their morale, bearing and conduct were admirable. They won nothing; so much was lost and a bleak legend was born.

The trenches of the 15th West Yorks, the Leeds Pals, were among those shelled before Zero Hour. Men were seated on the fire-step when a shell struck the parados, deafening everyone near with its explosion and filling the trench with smoke. One man was killed and to either side of Corporal R. N. Bell there were casualties. When the whistles shrilled for the advance, Bell recalled that for a brief moment he felt relief at getting out of the

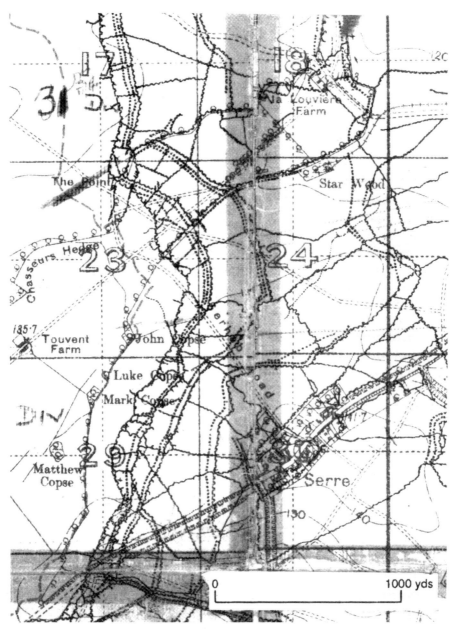

Map 8: SERRE: From the trench map entitled 'France sheet 57D NE Edition 2D'. Scale 1:20,000 (approximately 3½in to 2,000 yds). Ordnance Survey 1916. Trenches corrected to 7.9.16. (*E. K. Page, Liddle Collection*)

confinement of the trench under the shelling it was taking. The rattling of several machine-guns as the men scrambled out dispelled such thoughts. He tripped in a strand of wire but scrambled up to follow other men the short distance to the most forward trench leading into No Man's Land. Here the sights and sounds were dreadful and movement was virtually blocked by dead and wounded. Making his way with difficulty to the left, 'I found I was entirely alone, the rest of the Company seemed to have disappeared and although a momentary glance to the rear had shown waves of men of another battalion moving forward, nothing more was seen of them'. In this position of isolation, Bell watched a man appear and then crawl towards him before a shell landed beside him in the trench leaving the Corporal alone again. 'I have to confess that at this point quite an effort was required to keep my head since everyone seemed to melt away around me as if in a nightmare.'[28] On this day the Leeds Pals were to suffer twenty-four officer and 504 other ranks casualties; it seems little wonder that in retrospect Bell should use so graphic an expression as 'melt away'.

Second Lieutenant Robert Tolson fell in this attack upon Serre but for quite some time his family had no certain proof of their loss. Among the letters they received which sought to answer their desperate search for incontrovertible proof of their son's fate was one from a wounded Donald Duxbury in Lewisham Military Hospital. It did not bring helpful information, nor perhaps any comfort, but it held a point of detail and expressed an undiminished identification with the battalion: 'I am really proud to be a Leeds Pal – they went over with a great shout of "Now Leeds". It was grand but we have suffered terribly I hear.'[29]

If events in front of Serre were disastrous in the extreme, what can be said of the subsidiary or diversionary attack on the fortress village and salient of Gommecourt, north of the Third Army sector where no attack was to be launched? Geographically near to the frontage of the real offensive it may have been but there was nothing like the need in heavy artillery to destroy defensive works of the strength of Gommecourt. Was this known, and in that event was the expenditure of the men of two infantry divisions justified? If there were to have been sufficient troops for a diversionary attack against some weaker sector a good deal further north than Gommecourt, Douglas Haig would have found it difficult to justify this to the French, whose requirement that the British should make a major effort on the Somme had given birth and restrictive nurture to the whole concept of this British endeavour. The critic today is not under such constraint as he levels his charge, but artillery bombardment and every indication of infantry attack without launching that attack might have served the same intent, that of discouraging the transfer of German soldiers, materiel and mental concentration from Gommecourt.

The Gommecourt Salient was distinctive in configuration, like the prow of some ancient warship with its ram. The shape had in fact been taped and flagged for British preparatory training and then, sadly, photographed from the air by a German plane which had sneaked through the defensive cover generally so well maintained by the RFC. On the two faces of the Salient, considerable observation advantage lay with the Germans on the north-western face but their observation balloons were needed on the south-western front to see what was happening behind the British lines.

Gommecourt wood and park were thickly wooded and deep dug-outs further made them ideal for defence. The village itself was superbly fortified with entrenchments and there was no time for the British to undermine them. There was to be an attack from the north by the 46th Division and one on the south by the 56th. The head of the Salient was not to be directly attacked other than by simulation and the village would be snipped off and isolated by a juncture of the two attacks about 500 yards behind its rear defence.

Wet weather, drainage problems and the danger of German detection while the work was being undertaken interfered with plans to reduce the width of No Man's Land by a new advanced trench system. It was done more effectively on the northern sector than on the southern side but it still left an average of 400 to 500 yards to cross and, in the 56th Division, by troops exhausted by the work on their ill-drained sector. Nevertheless the Germans, as had been intended, reinforced their defences. The debit side of the balance sheet was that German artillery reinforcement was to bring fierce retribution on the troops whose scarcely concealed offensive preparations had drawn the enemy to defend this salient. The weight of British artillery was wholly insufficient to neutralise the effect of increased enemy firepower and however carefully timed was the British artillery plan for 1 July it was not going to offer the infantry the protection the men needed.

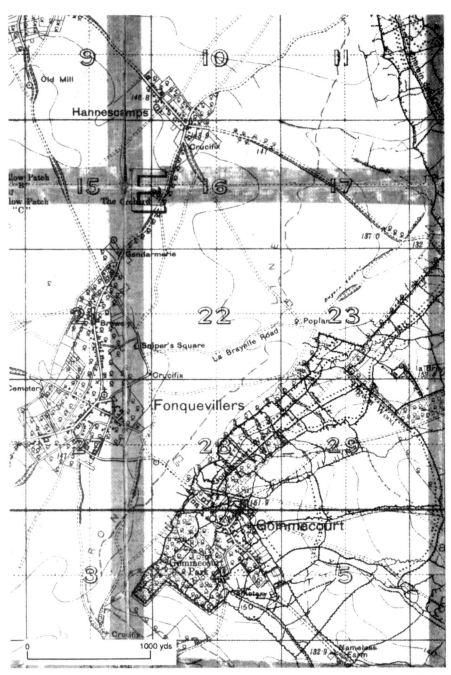

Map 9: GOMMECOURT: From the trench map entitled 'France Sheet 57D NE Edition 2D'. Scale 1:20,000 (approximately 3½in to 2,000 yds). Ordnance Survey 1916. Trenches corrected to 7.9.16. (*E. K Page, Liddle Collection*)

From the hours of assembly before Zero Hour, the British front line, communication trenches and assembly areas were heavily shelled. The 56th Division, London Territorials, did remarkably well in capturing the first objective, the three German trenches facing their assault on the southern shoulder of the Salient. In this they only failed to take one strongpoint in the third line. However, so intense was the German shelling that they could go no further, could not carry out the security measure of digging a trench across No Man's Land to protect the right flank of their success and were cut off from support from the British trenches by the German maintenance of a continuous heavy bombardment preventing anyone reaching them. The gallantry displayed by those who attempted to hold onto that which they had won has left an inspiring story. For all those of us who have not been through the test of battle it is humbling to read of the performance of all concerned. Duty, efficiency, composure, initiative, discipline, loyalty, individual and collective courage; how are they found in such combination under such circumstances? The answer must lie in a consideration of training, unit pride, discipline, belief in the cause, quality of men and officers and their interrelationship, welfare, sub-unit closeness and more factors still. Together they produced the high morale necessary to stand the test of battle and prolonged stress. It was there in the BEF in 1916, in adequate measure still there in 1917 and even in the Spring of 1918 when enormous demands were made on the reservoir of resilience, sufficient remained. Later in 1918, it was to prove the foundation of victory as in 1916 it had proved the bedrock against despair and disillusion.

An element in the support fire for the advancing 168 Brigade was to be the fire of two machine-guns each placed at a forward exit into No Man's Land of a newly-constructed dug-out ahead of the British front line. The NCO in command, Corporal W. G. Martin, had to direct traversing fire on the enemy front line before the attack and then lift onto the reserve positions. His diary records that at 7.30 a.m.: 'Mounted gun and opened fire at 2,000 yards on trenches E of Rossignol Wood. Heavy smoke screen obscuring wood and preventing observation. Fired 1,250 rounds till about 9.30 when heavy shelling all round position made it necessary to dismount gun. Rifleman Stephen assisted in this though exposed for the whole time. 2.30. Shell on observation post knocked down gun and tripod.' The gun was put back into action.[30]

The diary of Rifleman C. M. Woods (1st Battalion, London Regiment), who was in charge of an Aid Post at Battalion HQ, is succinct: 'Our fellows took Gommecourt Wood but, after sustaining heavy casualties, were obliged to return to the original front line. Two-thirds of the Division were wiped out. An Armistice was declared on our front in the afternoon so as to allow both sides to fetch in the hundreds of dead and wounded who were lying in no man's land.'[31] A 3rd Battalion London Rifleman, E. A. Cannon, wasted no words in his diary: 'Attack on Gommecourt Wood. Hell itself. Wounded in the right hand. 2/3rd (London Regt) unlucky. QWR's wiped out. Wood captured by us but we fail to hold on and have to retire at night. What a day.'[32]

In the Signals Section of the 5th Battalion London Regiment, so keen had been the competition to go forward with the first waves that lots were drawn among the Signallers. As a result, H. G. R. Williams, a Lance Corporal, was to remain with Advanced Battalion HQ. His station was in a communication trench adjacent to the dug-out HQ. He remembered the bombardment as being thrilling and awe-inspiring, convincing him that nothing could survive it. Smoke obscured their observation of what was happening ahead but the lack of prisoners or of signals of any nature was disquieting. Wounded making their way back or being carried back brought no information but increased the signaller's apprehension. Then a shutter signal was detected and read as 'SOS Bombs'. It was quite impossible to get any help sent forward. Williams recorded in his memoirs the unofficial truce to bring in wounded and his thoughts on the two signallers who had won the draw to go forward. One had sent the SOS signal and was to be awarded the Military Medal, the other had simply vanished, presumably blown to bits.[33]

Private Barber, also of the 5th City of London Regiment, was to be in the second wave of his battalion's attack, but through a trench periscope he had watched the first three companies go over, reach the enemy wire and try to battle their way through. He could hear the crack and whine of bullets across the top of his trench, see men 'dropping like ninepins' and then wounded men came back telling of being held up at the wire. 'I was never more frightened in my life. I prayed that we would not have to go over in the face of that murderous fire.' In fact a ball from an exploding shrapnel shell skidded down his back, opening up the flesh causing him to bleed copiously. His friends dressed his wound but it seemed to have shocked them too. He was sent off to find a Field Dressing Station and had still another alarming experience when he turned to find he was being followed by a line of Germans who had surrendered. They were lost and had no one to take charge of them. They would not be waved away and Barber's dilemma was only removed when a lorry picked him up to take him further down the line.[34]

The conditions of overcrowding which Barber was likely to meet on the stages of his journey away from the Gommecourt front may be judged from the diary of Major A. W. French RAMC of the London Field Ambulance. At Mondicourt, he was: 'Left to run Rest Station with only McHattie and Quartermaster Chapman. A rush of over 400 sick and "shell shock" cases coming in all day till two in the morning. All huts crammed with cases. I evacuated 1600 cases by Motor Ambulance Convoy.'[35]

Behind the whole battlefront, from Gommecourt to Montauban, the work of treating and evacuating casualties on that day developed on an unprecedented scale. The preparations had been thorough. There had been two earlier occasions of scandalous inadequacy, at Gallipoli in April 1915 and in Mesopotamia at the end of the year, and this must have concentrated the minds of those responsible for the planning. Nevertheless, the numbers of wounded to be treated – perhaps not far short of 38,000 – was well above expectation and yet behind the 56th Division as elsewhere, the Medical Service coped under such exceptional circumstances.

The northern flank of the Gommecourt Salient was attacked by the Territorials of the 46th North Midland Division. They were experienced soldiers but their experiences had not been gained in success. In 1915 they had been at Hooge and more significantly still at Loos in September. Not considered to have covered themselves with distinction at the latter, they were dispatched to Egypt in January 1916, but this order was cancelled even before the complete division had arrived in the Middle East. Most of them had thus had the variable privilege of a double journey troop-ship voyage in the Mediterranean before they found themselves responsible for the northernmost element of the 'Big Push' in France in the Summer of 1916.

It was intended that they should break into their flank of the Gommecourt Salient, secure their acquisition and then join with the 56th Division in pinching off the village itself. The Territorials had prepared an advanced 'jumping off' trench but all the ground between that line and their assembly positions was affected seriously by poor drainage, heavy rain, and old and new trench diggings. Nothing favoured the Division in the event. Their smoke screen was so thick that men became lost; then it cleared entirely and they were exposed; the muddy ground delayed the men; the wire was either untouched or churned up but not cut. The German infantry and artillery took devastating advantage of these British misfortunes. Even where perfunctory success was gained, it was isolated and unsupported. Here more than elsewhere on the battlefront, signalling procedures which might have reported a tenuous success and the need for urgent re-directed artillery action to help secure it, simply broke down. The results all round on this sector were calamitous. In the confusion, supporting attacks proved difficult to organise and even on this the first day of battle, the mud in the trenches here made all movement slow. The War Diary of the 6th North Staffords parallels the sad record of many units on this day with the additional significance of the smoke and the waterlogged ground.

> Immediately the smoke appeared the enemy opened heavy machine-gun fire and barraged our front line whilst the assault was in progress. This fire caused heavy casualties which occurred chiefly in the first four waves. The casualties so depleted the strength of the waves that very few men succeeded in reaching the enemy wire which was found to be very strong in parts. Owing to the smoke many men lost direction and were unable to see the gaps in the wire. Previous heavy rain had made the trenches into very bad condition especially the assault trenches which were from two to three feet deep in mud. This caused delay in the waves leaving the trenches.[36]

The Commanding Officer of the 6th Battalion South Staffordshires recorded smoke drifting parallel to the lines so that, halfway across, the men were in full view of the enemy. The CO, Lieutenant-Colonel Thursfield, also drew attention to the wire having been cut but not cleared, still remaining 'in such masses as effectually to prevent a passage'.[37] The Officer-in-Command of the 6th Battalion Sherwood Foresters, Lieutenant-Colonel Goodman, drew attention to the mud.

The greatest difficulty was the mud in the trenches. The communication trench was even more difficult to pass through than on the preceding days as the water was subsiding and thick mud was being formed. It was immensely difficult for the carrying parties to get along with their loads and the men were much fatigued. But the men were all very keen and did their utmost, and I am confident that all would have gone well had they not been impeded by the condition of the trenches.

Goodman's report detailed further problems beyond mud, congestion and officer casualties. He stated quite specifically that at 12.30 p.m. he had received orders to attack with two companies 'at 1.15 under cover of smoke' but at that time 'there was no smoke however, so I did not attack'. Another attack was ordered, also under cover of smoke and 'at about 3-30 p.m., a small film of smoke appeared, but as it in no way interfered with the view from the enemy trenches, I at 3.35 ordered the men not to go over the parapet.' Goodman's justification of the second countermanding of orders is a powerful statement with wide implications. Some might well consider the implications a conclusive indictment of the infantry tactics employed. The enquiring mind has again to be focused on the reasonableness or otherwise of the anticipation of the effectiveness of the British artillery bombardment. Of one thing there can be little doubt and that is the error of the ten-minute-to-Zero-Hour lift of heavy artillery from bombarding the enemy front line trenches to the bombardment of support trenches. The price of this error would be fully revealed in the casualty returns and the lack of initial success. In his case, the Colonel of the 6th Sherwood Foresters arrived at his judgement because 'There was a very heavy and extremely accurate barrage and also considerable rifle fire. I was and am quite satisfied that there was no possible chance of reaching the objective, and that no result could have been achieved.'[38]

With the Gommecourt Salient still resolutely held by the enemy and with only minor incursions into the German positions in the centre, there remained on 2 July but the successes on the right offering any hope of exploitation. Where the French had made their considerable gains astride the Somme and the British had done well at Montauban and Mametz, there may have been some prospect of a northward attack to take in the rear the

German positions which had effectively resisted the central advance of the Fourth Army. Such an opportunity was not taken. The position from which it would have had to be launched was cramped and the French might quite reasonably have considered that they had already played their part but perhaps more conclusively still, such an attack did not lie within the measured, siege-like approach of the Fourth Army Commander himself, Sir Henry Rawlinson.

Chapter 3

After the First Day: July to Early September

We should be aware that the events of the day and their implications would not be clearly within the grasp of Fourth Army HQ on the evening of 1 July. If a confused picture were to be the case in one particular sector, how much more would there be difficulty in assessing the general import of a series of pictures, some holding considerable elements of confusion. However unclear the picture, from Haig's viewpoint at GHQ, there could be no thought at this stage of relaxing pressure upon the Germans, enabling them, unharassed, to get their reserves into position. That way of thinking offered no hope of a breakthrough.

Rawlinson was in accord with the spirit of resuming the offensive but from a different philosophical standpoint. When Rawlinson, late in the evening of 1 July, issued orders for a resumption of the offensive as early as was possible in relation to the provision of adequate artillery support, it was to 'bite and hold', to draw in German reserves and progressively drain away the defensive capacity of his enemy. Haig, however, countermanded Rawlinson's plans to resume a broad-front attack on the left despite strong French representation in support of Rawlinson. Haig wished to exploit the success at Montauban rather than redress failure at Thiepval and elsewhere. Gary Sheffield is among those who judge that Montauban did present possibilities but it was clearly dependent upon a considerable French involvement and this had not been secured. In the light of the evidence of the first meeting between the British and French High Command since the opening of the offensive, which took place in the afternoon of 3 July, it does look as if the opportunity were illusory. Generals Joffre and Foch showed no great interest in exploiting the French success astride the Somme and disapproved of British intention to attack anywhere other than between Pozières and Thiepval which was of course well north of any substantial gains made on 1 July. A potentially awkward situation over the independence or otherwise of Haig's position was averted by the exercise of diplomacy all round but the net result was that any ideas Haig may have had for the taking of the enemy defences in the rear were not yet to be followed through.

Against a resumption of the offensive at Ovillers and Thiepval, the Germans held firm. La Boisselle, however, was taken on 6 July. The French, in conjunction with British attacks on their left, secured further limited objectives on their front and it is ironic that just as German resistance was stiffening, the French High Command was becoming the readier to exploit the success of General Fayolle's Sixth Army.

The divergence of British High Command thinking was at this stage to be illustrated in a paradoxical way, that is by the imaginative concept of the cautious Rawlinson and the scepticism this drew from Haig, the man who had been more hopeful of a breakthrough. Rawlinson wanted to launch Haig's requirement of a new major attack on the relatively narrow right wing but with troops assembled in the dark and then deployed well forward in No Man's Land to attack after only the briefest of intense bombardments in the half-light of dawn before they would be clear targets for the enemy machine-gunners. Haig doubted the capacity and experience of the Staff concerned to do the necessary planning and the discipline and training of the men properly to carry out the preliminaries. These matters, together with the problem of maintaining secrecy, were obviously determinants which could bring disaster and Haig saw less reason to see them as potential elements in a striking success. Haig, however, became convinced by Rawlinson's arguments, supported as they were by Rawlinson's Corps and Divisional commanders. The infantry attack was to be made on a frontage between Trones Wood and Contalmaison at 3.25 a.m. on 14 July. The five minutes of intense bombardment was to be undertaken as the four divisions of infantry advanced and it would be behind a creeping curtain of high-explosive shelling. Three cavalry divisions were to be in readiness to take advantage of infantry success but regrettably there was no French co-operation. French Command shared Haig's doubts about the early morning assault and, unlike Haig, remained fixed in their doubt.

Under considerable tension and with the aid of meticulously-laid tapes and placed markers, the infantry filed into their assembly positions in the dark, the front waves some 400 to 500 yards from the enemy. In some brigades, like the 8th, this distance was much further reduced, indeed for one wave reduced to appreciably less than 250 yards. In what was to follow so much was to go right but enough was to go wrong.

With a speed of success and relative economy fully justifying the innovation in tactics, most of the initial objectives were won, including the critical right flank of Trones Wood, the two Bazentin villages and their woods in the centre and Contalmaison Villa on the left. Then the impetus of the advance slackened, reserves being held back in anxiety over counter-attack instead of being pushed up to exploit the gains. High Wood and Delville Wood might perhaps have been outflanked, German supply to them nipped off instead of their being left to stand, as would be the case for so long, as bastions against frontal assault and as cover for counter-attacks. As for the cavalry, even its most forward unit, the Secunderabad Brigade of the 2nd Indian Cavalry Division, had found its move forward interminably delayed by mud, debris, shell holes and trenches to cross before it reached its appointed station, south of Montauban. Here it was still held back as Longueval had not been fully secured. As with Fourth Army Command's reluctance to send the Infantry reserves immediately forward, this XIII Corps Command decision concerning the cavalry, has been roundly criticised. John Croft has registered his judgement on both points:

> By 6.30 a.m. Rawlinson knew that the first objectives had been captured (in the main). There were plenty of fresh infantry who had not taken part in the initial assault and the Secunderabad Cavalry Brigade, having left their bivouacs round Meaulte near Albert at about 1.30 a.m. had watered and fed their horses at or forward of Bray-sur-Somme only

seven-eight miles from the breakthrough of the German second line. They were ready for operations for the rest of the day. It was now that several hours could have been saved. During the morning infantry commanders were waiting for the cavalry to arrive, although nothing had been done to speed up their movement for example, by clearing up the road. It took the Deccan Horse four hours to cover the six-seven miles to Montauban.[1]

In the early afternoon the Secunderabad Brigade was allowed to send out patrols but no more. It was not until 7 p.m. and with little daylight left for mounted action that the Brigade was sent forward towards High Wood in co-operation with an infantry attack. From the air, Lieutenant Stallibrass observed some details of cavalry action which at this stage were to be of little material importance in the balance of the battle but in terms of the history of the 20th Deccan Horse and the 7th Dragoon Guards were a matter of treasured pride. Flying at 1,000 feet and later at only 500 feet, from 6.15 p.m. to 8.27 p.m., Stallibrass had seen cavalry move up the road from Montauban towards Bazentin le Petit and then East along a road to Bazentin le Grand but when shells dropped nearby they retired to the first village. He continued his log, tracking their movements. 'Having trotted along the E edge of Mametz Wood they dismounted in troops, at a point half way down the E edge of Wood.' Stallibrass then described the movement up in support by the 20th Deccan Horse and another body of cavalry to a crossroads south of High Wood where they dismounted and took cover.

From here a mounted troop was sent out NE from this point. They came across the Hun infantry in a field and a small scrap took place when a few prisoners were taken. A large force of Hun infantry were entrenched in a road running SSE from High Wood. Fortunately a British aeroplane from No 3 Squadron spotted the infantry and descended to 500 feet and flew up and down the line strafing them with a Lewis gun. In the meantime a dismounted party had approached High Wood but later returned. All the Cavalry retired.[2]

An infantryman of the 8th Bn Suffolk Regiment, Lance Corporal Crask, had witnessed the movement forward of the cavalry. He commented not unsympathetically in his diary on their passing him at the gallop. 'Unfortunately they are of no use and suffer very heavy casualties without getting near the Boche from the fact that their horses cannot pass over the debris and the barbed wire that is lying about.'[3] Crask's contemporary judgement is not echoed by John Croft who has written: 'There was no cavalry massacre in front of High Wood, since the 7th Dragoon Guards only lost one officer killed and another wounded, two other ranks killed and 20 wounded and 14 horses killed and 24 wounded.'[4] The extent of the opportunity lost by the way the cavalry was or was not employed on this day will remain a subject for academic debate but is probably not one of the most significant issues left over from the battle.

If the achievements of 14 July were to have been important, the failure to develop them was of still greater importance. It fixed for the future the nature of a battle which the opposing High Commands both saw as vital. Haig had hoped for a breakthrough and it had not been secured. The associated aims of so committing the Germans to active defence on the Somme that their threat to Verdun was diminished and more particularly of exerting such destructive pressure on the German army that it would significantly erode their continued capacity to hold a large area of France and, by extension, of Belgium, these aims assumed self-justifying primacy. For the Germans, until the shortening of their line to new, massively-prepared emplacements was ready, no ground was to be conceded. Every British attack was to be matched by counter-attack. As has been mentioned, it is not easy to see why the enemy response in a battle of attrition should be so neglected as if an initiative in incompetence were uniquely practised by the British and French High Commands. For all the imaginative planning before 14 July and the limited victory of the day, it was clearly going to be a long, long haul. For a little more than a month, Haig held on to some hope of a real breach but not thereafter until mid-September, and no one subsequently, even in the unreal environment of hindsight, has come up with a convincing alternative to attrition as the means by which the BEF could most effectively have waged war against the Germans in 1916.

In the four months of the battle which remained, the number of battalions of infantry, batteries of artillery and field companies of engineers which were drawn into action on the Somme was legion. Reference can be made to some but there is certainly a need to link the troops of two of the Dominions to two very particular locations. July 14th had left two vital objectives in enemy hands, the capturing of which would become lastingly associated with the country of origin of the troops concerned. On the right flank of the new salient created stood Delville Wood for which men of the South African Brigade were already engaged; on the left, Pozières village and ridge, would be the scene for an equally famous Australian contribution to the battle.

Between 15 July and 3 September, South African units, above all, were involved in the progressive capture, consolidation and retention of Delville Wood. The woods of the Somme are again today often a closely growing light-filtering world of a variety of trees, tall bracken, coiled piles of bramble and thickets of hazel where progress from one part to another is intensely difficult unless using the grassy rides which Delville Wood and some of the other woods had in 1916. If we were to add to such a semi-natural picture the uprooted trees and severed branches, the trunks torn by shelling, the craters, the hidden trench emplacements and dug-outs, the staked-out hedges of barbed wire, the shallow communication ways through undergrowth and subsoil and then the smell of explosions, gas, urine, excrement, wet decaying vegetation in hot sun and the unburied dead, we have still considered neither the sounds from within so closed a location nor the fearful sense of isolation for men tenuously holding some post or trench only fitfully in communication with battalion HQ, wherever that might be. Field telephone wire could never be dug deep enough for immunity from shell fire and the hazards facing a runner within the wood or to and from the wood, made his task unenviable. It will readily be recognised that High Wood for example presented some of the same awfulness as did Delville Wood and that it was not exclusively South African troops which fought in the wood where their striking memorial now stands. It must also be appreciated that high endeavour was manifest elsewhere during the days when this wood was a scene which even a good book like that of Ian Uys finds difficulty in depicting.[5] It may be that this book relies heavily on testimony by recall but there is, as with so much 1914–18 recollection, such a graphic certainty in the memories of witnesses to Delville Wood that the reader is left with a convincing image. How is the unimaginable conveyed? Victor Casson (1st Battalion, South African Brigade) tried: 'McGregor and I retreated to our original funk-hole. At this stage the wood was subjected to a rain of shell fire, the whole wood appeared to be hit by an earthquake. The wood heaved and shook, blowing up trees and men. Mutilated bodies lay everywhere. The dying and the maimed calling out for water and help – but there was none to be had. It rained hell-fire and steel; the whole wood was subjected to massive shell fire on the ground and in the air.'[6] As powerful an account is that given by Nicholas Vlok, a private in the 2nd Battalion who owed his life to a Lieutenant Tatham who supervised and accompanied his being carried out of action through an artillery barrage to a dressing station.[7]

Hugh Boustead's recollections of several days in Delville Wood during this period echo those of Casson but he adds something which must be of more than personal relevance. On being wounded, 'my main relief was the chance to get some sleep. For five days and nights we had hardly slept at all and at times I was conscious of a longing to get hit anywhere to be able to sleep.'[8]

Australian troops had had a shared responsibility for the diversionary attack at Fromelles on 19/20 July and it had been a singularly unfortunate introduction to offensive operations on the Western Front. Within a few days, much further south, an Australian division on the Somme, the 1st Australian Division, was to be entrusted with the task of taking the fortified village of Pozières. It was an operation which was to commence at 12.30 a.m. on 23 July, so the darkness provided a challenge just as was presented by the strength of the objective. Again an assembly in No Man's Land was essayed and initial success was achieved, though not evenly along the line of the attack. The gains were consolidated and the attack renewed in order to complete the capture of the village. Intensely heavy German shelling on 25 July seemed to presage a counter-attack. This was not, in the event, delivered, but the troops of the 1st Australian Division had been through a searing experience, one to be shared by other Australian units drawn into the struggle for Pozières and its ridge. There had been heavy losses and the British Official Historian who had praised the independent initiative shown by small sub-units of men in clearing the enemy from some positions in the village, nevertheless attributed the severity of these losses in some measure to Australian inexperience as well as to their 'reckless daring'.[9] There may be a measure of truth in this verdict which seems at one and the same time both patronising and a tribute, but most Australians, then and now, view it rather differently.[10]

The physical work of serving the Australian guns is well captured in the diary of Gunner Brownell. For 23 July he wrote: 'After two hours sleep we got up at midnight to prepare for our part in the attack that was to commence at 28 minutes past … we kept up a heavy rate of fire until 3.30 and then fired at the rate of four shots a minute which we kept up till 6 a.m. Managed to get a couple of hours rest.' On the following day, he spent some time up at the observation post but on 25 July it was 'Going like mad since early morning as the Germans have been counter-attacking. Have fired about 1,000 rounds since 3 o'clock this morning.' They were then subjected to high explosive shelling followed by gas shells and on the next day there was a great deal of repair work to be done on their field telephone line.[11]

As the 5th Battalion formed up in their waves in No Man's Land waiting for the bombardment to begin, Ben Champion noticed that the thunderous crash of the bombardment caused the recumbent figures to creep together instead of remaining at four-pace intervals. His own tension was manifest by an inability to stop urinating. Though the battalion followed the barrage closely, the men were an instant too late and the enemy machine-guns were manned, inflicting some casualties. Their objective was nevertheless taken and the trench hurriedly reversed but of course the Germans were now easily able to direct shelling upon it. Its repair, the digging of a communication way to the rear and then forward sapping, were all done under fire. Of their being relieved and straggling out of their position, Champion recalled: 'What a mess of a battalion. We felt very sad for by the look of it we had lost more than half of our men.'[12]

In the same battalion, J. F. Edey's main memory of Pozières was feverishly digging out his mates entombed by shelling of their trench. 'I was alone and had to start digging them out by hand. It was impossible to use any implement. All I could do was to scrape down till I could locate a face and then continue till I could locate another and so on. I eventually located nine and then I had to start digging them out. Some of the poor chaps were in terrible pain with parts of their equipment sticking into their bodies.' A short while after the rescue was completed, Sergeant Edey was himself wounded.[13]

An Australian account which does support the claim that inexperience contributed to the casualties, is also from a soldier of the 5th Battalion. E. W. Moorhead has recorded that they had got lost on the way up to the front line and did not know what they had to do once they were in No Man's Land. With yells of 'Come on Australia', oaths, cooees, 'in a wild mob we gasped and tore in the direction we thought the enemy lay...'. In his sector, they took an unoccupied trench. 'Now, again there was confusion, disorder, and lack of discipline. Officers differed and argued.' A second trench was taken at the charge; again in Moorhead's sector it was undefended. Further argument ensued. 'A Captain filled to the neck with rum overrated all other officers, finally blew his whistle, roared "Charge Australians" or some such phrase and dashed ahead again. Finally the survivors came back in a panic, calling out that we must retreat, we're all cut up, the Germans were on us etc.' Even after the men around Moorhead were given orders by NCOs who in his words 'kept their heads', it was to improve for defence a ruined communication trench which daylight showed they had been digging in the wrong place. The work was abandoned. In an exposed position, cut off from support, there were more hours of shelling and counter-attack until they were relieved. 'We finally got out into the road near Contalmaison and filed down it in small parties, dirty, unshaven, worn-out, dusty and nerve shaken. It felt like getting out of hell.'[14]

Not just for Pozières Ridge but for Delville Wood, High Wood, Thiepval and other objectives, the struggle continued through August and into September. Some bitterly contested objectives were won and held like the sector of Delville Wood which, till early September, had remained in German hands, but before dealing with the plans for the resurgence of a major offensive from 15 September, it would be appropriate briefly to look at the experience of three people who may stand as representative of so many more engaged in kindred work, Major L. G. Hawker VC in command of No 24 Squadron at Bertangles, Lieutenant I. R. H. Probert with a battery of 18-pounder guns near Trones Wood, and Alice Slythe, a Territorial Force Nursing Service Sister in a hospital at Warloy-Baillon.

In Lanoe Hawker's papers there is a copy of a signal he received on 21 July from his Brigade Commander. 'Well done No. 24 Squadron in fight last night. Keep it going. We have the Hun cold.' Hawker, who had already earned the DSO and then the VC and was Britain's first true fighter scout pilot, showed in his letter to Beatrice the girl he hoped to marry, tremendous pride in the achievements of his squadron. 'Four of my chicks took on 11 Huns and downed no less than 4 or 5 of them!!! And yesterday we got 2 more. I was out myself yesterday and joined a tidy little scrap with 5 of them but nothing much happened as my gun wasn't working properly.' Then, three days later, on 25 July, 'Beasties doing very well thank you. Grand old battle – sort of high Fleet action with the accent on the high' – on 20th, '4 versus 11 – lasted nearly half an hour and 4 or 5 Huns done in. Some effort, one fell in flames, one caught fire on the ground and 3 or 4 fell "out of control" and that's what the trenches report not our own tale. They had another sharp one next day 5 v 10 of their best scouts – equally bloodcurdling but so far back that no one saw it … They met 5 others later, also me, and we had a mild dust up. My gun played the fool and spoilt my aim, which was annoying but they didn't seem to like it.' At the end of July, Hawker reported the low clouds, misty and very muggy weather: 'very tiring sort of weather to do any work.'

Number 24 Squadron was the first RFC single-seat fighting scout squadron. The work of its machines, nineteen of the new DH2 Pusher Scouts and two Morane Scouts, was to maintain British superiority in the air, preventing German aerial reconnaissance and ensuring that RFC reconnaissance, photography, spotting for the artillery and contact patrols, the sort of work undertaken by the Morane Saulnier (Parasols) for which Stallibrass was an observer, could be carried out. Administrative work and RFC higher command disapproval of commanding officers being engaged in operational duties, reduced Hawker's combat flying but he did make unauthorised flights in cases where he felt he might reduce the pressure on his men. In his operational orders, 14.7.16, the attention given to countering the tactical advantages held by the enemy was clear. 'Every machine must carry one drum of Buckingham Tracer Ammunition and pilots must watch for a suitable opportunity to strafe the balloon which does a great deal of harm to the infantry' and on another occasion, 23.7.16, 'If HA [Hostile Aircraft] are active, patrols must stay out as long as possible.' The CO had a shrewd understanding, even in July, of the nature of the battle they were fighting. 'We are getting a lot of our own back now, now we've got the shells, and I suppose we'll just go on pounding away till he breaks to pieces,' he wrote to Beatrice.[15] It may be added that his scientific approach to the task he had in hand was not lessened by his overall appraisal of the battle. He prepared notes for the guidance of his new pilots – 'The De H Scout. Fighting and Flying' – and then in October the broader base of his technological thought was encapsulated in a document entitled Some notes on flying as affecting (aircraft) design.

In August, the Squadron Commander recorded that 'the Hun is very wary and nowadays it is extraordinarily difficult to get to close quarters' but the reward of earlier success was noted too. 'We raked in 2 more decorations the other day, making a total of 1 DSO and 5 MC.' In September, concluding a letter almost entirely devoted to a dog he had acquired, a mixture of bulldog, Great Dane and pointer, he returned to the achievements of his squadron during the battle, twenty-eight enemy aircraft shot down by the end of August. The responsibilities he was bearing were however weighing upon him. In the RFCs communiques for September, No. 24 Squadron's casualties are listed. On 3 September, Second Lieutenant H. C. Evans is reported as missing; on 8 September, Second Lieutenant A. E. Glew is reported killed; on 9 September, Lieutenant N. P. Manfield as missing; 11 September, Lieutenant L. R. Briggs similarly; and likewise on 14 September, Second Lieutenant J. V. Bowing. Some idea of the scale and detail of the fighting on 15 September is succinctly captured in the RFC Communique for that day. Concerning the work of No. 24 Squadron:

Lts Byrne, Mackay and Nixon, whilst on offensive patrol near Morval, encountered 17 hostile aeroplanes at various heights. They dived into the middle of the hostile formation and attacked. Lt Byrne got to very close quarters with one machine, which burst into flames and was seen to crash. He then attacked a second machine, which was driven down and crashed in a field. Lt Wright also of 24 Squadron, attacked a hostile machine over Flers, into which he fired half a drum. The German machine went down vertically and was seen to crash.[16]

1. A Platoon of Liverpool Pals. Number 12 Platoon 1st City Battalion (The 17th [Service] Battalion) The King's (Liverpool) Regiment, in barracks at the Watchworks in Prescot, 1914. (*E. W. Willmer, Liddle Collection*)

2. Lime Street, Liverpool, 20 March 1915 and the 1st City Battalion (The 17th [Service] Battalion) The King's (Liverpool) Regiment, marches through its city. (*E. W. Willmer, Liddle Collection*)

In Loving Memory
of
William Haldane Round,
Captain, 7th (Robin Hood) Battalion
Sherwood Foresters,
Killed in action at Gommecourt,
July 1st. 1916,
Aged 23.
" Gone West."
(His last Message.)

The Rev. and Mrs. W. Round
and daughter return grateful thanks
for all the very kind sympathy shewn to
them in their great sorrow.
They regret that it is impossible to answer
at present all the letters they have received.

New Radford Vicarage.
Nottingham.

3. Killed in action at Gommecourt, 1 July 1916, aged 23. (*Liddle Collection*)

4. Wakefield and district learn the scale of the local losses. (The Wakefield Express, *15 July*)

THE DEATH ROLL.

LITTLE BOY ORPHAN.

A PATHETIC BURNLEY CASE.

One of the bonniest little boys anyone could wish to meet has been made an orphan through his father being killed at the front. The little fellow is Wilfred Jackson, of 128, Sandygate, Burnley, and he will not be five years of age until November next. Only last April his mother—who had been an invalid for about two years—died, and on Monday morning official news came that his father, Pte. Thomas Jackson, of the 8th Batt. East Lancashire Regt., was killed in action on July 15th. Pte. Jackson, who was 32 years of age, was formerly a weaver at Messrs. Blakey's Sandygate Mill, and enlisted in November, 1914. He came over from the front in April for the funeral of his wife, but unfortunately he could not arrive

PRIVATE T. JACKSON.

5. Casualty at the Front and a loss at home. A recently-widowed Burnley soldier, Thomas Jackson of the 8th Battalion East Lancashire Regiment, was killed in action on 15 July leaving his four-year-old son, Wilfred, an orphan. Here the local newspaper features the sad story. (*In 1991 Wilfred Jackson came from Burnley to bring the documentation of his family tragedy to the Liddle Collection*)

THE MAN WHO STAYED AT HOME.

6. Ready, if not ferocious: a 'Leicester Tiger', Private G. A. Dawson. (*Liddle Collection*)

7. 'And gentlemen in England now abed
Shall think themselves accurs'd
They were not here,
And hold their manhoods cheap whiles any speak
That fought with us upon St Crispin's day.'
An artistic expression by a man in the ranks scorning those who had not volunteered or who were even then seeking to evade the new Military Service Acts. (*G. A. Dawson, Liddle Collection*)

8. A square in Albert, the *Place d'Armes*, before and during the Battle of the Somme. (*Liddle Collection*)

9. For many soldiers, sojourning in the wilderness of the Somme, the precariously leaning Virgin and Child atop the tower of the church of Notre Dame de Brebières in Albert became a symbol of their war experience in France. The man who took this photograph had travelled more than 12,000 miles to reach Picardy. He would return home to New Zealand, his photograph identifiable proof of his service overseas. (*A. Wilson, Liddle Collection*)

10. From the left, General Sir Douglas Haig, Commander-in-Chief BEF, Sir Charles Monro (whose responsibilities lay further north with First Army), Colonel Perceval, a staff officer, and Lieutenant-General Sir Hubert Gough, commanding the Reserve Army. (*National Army Museum, 73957*)

11. July 1916 and much to consider: General Sir Henry Rawlinson, in command of Fourth Army, at his Headquarters, Querrieux Chateau.

12. Necessary training but circumstantially different from the reality. (*G. A. Higson, Liddle Collection*)

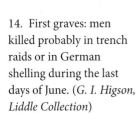

13. A packet of cigarettes for every man: officers of the 17th (Service) Battalion, The King's (Liverpool) Regiment, ensure that this 'comfort' is provided for the tension of the last few days before the assault. (*E. W. Willmer, Liddle Collection*)

14. First graves: men killed probably in trench raids or in German shelling during the last days of June. (*G. I. Higson, Liddle Collection*)

S.S/103.

O.B./630.

ORDERS
regarding the sending of Messages within 1,500 yards of the firing line.

1. Messages sent by buzzer on any circuit which has an " earth " within 1,500 yards of our front trenches, are liable to be overheard by the enemy.

2. As a circuit, even if metallic, may be earthed, either through damage to the conductors by shell fire or other causes, it is necessary to ensure that as far as possible messages transmitted shall not give information of value to the enemy.

3. No written message is to be sent by buzzer from or to any office in the zone 1,500 yards from the front line trenches without the sanction of an officer who must sign the message as being authorized for transmission within the dangerous zone.

4. Every station working buzzer in the dangerous zone is to be given a station call which will *not* be the recognised signal call of the unit. These calls will be allotted by Divisions.

5. Names of units are not to be " buzzed " in any messages. Only the code names of units as laid down and published by Corps and Divisions should be used.

15. It was necessary but not always possible to ensure that messages transmitted by an earthed Morse buzzer were not offering 'information of value to the enemy'. On one critical occasion at the very least, such a security breach occurred. (*I. R. H. Probert, Liddle Collection*)

16. A German photograph of British prisoners-of-war being escorted to the rear through Fremicourt, July. (*From a German photographic publication* An der Somme, *Munich 1917*)

S e r r e

John Copse
(in hollow)

17. A section of an official panoramic photo, taken in June 1916, shows John Copse and Serre, the objective for the Pals battalions of the 31st Division. Here, Reg Glenn, who wrote the Foreword to this book, was to enter No Man's Land. (*Liddle Collection*)

18. A German photograph of Gommecourt Wood in July. (*From a German photographic publication,* An der Somme, *Munich 1917*)

19. A German photograph of the ruins of Gommecourt in July. (*From a German photographic publication,* An der Somme, Munich 1917)

20. La Boiselle: The entrances to a captured German dug-out, July. Above the lintel to the left of the unblocked entrance there is the end of a communication voice pipe. To the right of this entrance a gas warning 'gong' is suspended, and emerging from the entrance itself is the flue of a coke brazier following the angle of the stairs to release the poisonous fumes. As a result of shelling, the dug-out entrance to the right is partially blocked. Duckboards, a pick, a rifle, a bayonet and, above the trench, remains of pickets with their barbed wire, can be seen. (*From a contemporary watercolour by G. A. A. Willis, Liddle Collection*)

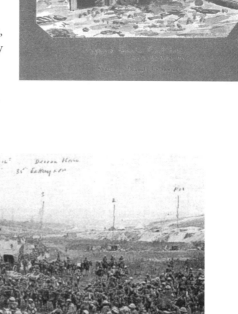

21. July 14th and the Deccan Horse await their move into action. The guns of the 35th Battery RFA (their positions marked 1, 2, 3, 4) are in action. (*I. R. H. Probert, Liddle Collection*)

contn:-

moved up in support along the road from
Dramety to Flatiron Copse where they were met
by the 6th D.G. + the White moved East along
the road N of Bazn le Petite + Bazn le Grand to the
cross Roads S. of High wood.

There they dismounted, + took cover behind
the belt of trees in a hollow S of High wood
From here a mounted troop were sent out
N E from this point they came across the
Hun infantry in a field, + a small scrap
took place when a few prisoners were taken
A large force of other infantry who had
spotted the cavalry were entrenched in a road
running SSE from High wood. Fortunately a
british aeroplane from No 3 Squadron spotted
the infantry, + descended to 500 feet + flew up,
+ down the line strafing them with a Lewis gun
This gave away the Hun position as they returned
the fire with many machine guns, + rifle fire.

22. Protection from on high: the log-book of RFC Observer T. L. W. Stallibrass, recording what he saw from his Morane Saulnier machine, soon after 7 p.m. on 14 July. He had been witness to another machine of his Squadron (No 3 RFC) machine-gunning a concentration of entrenched enemy infantry, which would otherwise have wrought havoc on British cavalry in No Man's Land near High Wood, the cavalry being unsuspecting of their imminent danger. (*Liddle Collection*)

23. Lanoe Hawker RFC, photographed at the time of his VC investiture in 1915. (*Liddle Collection*)

24. Attack Everything': the DH 2s of 'A' Flight of Major L. G. Hawker's No 24 Squadron RFC at Bertangles, July. (*Liddle Collection*)

25. The price of the eye in the sky: on this photograph, contemporary annotation by T. L. W. Stallibrass (No. 3 Squadron RFC) shows three men killed, two wounded and one unscathed of the six men clearly visible. (*Liddle Collection*)

26. German gunners of Field Artillery Regiment No. 27 beside a crashed RFC machine near Irles in September. (*State Archives, Military Section, Stuttgart (660/19/659)*)

27. 'My bivvy', edge of Delville Wood. Note the boots, water bottle and, in their roof-supporting role, the ammunition boxes around this New Zealand gunner's bivouac. (*A. Wilson, Liddle Collection*)

28. Sister Alice Slythe, Territorial Force Nursing Service. (*Liddle Collection*)

29. Sister Alice Slythe's hospital at Warloy-Baillon, an old people's home converted into a war hospital for serious chest and abdominal cases. (*Liddle Collection*)

30. Lieutenant Willmer of the 17th Battalion, The King's (Liverpool) Regiment received multiple wounds from a shell explosion late in the evening of 29 July. He was near the jumping-off trench for his battalion's morning assault on Guillemont. His batman, Anderson, bound up his wounds and remained with him, helping him at midday on the following day to make the effort to reach a sunken road to the rear. A Ford ambulance took him to an Aid Post where, at 12.45 p.m., he received an anti-tetanus injection. With the card shown here attached to him, indicating his dangerous condition, he was sent to No. 5 Casualty Clearing Station at Corbie. He was to survive. (*Liddle Collection*)

31. Bill Rothwell, before he became Sister Alice Slythe's patient with 'an enormous hole in his tummy, another in his chest, a fractured thigh, top of a thumb gone' and he had lain out, untended in No Man's Land, for three days and nights. (*Liddle Collection*)

32. German troops moving up to St Quentin halt for midday rest and refreshment from their field kitchen. (*Zinner, Liddle Collection*)

33. German soldiers at rest but making music. (*Zinner, Liddle Collection*)

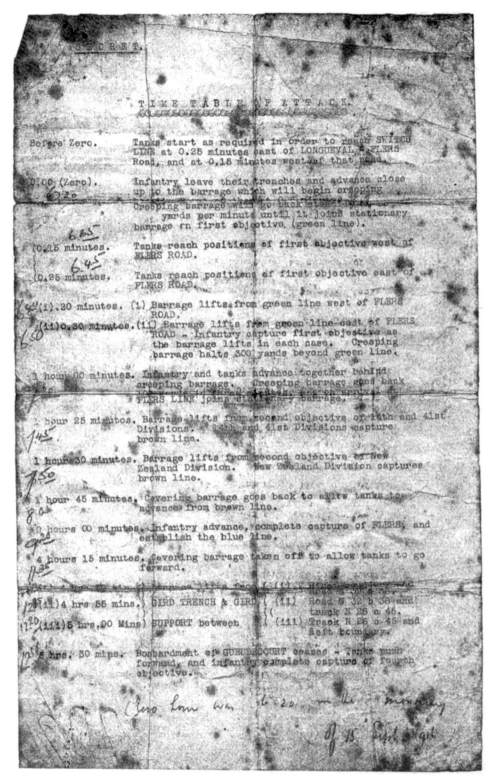

34. Infantry and Tanks: 15 September. The timetable order held by Lieutenant J. W. Staddon, 12th Battalion East Surreys. (*Liddle Collection*)

35. Flers, 15 September: recognition by the Divisional Commander that John Staddon, a Platoon Commander in the 12th Battalion East Surrey Regiment, had displayed conspicuous gallantry. (*Liddle Collection*)

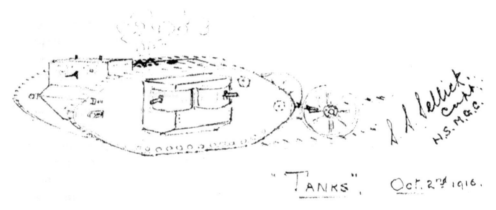

To Lieut. J. W. Staddon
12th E Surrey

I wish to place on record my appreciation of your *conspicuous Gallantry in leading your platoon up to + through* FLERS *15 Sept. 1916. — for your continuing energy . . . and example to your men .*

Major General.
Comdg. 41st Division.

NOTE—It does not follow that your name will be submitted to higher authority.

"TANKS", Oct. 2nd 1916.

36. Tank D 19, under the command of Captain Sellick, became ditched and did not get up to the start line on 15 September. On the 26th, when it was in action on the day Gueudecourt was captured, Sellick himself was wounded. He was taken to No. 2 Red Cross Hospital, Rouen. There, on 2 October, he illustrated the autograph album of RAMC Surgeon C. H. Milburn, with a drawing of the Mark One tank, so recently a well-kept secret. (*Liddle Collection*)

37. Delville Wood, looking towards Flers: a photograph taken immediately after the advance of 15 September. (*A. Wilson, Liddle Collection*)

38. Divisional achievement at Flers. The Fourth Army Commander congratulates the 41st Division. (*W. J. Polk, 10th East Surreys, Liddle Collection*)

41st Division.

I desire to place on record my appreciation of the work done by the 41st Division during the Battle of the Somme and to congratulate all ranks on the brilliant manner in which they captured the village of FLERS on September 15th. To assault three lines of strongly defended trench systems, and to capture the village of FLERS as well, in one rush was a feat of arms of which every officer, non-commissioned officer and man may feel proud.

It was a very fine performance and I offer my best thanks for the gallantry and endurance displayed by all ranks.

The work of the Divisional Artillery in supporting the infantry attacks and in establishing the barrages deserves high praise, and I trust that at some future time it may be my good fortune to have this fine Division again in the Fourth - Army.

39. Tanks trundle past a watching New Zealander. (*A. Wilson, Liddle Collection*)

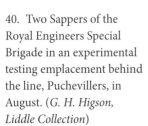

40. Two Sappers of the Royal Engineers Special Brigade in an experimental testing emplacement behind the line, Puchevillers, in August. (*G. H. Higson, Liddle Collection*)

41. Funeral procession for a German soldier. (*Zinner, Liddle Collection*)

42. General von Soden talks to soldiers manning a covered fire trench position at Thiepval in August. (*State Archives, Military Section, Stuttgart (660/19/613)*)

43. German soldiers beside a trench barricade in the remains of Thiepval Wood in July. (*State Archives, Military Section, Stuttgart (660/40/423)*)

44. A Scottish soldier in Whalley War Hospital, Lancashire, captures something of the Autumn essence of the Somme, in the autograph album of VAD Nurse Mildred Clegg. (*Liddle Collection*)

45. Philip Hirsch, an officer in the 4th Battalion the Yorkshire Regiment, on the Somme in September.

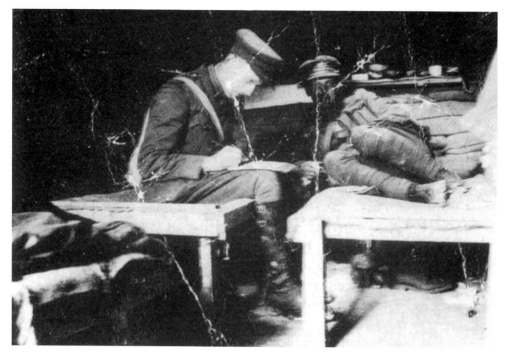

46. Office work under active service conditions. In a dug-out, the Acting Adjutant of the 4th Bn Worcesters, William Strang, prepares his report on the day's operations. (*Liddle Collection*)

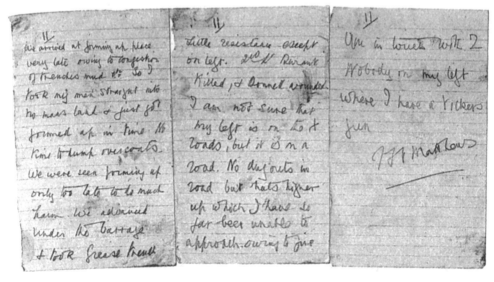

47. On 18 October, during the battle for Gueudecourt, a runner from Y Company, 4th Battalion Worcesters, managed to get this message from his Company Commander back to Battalion HQ. Y Company had established contact with Z Company, on its right, but the left flank was exposed and hence the Company Commander had a Vickers gun team here. The original Field Message is stained by water and mud. (*William Strang, Liddle Collection*)

48. Behind the German lines: October graves. (*Zinner, Liddle Collection*)

A devoted son, a faithful friend,
One of the best that God could lend;
We little thought when he left home
He would no more return;
But God has willed it otherwise,
And left us here to mourn.

In Loving Memory of

Corporal JOHN ROBERT (BOB) COULSON,

ROYAL MARINE LIGHT INFANTRY.

The Beloved Son of Rose Coulson, Surrey Place, New
Herrington, and Grandson of John Short,
Postmaster, Philadelphia,

Who was Killed in Action in France, on
November 13th, 1916,

AGED 19 YEARS.

MEMORIAL SERVICE in the United Methodist Chapel,
Philadelphia, on Sunday Night, February 11th, at 6 p.m.

49. Beaucourt, 13 November 1916, and a nineteen-year-old, among the last to fall in the battle. (*Liddle Collection*)

50. An ammunition column on the road to Longueval, riding through what had been Guillemont. (*Liddle Collection*)

51. General von Soden poses beside British shells which have failed to explode, Miraumont, Ancre Valley, end of August. (*State Archives, Military Section, Stuttgart (660/41/472)*)

MAJESTY'S SERVICE.

52. HRH The Prince of Wales's signature indicating his presence on the Somme. (*E. G. Bates, Liddle Collection*)

53. Private Victor King, 1st Battalion Royal Welsh Fusiliers, wounded and in hospital at Richmond, Surrey, in September. He was sixteen years old and had been hit in Delville Wood on 3 September. (*Liddle Collection*)

54. Just far enough from the madding crowd: the encampment of 209 Field Company RE at rest near Bresle behind Albert after the operations of 14 July. (*From a contemporary watercolour by G. A. A. Willis, Liddle Collection*)

55. The 1st City Battalion (The 17th [Service] Battalion) The King's [Liverpool Regiment], – Liverpool Pals – in December 1914, parading in Knowsley Park, the seat of the 17th Earl of Derby, their founder and patron. (*E. W. Willmer, Liddle Collection*)

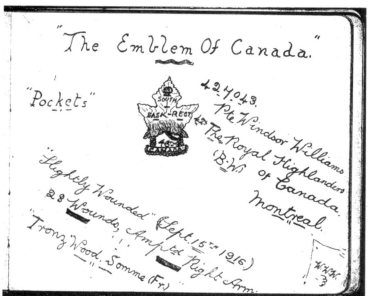

56. A Canadian, 'slightly wounded' and in No. 1 Temporary War Hospital in Exeter, illustrates the autograph album of Kathleen Codyre, whose older sister, Sarah, was a VAD Nurse at the hospital. (*Liddle Collection*)

57. Leeds Pals return in 1921 to the German trenches at Serre, their 1 July 1916 objective: evidence of a compulsion to return which drew Somme survivors even into the 1990s, seventy-five years after the trauma of their initiation into battle on such a scale. (*A. V. Pearson, Liddle Collection*)

Though his squadron was not to be suffering losses in October at the rate recorded above, he admitted to Beatrice on 22 October that he was feeling 'very depressed'. He explained what occasioned the depression. It was that he hardly knew anyone in the Squadron at this stage. Men were on leave, three or four 'home for a rest' and there were casualties, one 'shot down 2 days after he was made flight commander and I haven't recovered from the blow of losing him – he was such a nice lad as well as the best officer I have ever met'.[17]

Hawker himself had not got long to live. He was killed on 23 November in a prolonged combat with the formidable Manfred von Richthofen. His instructions to his squadron on 22 June had been 'Attack Everything' and independent evidence of the effectiveness of the work of the fighter squadrons in August is held in the official log of No. 8 anti-aircraft battery under the command of Captain J. J. A. Foster. On 2 August, twenty-seven enemy machines are seen whereas 193 British are recorded; on 3 August seventeen as opposed to 189 and of the 17th: 'Captain Foster brought down an Aviatick [sic] at 7.40 a.m.'[18] Hawker, his men and the men of other squadrons, had indeed attacked everything and it may be added it was an example paralleled by the pilots of machines engaged on different work, that of longer-range bombing behind the Somme like Hugh Chance whose log book for a raid on Gouzeaucourt on 15 September described a train being bombed at 500 feet, the station machine-gunned and his machine being 'hit by MG from ground. Both tyres punctured and longeron shot through etc.' Two days later, attacking Valenciennes, he came under anti-aircraft fire and his engine failed. He landed near Bourlon and was taken prisoner.[19]

In all, 308 pilots and 191 observers were killed, wounded or posted as missing between 1 July and 17 November, the vast majority of these men being casualties of the Somme offensive. Towards the close of the battle, the RFC's mastery of the skies came under serious challenge from new, faster German machines and the leadership of outstanding airmen. Over the whole battle, for the British there was a pilot wastage rate of 300 per cent. The toll in machines ran parallel, with 782 having been struck off charge in the squadrons of the BEF between 1 July and 17 November. A final statistic which might be listed here is the 19,000 RFC aerial photographs taken in the same period, again with a large majority relating to the Somme. In the sense of tackling with determination all that had to be done, the RFC had certainly fulfilled the spirit of Hawker's operational orders and there had been a price to pay in so doing.

Lieutenant I. R. H. Probert's diary documents his work with a Field Artillery Battery of the 7th Division. On 19 August, he took a party of twenty gunners to dig a gun position near the quarry in Caterpillar Valley. 'We found a partially built position so I took it over and we spent the rest of the day deepening the gun pit to make dug-outs and ammunition recesses.' He slept the night in one of the dilapidated trucks on the light railway. On the following morning the gun pits were finished; the battery moving in during the afternoon. An officer named Knight went up to the trenches opposite Guillemont 'to register a zero line. Ginchy church was too indistinct but we worked out a sort of line on the corner of the hedge at T. 13.' The Colonel and the Major inspected and approved the position. On 21 August, Probert went up to Trones Wood to observe. Other than a German shell hitting an ammunition dump on the road to the west of Bernafay Wood it proved a quiet day which was just as well as their field telephone line had been cut 'in about 15 places'. Probert's duties drew him back to the battery position and from there to the HQ of the Infantry battalion just behind Waterlot Farm. At 4.30 p.m. an infantry attack in Delville Wood was supported by a barrage and drew shelling from the enemy.

On 22 August, German 8in howitzers fired 'about 300 rounds' into Caterpillar Valley.

One shell hit my dug-out direct and knocked out Carberry who was standing in the road just outside. He had a bad cut in his face and a big bruise in his side which may have ruptured something. We took him across to the Dressing Station in the Quarry and he went straight to the Corps Dressing Station by Motor Ambulance. I sent his servant with some of his kit after him. Nearly all my kit was destroyed. Both our watercart horses were wounded, one badly and I had to shoot him.

On the following evening, as Brigade Forward Observation Officer, Probert took two signallers, a gunner and a four-man working party up to Trones Wood at 8.30 p.m. and almost immediately upon their arrival heavy rifle and machine-gun fire came from their immediate front, followed by an artillery barrage on their support lines. Communications were cut and soon it was too dark and the shelling too heavy to find and mend the wires, despite every attempt so to do. At 3 a.m, Bombardier Hayward arrived at the Observation Post having traced up the 105th Battery's wire and he took cover with them in the dug-out.

Thursday 24 August was devoted to getting head cover over the gun positions, fifteen long rails and then sandbags and earth. 'At 3.45 p.m. we started the bombardment of our front, 1 round per gun per minute. At 5.45 p.m. we increased to gunfire 15 seconds. 5.50 p.m. was zero and we lifted 300 yards and continued slow rate of fire until 8.45 p.m.' All but a single strongpoint in Delville Wood was recorded as having been captured by the infantry. On the following day this Artillery Officer went up into Delville Wood which he found 'full of dead and smells terribly', then he was himself spotted observing from a tree and shelled which ruined another Observation Post. They were 'crumped' out of another post, half-buried in the process and there were more casualties. 'Gnr Young was wounded in the testicles this evening by an 18 pdr premature.'

There could scarcely be a better illustration of the physical and nervous demands faced by gunners on the Somme that Summer than that illustrated by Probert's diary entry for the last day of August. The officer had got up to Trones Wood to organise the construction of a latrine beside the observation post. Even getting to the wood had been difficult because of an enemy gas shell and high explosive barrage. 'The trench through it [the wood] is knee deep in mud and very much knocked about. We at last reached the OP but it is quite impossible to dig in that clay and water.' They were then shelled by a 'new and particularly disagreeable gas shell' put in on the edge of Bernafay Wood. Probert tried to dodge this by going round the north end of the wood 'but they put a lot of shell in between through which we had to pass … We crawled into a hole in the trench and waited with smoke helmets on for about 20 minutes.' When he eventually got back to the Battery it was just as this came under gas shelling and also as Brigade HQ required them immediately to open intense fire ahead of the front held by the South Staffs. 'By this time the front lines were completely obscured by the thick smoke from the German shells and the Huns attacked.' Their battery remained under fire for ten minutes: 'One gas shell went clean through the shield of No 2 Gun killing Gnr Felton and blowing Gnr England's foot off and laying out the rest of the detachment.' Bombardier Grant then returned from Brigade HQ to tell Probert that one of the Battery's officers there, Knight, had been killed and Probert, in going to check this, found that Knight had been hit directly by a high explosive shell.[20]

Before leaving the gunners, it seems appropriate to quote another who may speak for many in showing an understanding of the war in which he was engaged. As early as 18 July, Captain Rory Macleod wrote to his father: 'Once we get beyond the trench system and get the Germans "on the run," there ought to be a chance for us, but we still have some way to go before we come to that. The Germans still have more lines of trenches left which we shall have to blast our way through first … At every attack we must "stand to" in case the infantry get right through. It is not likely to happen, as the German is a very stubborn fighter, but the hundredth chance might come along, for which we want to be ready' – and in a letter on 19 July: 'the only way we can hope to beat them is by keeping on hammering away at them with heavy artillery.'[21]

The hospital in Warloy-Baillon which Sister Alice Slythe reached on 14 August had been adapted from a hospice for the elderly. Some of the nuns who had staffed the hospice had stayed on to help. Sister Slythe's ward had ten 'other ranks' cases and a side ward for four officers. All her cases had severe abdominal wounds. The orderlies were untrained, the equipment deficient and 'You just muddle along with what you can get.' This hospital was to have, according to Sister Slythe's diary, a 46 per cent recovery rate but while acknowledging a Medical Officer's challenge that this was too low, she made a reasonable rejoinder that 'it's the journey that does for most of them'.

For a man seriously wounded in No Man's Land, the first factor in the question of his survival, after the degree of severity of his wound, was the speed with which he was found and brought to a Regimental Aid Post. The survival of sufficient stretcher bearers in his battalion or brigade was a consideration here. The evidence of men surviving several days in No Man's Land as Private Frank Hirsch of the 6th Cameron Highlanders did from 15 September, and Second Lieutenant A. H. Crerar of the 2nd Battalion

Royal Scots managed in October 1916,[22] is not rare but in general terms it is exceptional. The second factor was what could be done there and then for him in the sort of circumstances outlined in the diary of the Medical Officer, G. D. Fairley. Related to this was the degree of difficulty for his stretcher party trying to get round the traverses of crowded, littered trenches into a communication trench where movement might be just as difficult and from thence back to a dressing station where, if fortune were with him, he would get some degree of professional attention. The amount of time for such attention would be dependent of course on the flood of similar cases. At a dressing station, the severity of his wound would decree whether he would there undergo surgery, be sedated in a 'moribund' ward or sent on to the next stage behind the line. In this last event, his onward journey would now be by horse or motor ambulance to a Casualty Clearing Station. From here, according to planned arrangements for that location, motor ambulance would take him to a field hospital – perhaps tented, hutted or in a building like the Warloy-Baillon Hospice – or to a railhead for an ambulance train, or to St Omer for transportation by hospital barge. The trains and barges took the men to the coast or to Rouen. A wounded man's journey might or might not end there. The question of his fitness for hospital ship travel across the Channel and further ambulance train transport to UK war hospitals had then to be decided. For severe head, chest, abdominal and amputation cases and for those suffering wounds with the onset of gangrene, Sister Slythe's words of the journey at some stage 'doing them in' remain morbidly realistic despite the care, compassion and professionalism which was brought to most cases.

At Warloy-Baillon that Summer, one of the first problems was the flies. On her first day of duty, Alice Slythe found a 'brown blanket' covering one of her cases – 'a heaving mass of flies. In a week we'd reduced them pretty considerably but they were unbelievable. The men had to have mosquito nets.' When she showed her anxiety for news of progress in the battle she made an observation which goes far towards explaining why at this stage in her diary there is so little about the patients as individuals. 'For the benefit of any who may read this diary and say why don't you ask the patients [for news]? Let me point out that it is the exception for us to admit a man who is fit enough to think consecutively, much less talk. Often they have been lying out for hours and are even past the stage of being grateful or glad to be here – they just don't care what happens.' The depressing nature of the ward is matched by the oppressively heavy atmosphere of September days and nights. Querulously a man complained of the traffic vibrations in the room as convoys rumbled past. 'The atmosphere in the ward is indescribable. I've opened windows but the rain makes it so heavy.' With wry amusement she records some of the question and answer exchanges she has had with patients in delirium. Internal rearrangements in the hospital, a partition erected and painted, involved the move of her patients to a different ward. 'They are quite bucked to be out of the noise and the paint smell. I have told them they must behave as the new ward is HQ, this because I have fitted up my table in the corner with writing things and a German shell-case full of dahlias and a big wall pocket hung up for charts and odd papers.' Soon after this rearrangement, her wounded German officer patient was taken off to a Casualty Clearing Station. She had referred to him as the 'happy Schluter' and now wrote 'I hope he gets on all right. He expressed an earnest wish to see me after the war in Germany! I think not.'

Patients died and on one occasion there was 'an awful day'.

Two died this morning and two others I expect will. One dear Yorkshire boy who has been in Canada 5 years has given me his photograph. 'William Rothwell' – I generally got 'Bill' though. He had an enormous hole in his tummy, another in his chest, a fractured thigh, top of a thumb gone and he lay out for 3 days and nights. The last two he spent in a German dug-out into which he had crawled behind Courcelette and Martinpuich. He has a gold ring belonging to his dead mother and all the three days 'was watching that ring and hoping as how nobody would come and take it off me.' He's such a dear – goes to CCS tomorrow.

There is little question that what kept Sister Slythe's spirits up was her intense desire to increase her own experience of life, which in her current circumstance meant seeing all that she could see of military activity and a good deal that she ought not to have seen. She raided dumps of shell cases for souvenirs and she relished a lift from General Birdwood as she was making her way along a road to the Field Cashier at Senlis. The General was 'only sorry he could not wait to take me back but he was due at Pozières to give decorations. I told him to be careful. I don't think Pozières is a nice place to give decorations in.' Returning from Albert on one occasion, she saw a demonstration of poison gas and a bomb-throwing school at work. 'Altogether a well spent morning.' Hearing an unusual rumble of traffic noise outside the Hospice, she saw seven caterpillar tractors 'five with gun mountings. You never heard anything like the noise. I had to go down to the gate to watch them.'

An especially heavy bombardment was 'one of the finest noises I've heard'. Early in September, Major Bean, their Australian anaesthetist, 'brought in his brother Charles, a war correspondent, to see me tonight … He says that we have really done very well. We have the whole of Guillemont and Ginchy now' and soon after this there was talk of their hospital staff being 'filmed as Canadian nurses on the battlefield'. A Colonel Templeton was 'going to get a gun or two and rig up a film for Canada! We are to be in overalls as our uniform isn't quite the brass bound bright blue thing that Miss Canada wears. But I would have thought wide awake America would have known you don't find Sisters and guns falling over each other – even Canadian Sisters.'

The most thrilling experience she wangled during September was the successful organisation of an ambulance journey which took her towards La Boisselle. Over a ridge 'was a sight I couldn't have imagined. White lines showed the earth thrown up from trenches. A collection of short irregularly spiked bits of wood sticking up 1–5 ft out of the apparently ploughed earth and a few bits of brick was the village of Ovillers.' Similarly she described La Boisselle, Contalmaison and Pozières and while she watched, she was rewarded with the huge fountain of earth which was 'My first shell-burst!'[23] If everything about this scene were to have been extraordinary, the diary confirms that Alice Slythe, qualified and professional as she was, captured to a remarkable degree the adventurous spirit which animated so many women in the different branches of nursing and related work in France in the second half of 1916.

Chapter 4

The Fifteenth of September:
A New Major Effort and a New Weapon

I t is difficult to argue against the launching of a new offensive drive on the
Somme in mid-September. Inter-Allied co-ordination had been a prime
factor in the earliest planning for a major offensive on the Western Front,
one for which the British would take the main burden and now developments
that summer in Macedonia, Italy and the Eastern Front all pointed towards
the need to maintain the pressure on Germany. In addition to some evidence
from German prisoners, of course subjective, that enemy morale might be
weakening, aerial photographs were providing incontrovertible proof of the
construction of new, stronger positions in reserve. Such an undertaking,
if developed to completion, might remove altogether the prospect of a
breakthrough. Two further factors impelled forwards the argument for a
large-scale resumption of the offensive. First there was the availability of
new troops, including the Guards Division, and then the exciting possibility
of employing a new weapon, the tank, which at last suggested a way had
been found for a protected crossing of No Man's Land, getting through wire
and across trenches. Accordingly, deaf ears were turned to noises relayed to
Haig of political rumblings in London over the casualties incurred and the
lack of evident profit from such human expenditure. Rawlinson and Gough

were ordered to prepare plans which would use the new troops and the tanks to secure the breakthrough which militarily and politically would justify the endeavour.

Only secrecy can secure surprise but while this factor was paramount in GHQ and Army HQ thinking in the employment of the first tanks to see action in the evolution of a petrol-driven, armoured, armed, caterpillar-tracked vehicle, a huge question remained and that was how would it perform in action. There could be but one answer to this – battle testing. There were many interrelated issues – the early test necessary and one in which it might perform a decisive role was literally 'now', almost immediately on arrival behind the Somme, but the small numbers in which it arrived could mean its use in the very 'driblet' way against which there had been specific recommendation. Such numbers would render it ineffective and, worse, would concede its great asset, surprise. Should the High Command have waited then until tanks were in sufficient number for large-scale employment? This would have meant foregoing the testing and the great advantage they might give the Fourth Army now. In any case, were they to be mass-produced and a large apportionment of men drawn off to train as crews without the assurance that they would work in battle? It could reasonably be argued that September on the Somme would give them a better chance of proving themselves than October or November. If, retrospectively, eyebrows were to be raised here on account of the initial tank success in late November of the following year at Cambrai, it must be countered that the terrain further north was different, had not been so pulverised and the November 1917 Mark IV tank was a considerable improvement upon those employed on the Somme fourteen months earlier.

In 1916, Haig would have used them had they been available for 1 July; he was not going to miss the opportunity of using them now in September. In theory they represented the restoration of the potential of a breakthrough but their small numbers decreed that they should be used, Haig decided, in an infantry-support role to try to help the infantry deal with those places of strong defence which had hitherto defeated them. By this means, artillery, infantry and tanks could win the opportunity for cavalry to be pushed through. While at this stage not enough was known about the reliability of the engine, steering system and capacity to maintain motion across the

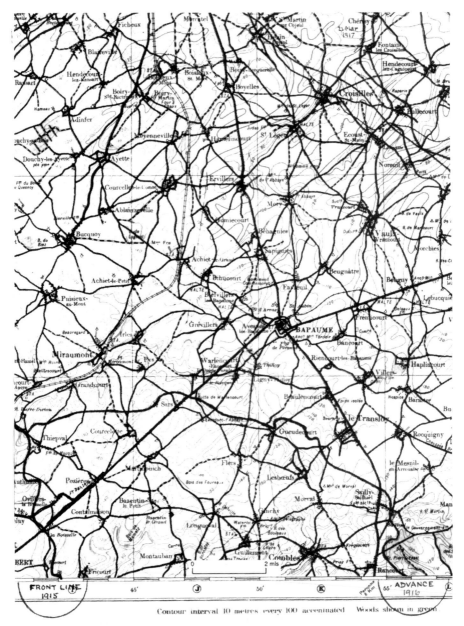

Map 10: THE SECTOR FOR THE 15 SEPTEMBER OFFENSIVE: From the Ordnance Survey Office 1915 map entitled 'France Lens IT'. Scale 1:100,000 (1in to 1.58 miles or 1cm to 1m) NB – there are hand-drawn front lines for December 1915 and December 1916 on this map. (*Liddle Collection*)

obstacles and cratered ground in the smoke of battle, the tank's low speed and vulnerability to a high explosive shell were fully recognised. It was essential by one means or another to secure concealment for the tanks until the last moment, to take advantage of surprise and to counter vulnerability to shelling. Infantry were to use the protection offered by a tank advancing on their immediate front and this was just one of the tactical factors to be incorporated in the planning. For an inter-arm, cooperative effort on the scale envisaged, at no level, from top to bottom, was there much time for familiarisation with the new weapon.

Rawlinson's plans, which were for operations extending over three nights and which required the tanks operating by moonlight and retiring behind the British line to concealment before dawn, were not acceptable to the Commander-in-Chief. He wanted no such 'bit by bit' advance but a decisive operation. In consequence, the Fourth Army Commander planned for a narrow front drive within an attack on his whole front – the drive would be for Morval, Lesboeufs, Flers and Gueudecourt. Most of the tanks would be used on this sector with the Cavalry in readiness behind, five divisions of them, ready to take advantage of opportunities ahead.

Despite the shortness of time, all the arrangements to give effect to the above had to be ready for 15 September, approximately a fortnight from the finalisation of the plan. The scale of the operation may be judged by the deception activity ordered for the whole of the British front right to the coast. It even involved troop movements through Dunkirk docks into lighters to simulate a seaborne landing behind Nieuport into German-occupied Belgium.

The time factor with regard to the tank is made abundantly clear when it is realised that from several strands of short-lived development the successful prototype was only demonstrated on 2 February 1916. The first organised unit for training of machines and men was established in the following month. Tanks were not available to this unit until June. The first tanks in France did not arrive until mid-August and, on the eve of the battle, twelve of the forty-eight tanks to be employed had not yet arrived at their assembly points. It might be mentioned here that, on about 10 September, tank trials on badly-cratered ground such as they might encounter, showed them capable of a speed of 15 yards a minute! There is one further element in the question of time available for planning. It has both particular and general application. It is far too readily assumed that new plans were drawn on a clean slate and that the drawing was done under conditions of uncomplicated, comfortable, contemplation – no attacks, counter-attacks, new developments, problems of men, materiel or circumstance, to say nothing of the equally immediate though geographically-removed factors of top-level political and military pressures from Britain and from France. The Fourth Army and the Reserve Army were engaged constantly in heavy fighting on each day of September up to the 15th and the operations which had led to the capture of Guillemont and Ginchy had been very costly. It may be argued that these operations, frontal assaults as they were, should have been more imaginatively mounted at an earlier date but a look at the map shows how Ginchy, Guillemont and Leuze Wood each defended each other's flank. There was no envelopment option open and certainly the concept of an attack having Lesboeufs and Morval as its right flank, objectives to be reached in one bound, could not have been attempted with the Ginchy, Guillemont and Leuze Wood fortified strongpoints held by the Germans.[1]

Many have poured scorn upon what they perceive as the isolation of the Staff, GHQ, Army and Corps. John Bourne's and Gary Sheffield's statistical analysis of the casualties among senior officers shatters the idea of a life of comfortable security at this level of command, and whether the charge of isolation were to be anywhere near as justifiable as is normally accepted is worthy of more debate than it receives. Certainly the idea that there were far too many Staff Officers doing far too little work, an idea almost automatically pedalled by Denis Winter from characteristically selective evidence, is one which belies the huge volume of work which necessarily had to be done. Many examples could be given to substantiate this point but just one will be used because of its particular relevance to 15 September. Among the papers of the Commanding Officer of the 7th Battalion, Durham Light Infantry, Colonel Vaux, is an Intelligence Report from Captain W. W. T. Torr of III Corps General Staff relating to the interrogation of the captured Lieutenant Richard Schade of the 181st Regiment. It is not just the thoroughness of the questioning which is impressive, it is that hindsight has proved the value of the information gained. Schade was captured on 18 August and the report was issued on the same day. He had been questioned on the enemy's intentions, on reliefs, support lines, order of battle, morale, effect of British artillery, opinion of British intentions, the sites of food, ammunition dumps, water supply and his Battalion HQ. Schade was also questioned upon the use of mobile machine-gun units and the 'development of the idea of initiative in the Germany Army'. The German officer's answers to these and other matters certainly have a ring of useful truth about them. Morale was stated to be very good, the men still getting 'hot meals in the front line brought up by carriers … The losses are heavy but reinforcements come up promptly. British artillery is very accurate but ammunition especially that of the larger guns [he particularly mentions the 9.2in] which were nearly all duds – is very bad.' As for British intentions, 'the enemy believe that our attack has only just begun and that we will attack in force again soon' but that 'south of Martinpuich there are strong redoubts and assembly trenches for the troops to retire into if necessary' and that 'the Flers line is very much stronger than their old front line'. When some of this information was confirmed by other interrogations and from aerial photography, there was going to be abundant co-ordinated planning necessary to secure success in the centre of the new offensive under consideration.[2]

The employment of a revolutionary new weapon was a further factor in staff work, made the more significant by the constraint upon time and multiplied by there being new divisions in the line. It may additionally be remembered that for the artillery the battle began three days earlier still, at 6 a.m. on 12 September when the preliminary bombardment commenced. It was a detailed complex programme tackling close, medium–range and distant targets of every description and it continued night and day without intermission. There was, however, a flaw in the programme. To ensure that the tanks did not catch up with and suffer from the British creeping barrage protecting the advancing infantry, avenues free from British shelling were left for the advance of the tanks. Robin Prior and Trevor Wilson have argued that this decision was misconceived, greatly responsible for infantry casualties and clamped a limitation upon the potential effectiveness of the tanks where the new fighting vehicle was advancing upon enemy strongpoints. Its weaponry was outranged and its speed inadequate to its task as it lumbered towards unharassed defensive positions. With the tanks rendered so vulnerable, they could scarcely accord protection to the infantry they were designated to shield.[3]

Haig's determination upon a battle of decision is made clear by his visit on 14 September to each Army Commander and his emphasis to Rawlinson that Martinpuich must be won on the first day of battle to assist the Reserve Army in its operation and his similar requirement to Gough, in command of the Reserve Army, that Courcelette must be taken during the first day.

Something of the expectation as well as the tension of the eve of 1 July seems to have animated many. It was felt at all levels of command and among the men too. The ambition of the plan, the scale and nature of the new resources, were certainly to give to 15 September a particular significance. It was a day to be ranked contemporaneously and in retrospect with 1 July.

As might have been expected, the worst time for one of the drivers of the tanks of the 'Heavy Branch Motor Machine Gun Corps', Bob Tate, was the early-morning waiting and waiting until the whistle blew to start up the engines. Tate's tank was crewed by seven men under the command of an officer who was seated at the front alongside the driver. 'It was tension, not fear. We had so much confidence in what we had been taught and in our tank – no, no fear at all.' Some of the men had been involved in laying out the white tapes the night before so the track to follow was made clear. In his recollections, Tate made no mention of the shell-free avenues which were planned to give the tanks a more secure progress with the British barrage as it moved ahead of the advancing infantry. As it happened, a German shell wrecked the wheels at the rear designed to assist with steering but this did not affect the performance of the tank nor did the 'hailstones' of machine-gun bullets except in the breaking of the glass prisms in the viewing slots.[4] As the tanks lumbered forwards they were watched and later variously described. John Baker, an RGA Gunner, saw them as 'big cases of steel running on caterpillar wheels ... like little forts with a big engine in the middle'[5] and Lieutenant G. B. de Courcy Ireland saw them as a 'wonderful new toy ... a kind of armoured car which spits forth machine-gun fire and six-pounders and goes over any obstacle'.[6]

Vic Huffam was in command of one of two tanks which became ditched in German trenches the walls of which collapsed as they were being crossed. The commanders of the two tanks (D9 and D14) 'climbed to the roof of our tanks and watched our other tanks go in, immediately behind a creeping barrage. It was a wonderful experience.'[7] Where tank success was reported with most dramatic effect was at Flers. An aeroplane was responsible for the renowned message 'Tank seen in main street Flers going on with large number of troops following it.' Lieutenant J. W. Staddon (12th Battalion East Surreys), whose conspicuous gallantry in leading his platoon up to and through Flers on this day was recognised by his Divisional Commander, has maintained that the British Army seen from the air was simply his 'platoon of German prisoners which I had parcelled together after directing the tank commander up the street. I was the only surviving officer to reach Flers, my last colleague falling in the wire in front of the village and my flare was seen by the air observer.' Staddon was badly wounded in the late afternoon and not picked up until the following day.[8]

Ten tanks had been allocated to the drive for Flers and seven made it to the start line. Four were hit or ditched but three 'pushed into or along the eastern edge of Flers, smashing machine-gun nests, breaking into fortified houses, and spreading panic among the defenders – most of whom fled towards Gueudecourt'.[9] Of these three tanks, the one which got furthest was D5, 'Dolphin', a machine-gun-armed 'female' tank, driven by Sergeant Edward Foden and under the command of Second Lieutenant A. H. Blowers. The tank was further crewed by Gunners Barnsby, Gutsell, Plant and Slodden with Privates Hodson and Thomas as gearsmen. The War Diary for D section, Heavy Section Machine-Gun Corps, relates for 'Dolphin' that she 'became ditched in Delville Wood which rendered Tail out of action' and prevented refuelling so that the petrol cans remained on the roof. Too late to deal with the first objectives, Lieutenant Blowers carried out the next stage of his operation orders and 'penetrated as far as Gueudecourt and engaged a German battery and the gunners of this battery disappeared into their dug-outs. Lieutenant Blowers, after waiting for a long while for infantry to come up, decided to return.' It was at this stage that a runner came up and requested help in dealing with a strongpoint south-east of Flers. In moving to tackle this strongpoint, 'Dolphin' was hit and set on fire. Two crewmembers were lost, Gunner Barnsby and Private Thomas. Blowers himself was seriously wounded and Foden, who had extricated one of 'Dolphin's' machine-guns, was hit in the ankle while returning the fire of an enemy machine-gun. Blowers, Foden and Private Thomas were decorated for their work on this historic day for the tank.[10]

Among the divisions newly employed on the Somme on this day, there were the Guards on the right, New Zealanders in the centre facing Flers, Scots opposite Martinpuich, and Canadians on the left to attack Courcelette and trench systems to its right and left. The 2nd Battalion Coldstream Guards was one of two battalions in the van of the 1st Guards Brigade attack. Sergeant Rumming's diary simply calls it 'a day of blood'. There is mention of a friend killed, 'the first of the TANKS went into action', plenty of aeroplanes and then 'got wounded at 3.30. Went to CCS then to Corbie next morning.'[11] Fortune had not been with the ten tanks allocated to the Guards Division and a cryptic reference to this is recorded in the diary of an officer, R. C. Bingham (Coldstream Guards).[12] 'It appears that those who were meant to go went all right, but most of the others only poked their noses into Ginchy and then stopped.' In fact five of the ten developed mechanical trouble or became ditched and so did not arrive at their start lines and problems neutralised any effect developing from the movements of the others. The Bingham diary discloses one aspect of the problem – ground so slimy and boggy that at Ginchy it was difficult even to walk – but mechanical troubles and loss of direction were the main factors. The Guards had suffered heavy casualties in achieving not much more than their first objectives. On their front there was never any question of a breakthrough being within reach. Welsh Guardsman, W. A. F. L. Fox Pitt cautioned his father against War Correspondent exaggeration of the achievement of the tanks: 'Two tanks did very well but on the whole they were a failure. They were much too slow and the infantry passed them in their first rush.' Assessing their speed over the cratered broken muddy ground at up to three miles an hour, Fox Pitt makes the telling points that 'if they were a bit faster and not so liable to get engine trouble [they] would fairly put the wind up Fritz'.[13]

Grenadier Guards officer Harold Macmillan led his platoon into the attack and recalled a Corporal Newton asking him for a personal souvenir before they moved off. He gave him a silk handerchief which, nicely, was returned fifty years later. Their first objective was taken but with heavy loss – Macmillan being only slightly wounded. He was now ordered to take men forward from the newly-captured position to deal with a German machine-gun team the fire of which was threatening any further advance. In so doing he himself was badly wounded in the pelvis. 'I could do nothing except roll myself down into the bottom of a shell hole.' He called the position where he found himself 'very curious', between the captured trench and the one unsuccessfully attacked, potentially a victim of 'shorts' from shelling by both sides. 'I was there all day and had been reading a book in Greek which happily I had in a pocket. My wounds were not awfully painful then.' He was picked up that night but the severity of his wounds belied the impression given by his description of the experience. 'I was in and out of hospital for about two years, yes over two years.'[14]

The New Zealand Division was on the Corps frontage to the left of the Guards with objectives related to the successful assault on Flers by the 41st Division. None of the four tanks assigned to the New Zealanders proved useful initially but the infantry kept so close to its barrage that the men got through their first objective in good time. One battalion, the Otago, had actually moved just in advance of the 6.20 a.m. Zero Hour, suffering some losses from the barrage but also gaining an advantage against their opposition. Further progress was then made but irregularly and against sterner resistance. Two tardy but welcome tanks valuably assisted at this stage in flattening wire and dealing with enemy machine-gun emplacements. The Official History of the Otago Battalion records that the enemy in Crest Trench, as it was being stormed, fought to the last instance and then surrendered and 'asked for mercy'. The account avoids any equivocation over the fact that they did not receive it.[15]

The 15th Scottish Division captured Martinpuich which had been a particular requirement laid down by the Commander-in-Chief. What the 6th Cameron Highlanders Machine-Gun Section had done towards this end was described in Sergeant James Campbell's letter home. The letter nicely illustrated the teamwork essential in the efficiency of any small unit operating under such circumstances. With the death of their Commanding Officer, Lieutenant Simpson had taken command and at 2 p.m. had informed the Section that the battalion was to attack and take Martinpuich.

We went over the top ten minutes later and hadn't gone 100 yards before a big shell burst right amongst us killing Bill Lambie and severely wounding Geordie Thomson and Harry Rankin. I left a Company man to dress them, took the gun and carried on with the Company. Just afterwards I saw Andy Hardie and his gun on my right but I lost sight of him next minute. We got into the village with practically no opposition and started to clean out the dug-outs. From one huge dug-out we got over 100. I got Baldy Young here with the two A Company guns and took the four guns right through to the other side of the village. Here we found some of the Company boys digging in and I got the four guns distributed in the line. Just afterwards Lt Simpson sent my two guns out on patrol. We went out for about 100 yards but as our own barrage had not lifted we got shells around us.

They were recalled and 'had to double round to the right flank of the village. On the way I passed Old Adam in position and gave him a wave. Geordie Spence was with him.' In fact their right flank was exposed and the Germans counter-attacked. 'We had an hour's hard work but they didn't get nearer than 50 yards and they paid dearly for the attempt.'[16]

Private Frank Hirsch of the 6th Cameron Highlanders, actually awaiting news of being commissioned, paid his own heavy price in this action. He was severely wounded by shellfire, but survived three nights and four days before being picked up. Hirsch's understated letter of 23 September, addressed simply to his father, sought by this means to avoid alarming his mother. 'I'll try to tell you a bit about what happened to me during that nightmare but first, on my honour, though it's perfectly miraculous, believe me I have no chill or poison in the wound. I am only afraid that you will still think I am not quite right, but believe me Dad, I'm absolutely alright and would be as happy as the day is long if I had not to remain on my back. You see femurs are tedious things to mend.'

In later recall, Hirsch mentioned drinking rainwater off twigs, getting rid of his equipment, making a tourniquet from a garter, trying to crawl, being tossed in the air by an explosion, pretending to be dead when thinking Germans were approaching, and on being picked up by stretcher-bearers, one attempting to shield him as another shell exploded. He remembered too being given morphia at an aid post and the blue cross indication of this marked on his forehead. How fortunately his misfortune had ended.[17]

In this sector the artillery work had been effective, greatly assisting the infantry. Two tanks, still in action though making slow progress, had ultimately played a striking part in putting the enemy to flight. It was the variable performance of the tanks which make the contemporary observation of a cavalry officer, Edward Ramsden, so representative. The tanks are 'really marvellous though there are many different views as to the good they did and there is no doubt they can be greatly improved'.[18]

On the right of the 15th Division, High Wood, an objective long sought, at last fell. On the left, the Canadians made for Courcelette. The role of the 24th Battalion was in support, bringing forward ammunition, barbed wire and supplies to the assault troops. Private M. M. Hood of the 24th was impressed by what he saw of the tanks and in particular by one which assisted in the taking of a fortified sugar refinery. He noticed the tank's name *L S* (for Land Ship) *Creme de Menthe* as it went right up to the sugar refinery, its guns firing, and then 'it seemed to lean against one of the walls which collapsed and the monster tore into the fort, while we could see the Germans streaming out offering an excellent target to the riflemen in the shell holes'.[19] The letters of a Canadian artillery subaltern reflect the concentration of effort for 15 September and subsequent days. 'We are having a strenuous time and I am horribly tired, so my letters will not be anything except to let you know I am well. Please send me an identity disc for my wrist.'[20]

The Canadians had fought well for what they had gained but, as elsewhere, in no sense did they threaten a breakthrough on their front. In his biography of General Byng, in command of the Canadian Corps on the Somme, Jeffrey Williams recorded that Byng ordered his Staff and each division to make detailed studies of every aspect of the offensive battle and to analyse the recent actions fought by the Corps so that the reasons for the lack of success might be learned. The staff work would be done, the Canadians would learn, and Byng, quite incredibly named by Denis Winter as one of Haig's 'sheep', would lead them to success in 1917 and 1918.[21]

Indubitably the tanks had not brought near any prospect of a decisive breach on 15 September. They had neither the mechanical reliability nor the speed. Furthermore, the crews could scarcely be expected to be sufficiently well-trained and experienced fully to extend the limited potential of these first machines. Tank, infantry and artillery co-operation was at an incubator stage of development. As on 1 July, determination had to follow on from disappointment. The pressure on the Flers Courcelette front was maintained until 22 September as rain worsened ground conditions. The work of the Sappers, supported by labour battalions, in road maintenance and repair, was constant. All other communications, including the light railways, were requiring attention. Answers had to be contrived for the drainage of flooded trenches and gun pits. Captured positions needed this too and the issue of drainage may be one of the explanations for the failure to initiate tunnelling work to undermine stubborn strongpoints in the weeks following upon 1 July.

The range of work carried out by the Royal Engineers preparatory to the Somme is made clear in the recollections of a former Sapper. The improvement of communication trenches was a major task but there were machine-gun and trench mortar emplacements to construct and roads to repair. In one instance a vital road was cut in several places by trenches and hence bridges over the trenches had to be made and given the strength to take field artillery traffic. The work had to be carried out night and day and, despite efforts at concealment, attracted shelling which ruined what had laboriously been erected. During the first weeks of July, Sergeant Heptinstall had an infantry party under his command to bring forward to Sappers in the line all that was needed in the way of barbed wire, screw pickets, tools, sandbags and explosives. Later in July, captured positions were more professionally consolidated than had been possible on the day of capture and communications cables were more deeply buried for their security. After the building of a POW cage, Heptinstall's Field Company was moved further north and so he escaped the problems which the Sappers had to tackle as rain worsened ground conditions in the second half of September.[22]

Sappers of the Special Brigade had the onerous task of carrying and installing cylinders for the release of gas. As Sergeant Dawson of F Company made clear in his diary, they could be closely involved with another weapon, the employment of which needed the favouring of fate.

2 September: All night we spent in the place for the liquid fire engine.
3 September: British still bombarding heavily. Everything got ready
              by 11 for the attack at midday. The oil cans went off all

right but a trench mortar landed on Page's guns set two on fire and he was buried and burnt and died soon after. The Black Watch went over the top and lay out in front till the liquid fire was finished then they went forward. We helped them over the top. We did not know what happened.[23]

No individual Sapper's recollections or private papers would illustrate the full range of work. Quite apart from the particular but varied nature of RE Signals work, of field survey for mapping, flash-spotting and sound-ranging of the enemy's batteries, of the operation and maintenance of the light railways and of the work of the Special Companies in the release of gas, smoke and liquid fire, the work of an ordinary RE Field Company could include the installation of coke-burning stoves in a tented field hospital or the construction in sections of lengthy bangalore torpedoes then to be emplaced in the enemy's wire to blast a hole through it for a trench raid. On the Somme, as a wet September was followed by similar weather in October and worse in November, the overriding task of the Engineers was drainage. Trenches flooded, their walls collapsed despite revetment and a porridge of slimy mud began to engulf all movement. The installation of pumps and the digging of new channels had to be attempted but rain, shelling and traffic sank the battlefront and support areas into a slough of despond which would only change in character as the New Year brought temperatures to freeze the ground.

In the last week of September and in particular on the 25th, significant but limited gains were won on and around the Flers Courcelette frontage. Morval, Lesboeufs, Combles and Gueudecourt were taken and in that same week of the Fourth Army's renewed offensive, the Reserve Army struck at Thiepval and the defences of its ridge which extended from Schwaben Redoubt on the left to captured Courcelette on the right.

Diary and letter descriptions for each of these fronts do much to indicate the nature of a common problem. First objectives were now being secured but taking advantage of them was a very different matter. Even when breakthrough possibilities were fleetingly glimpsed, the closing fog upon communications, the absence of reserves immediately to hand, and the

German will and capacity to restore a threatened position, combined to close the door.

An officer in the 1st Guards Brigade Machine Gun Company, R. C. Bingham (Coldstream Guards) wrote on 27 September: 'Our orders were to take Lesboeufs. This we did after a perfectly splendid attack', which he then described. 'The whole attack worked like a clock … We had reached practically open country. There was not a German within 1,000 yards though a few were to be seen digging in a sunk road in the distance'. These men were seen off by a few shrapnel shells 'but there was no one behind us to carry on through.' Bingham was very clearly annoyed. 'A Brigade of infantry could have marched up the Ginchy-Lesboeufs road in column of fours and gone as far as they wanted.' The blame is laid on there being no one from Brigade or Divisional Staff up with them to see the opportunity and for this reason, or for whatever reason, there being no reserves at hand. As Bingham described the event, the Guards got no further and the Germans began to 'trickle back' and to shell the captured village causing casualties as well as closing opportunities.[24]

On 24 September, 25lb lacrymatory gas bombs were fired by Stokes Mortars up to 600 yards into Thiepval to play their part in the capture of this stronghold. Private Crask, a signaller of the 8th Battalion Suffolks attacking here, remained initially at Battalion HQ. His diary recorded for the 26–27 September: 'The Battalion takes the village after two hours very severe fighting. They encounter the Boche in heavy numbers, take a lot of prisoners but we fail in our objective the Schwaben Redoubt.' The Colonel went forward to establish an advanced HQ but when the signallers followed so that communication could be made with Brigade HQ, 'the Boche laid down a tremendous barrage on all the ground that we have captured thus isolating all the forward troops. We signallers fail to get through this barrage – absolutely impossible for anybody to live in the same.' Their officer was badly wounded and Crask made 'a rough tourniquet around his thigh, put him on my shoulder pick-a-back style and carry him back until I meet an RAMC stretcher party'. He rejoined his diminished party of signallers and throughout the night, in turns, they try to get forward to the advanced Battalion HQ but none succeeded. 'They try all ways, along the trenches, over the top, along the sunken road and even try to encircle around the barrage.' Not until 6 a.m. was contact established between Battalion and Brigade HQ. Intense enemy shelling was resumed and the line was broken time and again, giving the linesmen their regular unenviable task of finding and mending the break under fire. The battalion was completely without rations for the day, 'so we have just to grin and bear it'.[25]

Crask's philosophical acceptance, clearly imposed upon him, was shared in a more natural sense by the remarkable officer Edward G. Bates, whose letters betoken a positive relish of the daunting circumstances endured by his battalion, the 9th Northumberland Fusiliers. On 25 September, he described how a patrol in No Man's Land had come upon an enemy patrol and at 5 a.m. in the mist there had been a successful bayonet encounter. He described it as 'unforgettable'. It seems likely that he killed or seriously wounded two or three men. The event was followed by a celebratory dinner in the Officers' Mess. The next day was spent in the front line and then the following night 'over the top with a "Howay the Lads", "Give the beggars hell".' On 29 September, he wrote home of hoping to last out without becoming a casualty but he noted that he was not in the list of Military Cross awards. 'I'm quite content as long as my work gives satisfaction to everyone, including myself.' The retribution of the censor, it seems, was almost suicidally invited on 4 October when Bates wrote: 'Just another bit of "secret". My Division and two others attack Gommecourt on the night of October 9-10 ... My Battalion is the first to go over the top. Good. If successful this advance will straighten out the Salient ... We are to be supported by tanks and cavalry so it will be some stunt.' In the event the stunt did not come off and this officer's family was regaled with an account of why, 'if you were a soldier, you would soon learn to bayonet a German', which might have been a well-founded observation because, in discussing Zeppelin raids in the same letter, Bates observed: 'I heartily agree with you. The Huns deserve to be burnt alive.'[26]

All of Bates's resolve, if not his stark enthusiasm, was required of the men engaged in the last days of September fighting to secure Schwaben and Stuff Redoubts and their trenches behind Thiepval. Denis Winter made much of what he called the 18th Divisional Commander, Ivor Maxse's, demonstration here of what Haig should have been doing and Winter outlines the thoroughness of Maxse's planning. He sees Maxse as 'the conductor weaving together the diverse instruments of an orchestra to achieve harmony'. In Haig he sees only 'obtuseness' and, in page after page of his book, much worse. Maxse's attack, 'was, of course, a complete success and supplied a textbook demonstration of how force was best able to break the crust of the strongest defensive position'.[27] The trouble with this eulogy of an undeniably distinguished senior officer whose reputation for the training of his men was winning deserved recognition, is that the attack of the 18th Division on 26 September was not a complete success. We have already had an illustration from Lance Corporal Crask of the desperate communication problems which ensued and in fact the fine achievement of taking Thiepval village was not completed until the following morning and a key objective, the Schwaben Redoubt and its trench system, was not fully taken when this sub battle closed down on 30 September. In the fighting, the 12th Battalion Middlesex had lost eighteen of its officers (ten killed) and 293 men (sixty killed). As the Divisional History records: 'The task allotted … had not yet been fully accomplished. Schwaben Redoubt and the intricate network of trenches surrounding it were still a thousand yards away across a slope of broken ground held in great strength by the enemy.'[28] The redoubt itself was taken on 14 October. Picking out of the air illustrations of how things might have been done, swiftly, effectively, economically, achieving 'a complete success' all along the line, if only a well-connected, devious dunderhead were not to have been in overall command, is malevolently vacuous – the illustration given for this is as spurious as the argument itself.

Chapter 5

Through October into November
and a 'Slough Of Despond'

Through October the Germans were allowed as little respite from attack as the weather permitted. Along the whole line, just southwest of Lesboeufs to Gommecourt in the north, new or the old uncaptured objectives were attacked. These were the battles of the Transloy Ridges and the Ancre Heights. Difficult tasks were made the more so as October rains clogged movement in the reserve and support areas while, further forward, conditions degraded into dire straits. Once again there were some limited successes but even when ingenuity was added to bombardment – the aerial projection of oil drums which exploded in flame and smoke as they hit the ground or the use of the electrically-fired Livens Projector to throw a 60lb phosgene gas bomb up to 1,500 yards – no gains were won cheaply.

Thought was certainly being directed to learning from experience; 167 Infantry Brigade Staff was not alone in following up actively such a process. On 14 October, the Brigadier required the COs of the four battalions to report within a week on nineteen listed topics where the Staff felt there were lessons to be learned in order that the Brigade might 'profit by the experiences we have gone through'. Among the points to be considered were the improvement of communications in battle, the suitability of assembly areas, the best way to move men forward to the front line and the way infantry might use the protection of their own artillery barrage more effectively. Matters of fine detail were to be examined: whether the bombers should have recourse to a bag of grenades or should each man carry two grenades with him into the attack; was it sound to take greatcoats into an infantry assault and leave the packs behind?[1]

When a battalion went into battle some officers were of course still not freed from administrative duties. William Strang was acting adjutant of the 4th Worcesters in their fighting at Gueudecourt on 18 October. Graphically illustrative of his duties and the circumstances under which they were carried out are the mud-encrusted, water-bleared messages he wrote or received in his Battalion HQ dug-out. His diary too is a document remarkable for its insight into his fellow officers and into his own state of morale as they were exposed to the stress of a prolonged period in the line.

On the 18th, in an attack on a wide front, mounted from ground which was a flooded morass of shell holes and trenches, and which ended in overall failure, the 4th Battalion Worcesters was one of two battalions which took its objectives. The diary, subjectively, sets the scene among the officers. One named officer has just been removed, his offence not known, his inebriation a byword among his colleagues. He is to stand trial by court martial but was a 'man of great charm, of gentle birth, brilliant capabilities and a fine soldier. A man one could respect in spite of his obvious failing.' His replacement is a very proud man. 'Men are not men to him, but members of this or that class.' Another officer is sickly and doleful in appearance but behind that there was a 'keen and accurate mind and a strong calm will. He is never excited and never hurried and he knows how to use his men.' Strang acknowledged that he himself had a great longing for the end of the war and a 'happy peaceful industrious useful life at home out of this nerve and flesh shattering hell'. His morale was 'pretty good at the moment but it may go crack when it comes to the test. But I am no worse than most other people. We await the 18th with mixed feelings. May the old 4th [Bn] do its job and may it not be hit too hard.' On 16 October, the men have to endure a bombardment of their trench, 'shells, shells, shells. Thank the Lord for this dug-out of ours.' He maintains his morale is still good except for short periods but he does not like the 'sight of death and corruption. There is no peace about sudden death, but contortion and tearing of flesh … life is sweet, I want to live, live, live.' Letters from home arrive and they cheer him considerably. He continued his diary at 1.30 a.m. on the day of their action, 18 October. Other officers were asleep in the dug-out and the rain outside teemed down. The men had moved off to their assault positions but as they slipped and got stuck in the trenches there were inevitable delays. Zero Hour was at 3 a.m.: the Worcesters were to attack at 3.45 a.m.

The field messages vividly convey urgency, emergency, need for information. The 'Pigeon man' must be ready by 3.40 a.m., then at 4.40 a.m., to the Officer Commanding X Company, 'You are to hold the trench occupied at all cost' – at 4.58 a.m., to the same source, 'You must hold on, forming defensive flank'. Contact is lost with this company and Strang sent runners off with messages to other company commanders who may have information of X Company. Prisoners were being brought in at 5.35 a.m. There was no news of X Company. The officer in command of the Trench Mortar Battery was ordered to report to Battalion HQ as soon as possible. He was instructed to bombard an objective not yet captured. The Commander of Y Company was told: 'You have all done jolly well and the position must be consolidated and held at all costs.'

A company commander reported that his earlier messages had not got through because the first runner was missing, the second buried, and the third wounded. One example of those messages received must suffice:

We arrived at forming up place very late owing to congestion of trenches, mud etc so I took my men straight into No Man's Land and just got formed up in time. No time to dump overcoats. We were seen forming up, only too late to do much harm. We advanced under the barrage and took Grease Trench. Little resistance except on left. 2nd Lt Durant killed and Donnell wounded. I am not sure that my left is on the X roads but it is on the road. No dug-outs in road but huts higher up which I have so far been unable to approach owing to fire. Am in touch with Z. Nobody on my left where I have a Vickers Gun. T. F. V. Matthews (Officer Commanding Y Company).

The battalion had secured its first objective but suffered heavy casualties in trying to go on further. Their relief by the 87th Brigade took twenty-seven hours and those hours must have seemed interminable after such prolonged physical and nervous endurance. Of this, Strang's diary leaves no doubt. 'I was nearer dead beat than I have ever been in my life before. The last mile past Longueval was a perfect torture. My feet seemed suddenly to become tender all over and lost all spring and when I was once stuck in the mud shin high I had hardly the strength to get myself clear.'[2]

If physical movement was so seriously penalised by the combined effect of weather, the nature of the terrain and the military activity upon it, to say nothing of sheer weariness, then there was a further Autumn penalty. Mist, fog, low clouds, poor light, rain, were all enemies of aerial observation and the work of those in ground observation posts was frequently disadvantaged too. An enemy palpably strong was not always easy to locate precisely. The gathering of fresh intelligence by aerial photography and then the updating of maps were essential parts of all military planning and this work was difficult on some days, impossible on others. Of course the virtual disappearance of recognisable features on the ground as they sank in a sludge of mud, pulverised brick and waterlogged craters, added to the problems. Villages were scarcely more than pinkish stains in an otherwise monochrome grey/brown squalor though the outline of roads survived helpfully to mark their presence in the past. The logic of this, however frustrating to those interpreting prisoner gleanings that German morale was creaking and might crack under more pressure, was that no more could be done until the ground dried or froze and the weather improved.

The Third Army was released first from its attacking responsibilities on 17 October but in the centre and the south of the battlefront, the Reserve Army and Fourth Army respectively were required to continue to exert pressure if the weather were to allow it and so they did though the weather scarcely did allow it. It should be noted here that some units were showing increased sickness returns which did not bode well for the maintenance of the offensive.[3] There is a significant reference in a letter dated 2 October 1916 to his parents from Captain Philip Hirsch of the 4th Battalion Yorkshire regiment: 'an officer, unhurt, but taken away on a stretcher "absolutely broken"'. On the same day Philip Hirsch had written to his badly-wounded brother, Frank, recognising and sympathising over the pain he must be suffering, and adding 'we've done damn well, but we've had it in the neck. Perris was killed poor lad and six others all together.' It might be added appropriately here that this Green Howard was still pleased that he had two bayonets and a bomb to bring home as souvenirs.[4]

The 2nd Battalion Lancashire Fusiliers was involved in a desperately costly attack in late October against strong complex positions of the Transloy Ridges, beyond and between captured Gueudecourt and Lesboeufs. A company commander, Lieutenant V. F. S. Hawkins, wrote such a vivid account of this harrowing experience that it reads as if it were a 1916 diary. Before the battle the Fusiliers had carried forward bombs, tools, stores and barbed wire in an extended day's march over quagmired open ground and were weary in the extreme. The last stage of the journey was in pitch darkness but having reached the dropping-off point, their battalion HQ, they still had their return journey to endure. With no rations having been brought up for them, they were instructed to make use of their iron rations.

The company commanders were now ordered forward to battalion HQ for briefing before the attack. Hawkins had the opportunity of seeing that their jumping-off trench was more like a narrow ditch and to complicate matters further, just to their right flank was a barricade separating them from a small pocket of enemy troops, isolated but active in defence of their beleaguered position.

There was much to do: orders to be given out to the company, flares, wirecutters and rations to be collected, then the midnight move up to the front line. They were in the assembly positions at 6 a.m. During the British bombardment some German soldiers filtered in to surrender, creating misplaced optimism. Watches were synchronised, the assault ordered for troops on their right for five past two in the afternoon. The noise of the British bombardment and German counter-barrage intensified with enemy machine-gun fire also menacing them directly to their front. At zero hour for the Fusiliers, some of the men went off early:

All the machine-guns in the world seemed to be firing at us. One subaltern and many of the men were hit within five yards of our line. My orderly and I went like blazes and almost at once found ourselves well

away in front of the company, all of whom seemed to be lying down. I
yelled to the nearest platoon commander to get his platoon on the move
again. He was lying just behind me. But that was no good. He was dead.
Another sergeant on my right was also dead. I shouted at all the men I
could see and got up to take them on. In fact they were all dead. Almost
immediately I found myself sitting on the ground facing the wrong way
with a largehole in my thigh. Of the 100 men in the company who had
started the attack, 80 were already dead but (of course) I did not realise
this at the time.

The account continues in relating how Hawkins ordered a less severely
wounded officer to take command of the company. With the help of his
orderly, who had cut his trousers off to get a field dressing on his wound
while Hawkins had used his tie as a tourniquet, the officer attempted to
crawl back to their jumping off position, the hole in his leg filling with the
potential disaster of poisonous mud. There was good work by stretcher
bearers, two of them 'old friends and old soldiers one of whom kept patting
me on the head and telling me "I was alright now"'. Nevertheless there was
delay in his getting the necessary attention to his wound and Hawkins was
certainly lucky with his life and leg being saved by the skill and dedication
of a surgeon and his attendant nurse.[5]

For all the sterling endeavour the Fourth Army expended in the sector of
the Transloy ridges, General Joffre expressed dismay at the limitation of the
broad-front offensive he wished to see maintained. His letter to this effect
drew a sharp reply from the British Commander-in-Chief. In any case, the
weather was to decree that there should be no major attack in late October
as rain drenched the last week, drowning the prospect of a resumption of
the offensive. The renewal of the Battle of Ancre, to be launched by Gough's
Reserve Army (renamed the Fifth at the end of the month) was postponed on
several occasions as Staff waited for reports of some drying out of the ground.
Meanwhile, on the front of the Fourth Army, the attempt to maintain smaller-
scale co-ordinated operations continued into November. The bitter essence
of these operations is conveyed in a single sentence in the Official History.
'Struggling through mud and water, the 2/R. Berkshire and the 1/R. Irish
Rifles lost the barrage and were stopped by rifle and machine-gun fire after

going 70 yards.'[6] The balance of the equation between continuing to exert destructive pressure on a foe who might be weakening, and expending men, munitions and morale from one's own finite resources, was judged by the British High Command in 1916 in favour of the continuance of the offensive. Today, comfortably removed from the eye of the storm, we may well consider this ill-judged. Too much was being asked at too great a cost for too little gain and it was not yet over. The Fourth Army maintained offensive operations on a limited scale and faced counter-attacks until the afternoon of 16 November.

After further hesitations over ground conditions, Gough's offensive north and south of the Ancre was fixed for 13 November. It was designed to reduce the German salient created by Allied gains in the south. Familiar objectives were to be re-attacked in three stages. With their defence systems extending laterally of course, Serre on the far left and then Beaumont Hamel, Beaucourt in the centre and St Pierre Divion on the right, were the designated fortified locations to be assaulted and success would secure two vital bridge crossings of the Ancre. It was a limited operation and this allowed for a concentration of the Fifth Army's reinforced artillery. The artillery plan had the essential elements of a trench raid box barrage on a far larger scale in that the area selected for the attack was to be isolated by a bombardment cutting off all routes of reinforcement and, in so far as was possible, all communications. A further sophistication of the artillery preparations was the attempt to accustom the enemy to an intense storm of shellfire which in fact presaged no infantry attack and then on 13 November such an attack was to be mounted with a further variation in the barrage to protect the infantry as they moved forward.

A moonlit night aided the infantry in getting into position. In the early hours, damp cold fog materialised. It added the element of uncertainty about orientation which was far from ideal for men who had endured the miserable ground conditions and the tensions of the postponements of an attack for which they had several times had to prepare themselves inwardly against natural apprehension. The fog was of course a two-faceted factor in that it added to the element of surprise and confusion among the Germans. This was certainly the case south of the Ancre where, despite some loss of direction by infantry in attack, the objectives were secured and for no heavy cost.

Immediately north of the Ancre, the Royal Naval Division (RND) (the 63rd Division), experienced at Gallipoli but not on the Western Front, was undertaking its first major battle in France. From official and from personal contemporary evidence it is abundantly clear that officers and men had been well briefed in advance of the operation. The War Diary of the Hood Battalion records that 'the objectives had been explained in great detail to all ranks. The ground had been studied and most of the officers had crossed the Ancre to get a better view of it and to see better the line of advance. The greatest trouble has been taken in explaining the nature of the ground and the movement of the barrage and there is no doubt that the subsequent success of the attack by the Battalion was due to this, particularly as the attack was timed to start in darkness – accentuated by a Scotch mist.'[7] Jack Bentham, a Sub-Lieutenant in the Hood Battalion, recalled that conferences were held daily and all officers and NCOs were given small specially-prepared maps of the plan of attack. This was all consistent with the thoroughness of their commanding officer, Bernard Freyberg. 'Nothing was overlooked and everyone knew exactly what to do.'[8] The detail certainly is remarkable. The Battalion War Diary provides information that the men with wire cutters were to wear a yellow band on their left arm so they could be readily recognised. It was also laid down that a rum ration, carried in Perrier bottles, should be issued to the men an hour before Zero. 'This was found most beneficial.'

Progress was slow as the men moved to their assembly positions, put on their greatcoats and settled down to rest and wait. The officers synchronised their watches at 4 a.m. and the men were woken at 4.30 a.m. Rum was issued, coats taken off, rolled in bundles of ten and left. At 5.45 a.m. British shelling, which had been kept up through the night, became an intense barrage and the men moved forward in waves from the four lines of white tape which marked the jumping off point of each wave. The first wave was 'right on the heels of the barrage which could only be discerned by little spurts of flame'.

A combination of factors, including 'the eagerness of the men' and the darkness, led to the waves becoming mixed up but the enemy's front line was taken. Of the officers, four had been killed and nine wounded, of whom one was Bentham. Six German officers and about 600 German 'other ranks' were taken prisoner. Bentham's recollections of the assault until the moment when he was wounded are of 'throwing phosphorus bombs down the dug-outs which forced the inmates to come up and some of my men bayonetted them as they did so. It was not that they were that way inclined but that they had lost all semblance of civilised beings.' In such a way, Bentham described the heat of the battle and instinctive human response to its stress.

Colonel Freyberg, now leading a mixed force of men from his own battalion, from the Drake Battalion (RND) and from the 1st Battalion Honourable Artillery Company, had moved on towards the second objective, Beaucourt, before the shelling of both sides forced a retirement to a position he ordered consolidated among the shell holes. The CO wanted to take Beaucourt but the British barrage did not lift and he was informed that this was because the situation on the left was as yet unclear. On the right, actually at the crossing of the Ancre, contact had been made with the 1st Battalion Cambridge Regiment so an important link had been established there. However, for the afternoon and night, there could be only the holding of what had been taken and the organisation of an attacking force from the men he had and those who had joined him from his left, or were sent up to reinforce him.

In the morning, the order to attack was given and at 7.45 a.m. Freyberg led forward a mixed body of men from battalions of the Royal Naval Division and from other units. The Second-in-Command of the Hood Battalion, Major L. Montagu, in a letter written six days later, described what happened. He saw Freyberg jump out of his trench and wave the men on, Montagu and three men beside him followed. They came under heavy small arms fire and the first wave stopped three times. Freyberg was knocked clean over by a bullet which hit his helmet but he got up again.

I and my runner dived into a shell hole and waited about half a minute. I said I would go back and get some more men out of the trench and crawled about ten yards back to do so. Then about a dozen men came out and I got up and waved the rest on, they all followed. We soon got in to Beaucourt (of course absolute ruins) and found that the Germans could not face our men and were surrendering in hundreds. It was an amazing sight, they came out of their holes, tearing off their equipment.

Freyberg arranged the consolidation of the village and there was even some opportunity for refreshment and celebratory conversation before fearfully heavy German shelling fell upon their immediate vicinity. They were awaiting a counter-attack when 'I heard Freyberg say: "Goodbye Montagu" and then: "Steady Hood" and I saw he was hit and going a very bad colour. He asked me if I had any morphine he then produced a tube and asked me to give him some, I gave him ¼ grain and labelled him to say I had done so.' The CO had been wounded in the neck and was bleeding profusely. Montagu had been wounded too, another man killed and one wounded. To Montagu's surprise, Freyberg did not die. In fact he continued to give instructions until he asked his Second-in-Command if he could walk to an Aid Post. Under shellfire, the two men completed the 300-yard journey back, the worst part for Montagu being the wounded men they passed, imploring him for help.[9]

Freyberg's leadership and personal gallantry were to result in the award of the Victoria Cross. The capture of Beaucourt was a fine achievement and there was pride as well as humour and diffidence in a Royal Naval Division Sapper's letter home on 21 November. 'We haven't been able to write at all lately. We have been "pushed" and are now out of it for a bit with good hopes of leave … Did you see about us in the Daily Mail – old Sea Dogs etc "Bosh" isn't it?' Sapper Davy, like so many before him, was greatly impressed by the size and elaborate nature of a captured dug-out very well stocked with food and utensils. 'There certainly is no sign of shortage of beef butter bread jam chocolate Rum or rifles bombs respirators or indeed anything necessary for war.' There was however a balancing cheer to this almost alarming evidence refuting claims of the enemy being stretched to breaking point. 'The prisoners look strangely white as if they had been living for months below ground. They looked sort of dazed and scared.'[10]

On the left of the Royal Naval Division, the 51st Division faced the Y Ravine Salient and Beaumont Hamel. All that Second Lieutenant Cheyne of the 5th Gordon Highlanders wrote for this day in his diary was: 'Attack on Beaumont Hamel. Take 3 lines of trenches. Officers killed – Major Napier, Capt Stephen, 2nd Lts Wilson, Sykes, RM Ferguson, John Watt. Wounded Gilmore, Johnstone, Brackenridge, Gibb, Reid, Manson, Capt Robertson, R W Ferguson. Other Ranks killed 60, Wounded 130, Missing 249.'[11] From the 6th Battalion Seaforth Highlanders, Captain Gerald Stewart wrote home less starkly but with his own thoughts of the account in the *Daily Mail*.

> We have been pretty busy this week. You will have seen all about it in the papers before now I expect and know as much about it as I can tell. This Brigade [152] had the hardest job of the lot but I think we came out very well. Of course the casualties were pretty heavy but we did not have as many as we expected and a good many of them were slightly wounded. The biggest proportion was among the officers. I see Beach Thomas has some descriptions of it all in the Paris Daily Mail. He has drawn well on his imagination, as half of it is not true, but just what he thought it would be like.[12]

Fog and the difficulty of locating gaps in the wire, mud everywhere, and in one place a morass, added to the problems of keeping up with the barrage and then storming formidable defensive positions. Beaumont Hamel was taken but on its left heavy losses were incurred for little gain. Exhausted men of mixed units were literally floundering in mud on the very approach to their objectives. Men in forward positions were often in no contact with the rear and where communications did exist they were frequently broken and re-established only with the greatest difficulty. Attacks were cancelled and in some cases a withdrawal from inadequately-held gains was ordered. Gough's confidence that the position could still be improved overcame Haig's reluctance – Haig being in Paris at the Chantilly Conference of Allied Commanders. A renewal of the attempt was sanctioned by Haig even as Gough himself was receiving Intelligence of the expensive failure to which he was committing himself on his left front against Serre. He ordered a more limited advance for 18 November but one launched on the whole front of II Corps and V Corps from Serre in the north, then on either side of the Ancre and finally eastwards to positions held by the Canadians in front of Courcelette.

Comparisons are often invidious and those made about October/November conditions on the Somme invite refutation by cited alternative example but it would be difficult to imagine circumstances more disadvantaged than those endured on the last two days of the battle. Tired, chilled troops, with their reservoir of spiritual and physical resilience drained, were now required to cope with bitter cold, with swirling snow or sleet later turning to rain, drenched bodies already affected by inadequate blood circulation. Whether waiting in the assembly positions, moving into attack or pinned down in shell holes by enemy fire, this must have been misery in the extreme, for some, still further extended by wounds. The blanket of snow and the wind-blown sleet obscured observation, hindering recognition of familiar features. In these final days of a four-and-a-half month battle there is a conclusive uniformity in all the evidence of what it was like to be there. Even the constant grim cheer of Northumberland Fusilier Bates is checked: 'I cannot describe what it is like anywhere near the lines – camps, roads, villages, one sea of filthy mud and the line itself ten times worse!!! Ponds of standing water: what looks like a fairly safe crossing, in reality a 10 foot shell hole; trenches falling in and impossible to repair; men done up before they ever get under fire.'[13]

The subsequently famous pen of Guy Chapman, a subaltern in the 13th Battalion Royal Fusiliers, closed his diary entry for the night of 16 November with:

No. 1 Coy is badly knocked out. Lander and Young both badly wounded, CSM Dell wounded. Farrington killed. Sgt Brown not expected to live. Sgt Baker wounded. Westle, poor fellow, killed. Foley – the last of his family – killed, a lot of other good men, too many to speak of. The Coy. apart from the Lewis Gunners is 27 all told. It is impossible to describe the country. The impression is that some volcanic blast has struck it. Vegetation scarcely anywhere: trees are stripped of their branches. Many lie smashed and the remnant are bare poles. Houses of course are no more, a ruined heap of bricks sometimes will show you where they once stood but everywhere is desolate. By Beaucourt Station lie the skeleton of five waggons and their team, the grisly evidence of the tragedy of a Bosche ration convoy. There is a sickly stench, the mixed smell of exploded picric acid, gas, blood, putrifying corpses and broken bricks. Here and there lie the bodies of the fallen … The burial parties work without ceasing. 800 Englishmen and forty Germans were buried yesterday – evidence of what price the assaulting parties must pay for some few yards of ground. Damn Germany![14]

Sergeant Adrian Hill's artistic talent was expressed in letters home as well as in Field Sketching for military purposes. In the year following his service on the Somme, he was to be commissioned and to take up duties as an Official War Artist. Here, in 1916, the drawings in his letters capture aspects of Army life and the prevailing weather and ground conditions of the Autumn. (*Liddle Collection*)

The Regimental and Divisional histories of those units involved in the actual attack on 18/19 November reflect a similar picture. The Cheshire Regiment account for their 9th Battalion wastes no words: 'It was now dark and many men were lost in the mud and darkness. Eventually, four officers and a handful of men charged OGI. The enemy drove them off with bomb and rifle.'[15] The 18th Divisional History, in a matter of fact way, captures the tragedy of the loss of direction in the mist and snow which caused two companies of the 7th Queens to vanish 'entirely, being overwhelmed by machine-gun fire'.[16]

It was over. The weather had at last dictated a merciful closure of all offensive operations on the Somme. The British task of consolidation was now the overriding priority. Gun emplacements, roads, communication trenches and rear, support and front-line defences, urgently needed the work of sappers, labour units, pioneers and the men serving within these positions. Water supply, drainage, latrines, improved billetting arrangements, all this and more needed attention. Much that had necessarily assumed a lower priority for four-and-a-half months could now receive concentrated attention. Ironically the dryer weather which followed this first snow of the winter brought down the temperatures to degrees of frost and left them there so that the mud which had squelchingly defied spade or entrenching tool now rang as iron in retaliatory vibration against the wielding of those same implements.

Chapter 6

A Verdict

While the November battle on the Ancre was being fought, an Allied High Command conference at Chantilly was considering plans for a co-ordinated offensive on several fronts in the Spring of the following year. A key element in such an offensive would be a renewed Anglo-French drive on the Western Front. 1916 had seen the defeat of the Romanian component of the Entente but there was evidence elsewhere that the continued exertion of pressure on the Central Powers had sown the seeds of a military harvest which could be reaped in the Spring. Such thinking was far from being universally held in the corridors of political power where the perspective was frequently framed by an antipathetic view of the military mind. Ministers of State looking at the Somme through this lens saw their judgement irrefutably confirmed.

Lloyd George, in 1915 a member of the War Council which had approved the Gallipoli operation, was in November 1916 Secretary of State for War. He was deeply convinced that an alternative way had to be found to get into the heart of the Central Powers and bring about their defeat. The continuous battering at a bolted front door, as seemed to him the unimaginative, indifferently callous, even stupid, High Command directive for the Somme, convinced him of the inappropriateness of such methods, re-confirmed his vision of an Eastern approach and determined him on Haig's unfitness to command. This depth of political/military cleavage was given awesome significance by Lloyd George's assumption of the Premiership in December under circumstances which make quite as good a story as those which had seen Haig reach his position as Commander-in-Chief BEF twelve months earlier.

Lloyd George's sudden turnabout as Premier, his temporary conversion to the idea of victory on the Western Front through a new deliverer, Joffre's replacement as French Commander-in-Chief, General Nivelle, and the direct repercussions this would have for the BEF and its Commander-in-Chief in 1917–18, are not strictly within the scope of this book. They are, however, deserving of one's awareness in this chapter as it is basically Lloyd George's and Churchill's verdict on the Somme, carried forward into the present by some, that we must address in any attempt to evaluate High Command direction of the battle.

The two political Titans, by definition conditioned to be reactive to opinion, trends, shifting ground, disappointments and quite naturally to the search for scapegoats as well as alternative, cheaper, shorter visions of how the war might be won, were to set themselves up against the military men while the war was being waged, most particularly in the case of Lloyd George. In their perception, the 'Brass Hats' exercised their authority with a total lack of imagination and a callous disregard for the human material put into their hands to win the war. For their part, military High Command did indeed think differently, being convinced that at this time of great industrialised nations with mass armed forces being locked in struggle, the war had to be fought as they were fighting it, by attritional methods to deplete the strength and will of the enemy.

What irony there is in that while the military men were grimly proved to be right, the politicians, in keeping with the post-war spirit of the times, wrote the more convincing self-justificatory memoirs and histories of the war, identifying the 'villains' responsible for its shameful cost and length. A battle won with a pen, casualties limited to reputations and a proper understanding of the war.

As weary British troops embarked on consolidation of their positions from late November 1916, two things were happening which in different ways illustrate some of the problems which require consideration in approaching a verdict on the Somme in its centenary year. First, Haig was penning his official despatch on the battle. It is dated 23 December 1916. In it he deploys the benefit of hindsight – what he had learned from his experience in directing the Somme Offensive – to underplay his pre-battle hope of a breakthrough, and, till at least mid-September, his retention of some hope of that breakthrough. If hindsight for the historian is at one and the same time his weapon and potentially his Achilles heel, then so it must be for the Commander-in-Chief. Certainly Haig's failure to acknowledge in this official document that the first great offensive waged under his command had educated him in how this colossal struggle inexorably would have to be fought, – simply by wearing out his enemy – seems to diminish him as a man, but surely, if one were to believe him correct in his assessment, does the omission seriously diminish him as a Commander-in-Chief? In my judgement that is less clear.

The second point is that as Haig was writing his report, the Germans were pressing on with the preparation of the new defensive line to which they would withdraw from February to April 1917. Well before this, in Germany on the Home Front, the exigencies produced by the war in general, blockade in particular, and not least the strain of the Somme, were stimulating strikes, disturbances and peace protests.

The Somme had played a major part in undermining German High Command in the West though it was the opening of a new front in Romania which led to Falkenhayn's removal and Hindenburg and Ludendorff being summoned at the end of August to take over in the worsening crisis in the West. What weight may we place on this, on the withdrawal, and still later developments, in evaluating whether the British and French were indeed to have won the Battle of the Somme?

John Terraine maintained that the Somme in 1916, and Third Ypres in 1917, were essential elements in the August–November 1918 defeat of the German Army on the Western Front. His argument has been further developed in the tri-nation research of William Philpott's history of the Somme, *Bloody Victory* – '[Attrition], loathsome as it may be, worked.'[1] The historian made the further point that Lloyd George, who had been pre-eminently in a position to halt such procedure in prosecuting the war, did little so to do until deploring the means after the war. Philpott might quite reasonably have added, as many would, that he 'did nothing except consistently undermine in Westminster, Whitehall, with the Press and with French politicians and generals, the position and reputation of his own Commander-in-Chief BEF', but Philpott is unequivocal concerning the strategy of attrition, originating from the 1916 Battle of the Somme. Cumulatively, the effects of attrition combined with repetitive and increasingly frequent battlefield defeats were to bring on the German army's eventual collapse.[2] The issues may not be easy to quantify but, as marshalled by these two historians, and others distinguished in the field, the argument convinces the author of this book.

In the Introduction to this book, some attention was given to the place of the battle in the generational passage of our history: what the Somme has come to mean to us and the extent to which that was a true reflection of the actual experience of the battle in 1916 and its significance to the outcome of the war. Here, at the conclusion of the book, an attempt will be made to restrict the perspective to the original setting. Was it a necessary battle; to what extent was there choice available to Haig over its location and timing; what can be said about the manner in which it was waged and the awful price? Was it unjustifiably prolonged and, within the 1916 time-scale circumscribed; was there identifiable profit from such expenditure of human and material resources? To some extent the author's answers to these questions have already been indicated, but they need summary and attention given to the further fundamental question of how the men of the units which saw prolonged service on the Somme coped with the experience in terms of their morale?

The reality of the constraint upon Haig's freedom of action as Commander-in-Chief BEF, lay in the relative difference between the British and French material contributions to the Western Front in December 1915 when Haig was appointed to his command: in miles of front held, about 50 as against 400; in divisions of troops employed on the Western Front, about thirty-eight as against ninety-five. The disparity between the British and French commitment was so striking that there could be no question that the overall strategic direction would be in French hands. This situation, by definition paralleled in reverse for naval strategy, was formalised by the conclusions reached at the Inter-Allied Military Conference at Chantilly on

6–8 December 1915 and then at the end of the month by the instructions given to Haig by the Secretary of State for War, Lord Kitchener.

First, at Chantilly, Joffre had secured unanimous support for what amounted to his strategic overview – concentration upon the main, rather than subordinate battlefronts, co-ordination of planned offensives for those fronts to be launched as soon as possible and designed collectively to be decisive. On 28 December, Haig received his instructions from Kitchener and they made it unarguably clear that British troops were in France primarily to combine with the French to defeat the enemy: 'The closest co-operation of French and British as a united Army must be the governing policy …'[3] As John Terraine, long ago, consistently maintained, no matter what clauses followed about Haig not coming under French command, the reality of his terms of reference was caught in the expression 'the governing policy'. Hence we have a uniform inter-Allied consensus for a co-ordinated offensive and it can be inferred beyond dispute that Haig would work with the French design and timing of that offensive on the Western Front. Furthermore, it would follow that a much heavier burden of such an attack would fall upon the BEF because the nearing readiness of the New Armies would enable the imbalance of the Allied effort on the Western Front to be considerably redressed. The Chantilly Conference had quite specifically referred to the need for the 'wearing down' of the enemy by operations conducted by those powers which had reserves of men, all this materially to help a concerted effort. In the West this meant Britain. There was no longer a reservoir of French manpower on which to call, and of course there is irony in the fact that the number factor dictated that strategy would be French-determined and yet it also dictated that the price in men would have now to be paid by Britain to a far greater extent than hitherto.

We have to accept then that there was no disagreement that a major offensive was needed and no possible issue over the fact that the BEF would foot the larger proportion of the bill. It cannot be seriously maintained that Haig's belief that Flanders was where the ultimate decision might be won, made him obstructive over Joffre's insistence that the offensive should be well south of where the BEF had so far undertaken major operations. What Haig wanted to do was to convert the idea of subsidiary wearing-out fights before such a great battle took place into the drawing together for more profitable use of all the resources necessary for that larger endeavour. To this end, attacks immediately prior to the general action would be justified as they would distract the enemy and draw in his reserves committing them to operations of secondary consequence; attacks launched earlier would be profitless.

In conference discussion with Joffre on 14 February, Haig's point was conceded but the same conference also fixed the scene and the date for the Allied offensive – the Somme on 1 July. There is no need here to examine the reasons why Haig would have preferred Flanders: it is sufficient to say that Joffre required the Somme. Again there is an irony. Here on the Somme in an attritional battle, Joffre would be able to fix the British into playing a major part. Haig would be looking for something different, a front to be broken but, in truth, with no strategic objective behind that front. In Flanders there were two such objectives, Roulers and the ports of the occupied coast of Belgium. On the Somme there was nothing of similar significance.

In parenthesis, it is tempting to consider whether Haig's lack of recognition for French achievements on the Somme, at the time and subsequently, something for which he has been criticised, had its roots in the British C-in-C having to dance to the French tune, being uncomfortable with this and with the fact that, in military terms, the French were at this time dancing the better – their artillery programmes and concentration, and their infantry tactics in the assault.

On 21 February, the German onslaught at Verdun made an indelible imprint upon all Allied planning for the Western Front. Haig had not yet jettisoned all thoughts of Flanders but such thoughts were held now under inescapable restraint. Readily he undertook what he had so recently refused, the immediate taking-over of the line held by the French Tenth Army. In French perception, the Somme, by its relative proximity to Verdun, could assist in the holding of the historic city; Flanders certainly would have no such effect. At a stroke, Verdun added a preoccupying urgency to all planning for the Somme and it would determine that a date earlier than 1 July might be contemplated for the opening of this offensive, a date later could not be. Haig, on 26 May, had made his preference for a later date clear to Joffre but he was not ungracious in accepting the priority of French need over British readiness for the battle.

The battle then had been judged necessary by French-led, inter-Allied agreement. It was given British Cabinet endorsement conveyed to Haig on 14 April. The location of the battle was decreed by Joffre, the timing decided by both Allied intention and German intervention. Haig's role had been entirely proper – professionally rather sceptical but, from the reality of his subordinate position, seeking at this stage to raise the prospect above that of *une bataille d'usure* and of loyally concentrating the available resources for what was now a threefold concept – a major element in the co-ordinated Allied offensive planned for 1916, the very necessary rescue of an ally and the development of the possibility of a decisive breakthrough.

Concerning the way in which the battle was waged, the divergence between Haig and Rawlinson over the question of 'breakthrough' or 'bite and hold' has been stressed. In his book *British Generalship in the Twentieth Century*, E. K. G. Sixsmith suggested that Haig was in pursuit of 'true strategy' which of course sought surprise, and examined the nature of the ground to see which objectives, once taken, offered hope for exploitation. Even with the closeness of the opposing lines offering unpromising chances of securing surprise, we should remember that some strategic surprise was won. British military activity from the Belgian coast southwards did delay German realisation that the real effort was coming between Serre and Montauban and the Germans did not anticipate that the French would be able to take on any offensive role at all. A shock certainly awaited them on the French sector. Sixsmith is one of several authors who stress quite appositely that in the earliest stage of the planning for the Somme Haig had wanted an infantry advance led by lightly-equipped infantry patrols but his three Army Commanders had opposed this and Haig conceded their point. Sixsmith maintains that Rawlinson was more concerned with the means at his disposal and the method of attack and that while Haig was able to insist on planning for the swift seizure of some key objectives – Montauban for example – his inability to answer the problem of the enemy wire other than by prolonged bombardment led him largely to accept Rawlinson's tactical approach. Hence, a preliminary bombardment that was long enough and heavy enough would leave the infantry with the reduced task of taking possession of destroyed defences and consolidating them against counter-attack. Successive waves advancing behind a precisely timed artillery bombardment which would lift exactly as previously decreed onto the next target, would be the subsidiary infantry role in what was basically an artillery battle.[4] Capturing the first line of enemy trenches was not, however, to be the relatively simple task envisaged.

As recognised in all accounts of the battle, there was an insufficiency of guns, in particular of heavy guns, of high explosive shells and, we might well remind ourselves, that the instantaneous fuse, so essential for the destruction of barbed wire, was not available for 1 July. The artillery programme for the assault has been considered by many to have been inflexible and, given the known insufficiencies and inadequacies in the instrument of delivery, unrealistic. Furthermore, even if the plan were to have been the masterpiece claimed by a recent historian of the Royal Regiment of Artillery, General Sir Martin Farndale, there was a considerable variation in Corps and Divisional understanding of the programme, and in the capacity to implement it or willingness to implement it. The same must be said of the use of meteorological information and newly-developed techniques like reliance on the map for 'predicted' rather than pre-registered shooting. In the case of the New Army, the lack of experience at all levels in the science of gunnery was a very serious matter. Additionally, in the light of all this and the inability to locate and destroy German batteries, an insufficient awareness of the true strength of the German underground defence system and that the British bombardment was to be rendered still less effective by the high proportion of defective shells and worn or dated artillery pieces, there was still another fatal flaw. This was the failure to require the infantry to exercise speed, keeping up with the barrage and being in on the defenders before they manned their parapets. This was the only way in which some element of tactical surprise could be achieved and, as fate was to decree, it was also the only way there would be any protection to the infantry as the men were exposed crossing No Man's Land. With too much faith put in the artillery completely to fulfil its role in the battle and no widely-held confidence that New Army infantry could operate in any other way than methodically walking across and occupying destroyed positions, over- and under-confidence respectively were to combine in the production of the tragedy of the first day of the battle.

There was more. For reasons of artillery observation, the French refused to countenance an earlier hour than 7.30 a.m. for the infantry assault. This compounded the problem on the British front where the artillery had not done its work effectively and that which would be clearly observed was not the German positions but the British infantry in their approach of them.

Hindsight compels us to witness and re-witness in our mind's eye the awful inappropriateness of heavily-burdened men attempting to make measured progress across No Man's Land in successive lines of companies in extended order, with the artillery not having been effective in protecting them. The issue of some battalions, and New Army battalions too, having been trained in different procedures and carrying them out successfully, has to be followed up with, 'then why were not all the Kitchener men so trained?'

Contemporary source after source lays emphasis on the New Army's unreadiness in terms of training for the assault they would have to make – that is of course in contrast to their exhibiting an outstanding readiness in terms of *elan*. Were the battalions of the Regular Army and of the Territorial Force required to attack using precisely the same procedure? No, but by whatever means the men of the BEF attacked north of Montauban, success was minimal and the price still dreadful.

It is difficult to make a convincing argument that the New Army infantry, given the chance of May/June training behind the lines in France, could have developed a real proficiency in advance, by detachments, in the lozenge-shaped 'artillery formation' or by the Regular Army pre-war 'fire and movement' procedure to build up a firing line, platoons alternatively giving covering fire and then advancing as they themselves were given protection. High morale there certainly was but there was not the marksmanship to take advantage from such procedure and, in fact, the nature of the more elevated German positions, secure in their concreted depth also, was surely not going to be taken by such methods at this stage of the war with morale of the defender unbroken.

There is then a strong temptation to state quite simply that the German positions were too strong and the enlarged BEF not ready for the Somme when the battle had, for all the reasons previously stated, to take place. Battle experience in this 'new' world war was everything. By definition, Kitchener's men had not had Neuve Chapelle or Aubers Ridge or the experience of the Battle of Loos as a grim guide and if High Command and its staff did indeed have such experience, the insufficiently-tuned instrument at their disposal was going to have to be played and there was not the rehearsal time for learning radically new techniques before the performance – Verdun saw to that.

A counter-argument can be developed but it leads to a quagmire for the politician. If it were to be maintained that in the development of appropriate tactical training procedures for the men of the New Armies, first in the United Kingdom and then in France, the Army authorities had shown a slowness to adapt to the changed circumstance of warfare on the Western Front, the truth of this in general terms could perhaps be conceded but behind this lies the harsh reality of the Nation's unreadiness for the war in which it found itself. Partnered by and matched against huge conscript armies with their nations' industrial systems more readily placed upon a war footing, Britain was paying a high price in every direction as she embarked upon what was needed, the fundamental transformation of her society, economy, institutions and Government to meet the National emergency of a European and World War. Would she have been better prepared, indeed might she have been more of a deterrent to German ambition to make or risk war had she possessed that which was unthinkable to the pre-war Liberal administration, a conscript army?

Yes, the infantry tactics used on 1 July proved on most sectors disastrously inappropriate. Some changes were made, most notably in the hour of launching an attack and in attempts to infiltrate No Man's Land before the attack was delivered but the tactics remained vulnerable. It is surprising that Haig's belief in the possibility of breakthrough was not translated into allowing a night attack on 15 September after the initial success achieved by such timing on 14 July. It can be added significantly, even if depressingly, that when new tactics were developed by all three major antagonists on the Western Front, it still needed special circumstances for them to be effective – first, and little surprise here, in the development of a new highly sophisticated programme of bombardment and second, in serious flaws in the defence of the objectives being attacked. Such circumstances were certainly not present in the Summer of 1916 on the Somme.

Returning to the question of the readiness of the BEF for the battle, several sources echo the Official Historian's emphasis on the relative inexperience of some of the Corps and the Divisional Commanders in managing units of that size. In one important sense the lament is more anachronistic than a fair charge to be made against any individual or the Army as an institution – the sheer size of the BEF was unprecedented and there was by definition no earlier school of experience for the large number of senior officers required. This still leaves open the competence of those promoted to senior positions and here the Canadian historian, Tim Travers, brings some of his most savage criticism to bear upon the system of promotion in the 'old army' and upon Haig in particular. There is abundant evidence of the tensions which developed as a result of the Edwardian army having to digest the lessons of the Second Boer War and ready itself for war in Europe. The old ways survived in awkward juxtaposition with attempts to modernise, make more professional, and develop more technical competence. In such a setting, power, privilege and prejudice advanced the careers of some, arrested those of others. Those who progressed were not always those best fitted for the requirements of the new war. This of course was not a scenario unique to the profession nor to the period, as the world of industry, business, politics and education for example, across any time scale, could doubtless testify. Travers made the point that 'a still largely traditional officer corps [attempting] to fight a modern [technological/firepower] war as though it were a fully prepared and professional group of senior officers and staff, led to a strong tendency to cover up errors during the war, and to achieve alterations in the subsequent military record and then in the Official History'.

There is some truth in this but if this were the whole truth one is left to wonder how the war was won. It has been argued that victory was earned to an overwhelming though inter-related degree by the Royal Navy, also that the psychological factor of the scarcely-tapped resources of the United States was the key. British skill in the realm of propaganda is stressed too (with just a touch of irony) but there is the need to explain the absence of a collapse in the attacking endeavours of the BEF in 1916 and in late 1917, the absence of a collapse as its soldiers desperately defended in the March/April 1918 crisis and then surely its leading part in the three months of hard fought unbroken victory terminating in the Germans suing for an Armistice. Can the military events following upon July 1918 all be attributed to a shrewdness of German High Command policy in withdrawal, French resurgence, American troop arrival in strength and the work of the Australian and Canadian divisions?

Returning to the military direction of the 1916 battle, it is possible that more could have been made from the success at Montauban on 1 July in conjunction with the adjacent French achievements. Perhaps Gough's reserves should have been swiftly given the chance to prove themselves here. Rawlinson's decision to halt and consolidate on the first objective was, some consider, all the more regrettable as Balfourier's XX Corps on his right had also reached its first objective and was anxious to push on to Peronne if the British were also to advance. The northward direction of any exploitation developed here would have been a serious outflanking threat to German defences which were holding firm against frontal assault.

On two further dates, questions have to be raised over the seizure of opportunities or of the reality of such opportunities. On 14 July, it does seem that the cavalry was not in a position swiftly to exploit advantage, again on the right of the British advance. One is almost conditioned to deride the potential usefulness of cavalry in France and perhaps the opportunity of which some have written was but a mirage. Nevertheless the mounted arm was expensively, and hence it must be presumed, purposefully, maintained, yet here we have it ordered up too late and then from too distant an assembly station to have any real chance of fulfilling its purpose. This matter, of great moment or otherwise, lay within Rawlinson's command.

The other major consideration is over the employment of tanks on 15 September. Haig's eagerness to use the new weapon is unquestionable and even after their patchy performance in initial battle testing, his faith in them is confirmed by his striking request, two days later, for 1,000. The charge against him that he used the tanks when he had too few to make an impact and that in using them he was conceding their surprise factor for small reward, does not really stand up against the dual need to use all means available to achieve a breakthrough while the weather held and the fact that the tank had to be proved in battle before mass production could be requested, never mind sanctioned. Where he might have been bolder and intervened in Rawlinson's plans was in the failure to concentrate those tanks available and to use them in a favourable location in the role for which they had been conceived, breakthrough. Instead, they were carefully spread like some special seed that some might fruit. The role given them was to deal with strongpoints, not to force a way through. Perhaps their slowness and the small number which remained immune to mechanical disorder or becoming ditched made them unfit at this stage for anything more adventurous than was essayed but a case can be made against the way the tanks were initially employed and more particularly against the absence of proper artillery protection of their advance.

The time factor can be used on both sides of the argument. On the one hand, there was the urgent need to use tanks almost immediately they arrived because so much was at stake in the effort to achieve strategic initiative, and then, essential battle-testing too, and on the other hand, there was artillery and infantry unfamiliarity with the new engine of war, the small number available, their mechanical unreliability and the inexperience of the crews. All the latter considerations counselled caution, retaining the surprise factor, addressing the problems known to be there and then launching a tank-centred decisive operation.

There were other general matters where tactical thought was developed slowly, like the way in which Lewis and Vickers guns might have been more effectively employed in a mobile attacking role. The same might be said for the need to train and utilise Stokes Mortar teams, but the second barrel of the double-barrelled shotgun charge against Haig for the Somme – the first aimed at the infantry tactics employed – was the prolongation of the battle when, to some at the time and to many who have written about it since, the offensive was maintained long beyond the point of any profit whatsoever. Built into such an indictment is the presumption, frequently stated, that Haig and his staff at their comfortable HQ were totally removed from an understanding of the actual conditions under which the men at the front served and that polished-booted, red-tabbed Staff Officers, coping with the inconvenience of the map obscuring the whisky decanter, drew neat lines which determined the fate of the men towards whom they were callously indifferent. Haig's immaculate dress and stern gaze out of photographs, the setting for which is usually the steps of some splendid chateau, are mentally juxtaposed against images of men in the line and casualty statistics. Of course such visions derive from judgements already made, presumptions affirmed.

There is substance to the charge of the perceived remoteness of the staff once the important qualification is understood that the nearer the line staff work took place, the more difficult it was. Anyone who was momentarily to doubt this reservation has only to read *Staff Officer: The Diaries of Lord Moyne 1914-18*.[5] Walter Guinness, the first Lord Moyne, was to be engaged in Brigade and Divisional staff work in the second half of the war and his diary documents graphically the well-nigh impossible circumstance for such work when under heavy shelling in a forward position. As it happens, there is too, a delightful illustration of the prejudice he met against staff officers when he himself was simply a regimental officer on the Somme. On 23 August, he wrote of the Adjutant of his battalion, the 11th Cheshires, a man who was a university lecturer in Agricultural Chemistry: 'He hates and despises all staff officers, feeling no doubt that he has far more brains himself and says that there are many Double First men serving in the Armies who ought to be on the staff. With all his cleverness, however, his manners are such that what the staff might gain in brains, it would certainly lose in friction.'[6]

It has been argued that the gulf between GHQ and the staffs of subordinate HQ lay not least in a combination of Haig's closed mind and the fear he inspired. The nature of his taciturn personality and of his remote position at the apex of military authority certainly combined seriously to reduce access to him and there is little evidence to demonstrate that the men around him were endowed with exceptional ability or the capacity for innovative thought. On a point of detail, Haig's keenness to use the tanks scarcely suggests a closed mind but the command structure, inter-communication, the exchange and discussion of ideas, implementation of change, the co-operation of individuals and of Staffs, were not areas in which Haig and the senior echelons of command achieved distinction during the central months of the war. Near the top of the pyramid, there were men whose work subsequently seemed seriously adrift like Brigadier-General John Charteris, in command of Intelligence, who fed Haig unwarrantably optimistic reports on the decline of German morale, but the point has to be made more general – there was simply an insufficiency of well-trained Staff Officers for all levels of this work in the hugely expanded BEF. The disappointing quality of their work on the Somme too frequently reflects this and not just at GHQ. From every point of view there was truth in Lord Moyne's diary entry. Later in the war, New Army officers would increasingly break into the enclosed professional milieu of the Staff, but during the Somme, a natural prejudice felt by 'one of us', that is the Regimental Officer with his men in the line, against 'one of them', the briefly visiting Staff Officer, too frequently is evident. It was rooted in the different circumstances of their daily life and the idea of receiving orders from on high through the person of a polished superior being, who seemed to display an unfamiliarity with and a distaste for work at the sharp end of his orders. A discordant thought intrudes here: is this not a normal feature of 'life at the coalface' – how well thought of, is the Bishop on his rare visitation, the school inspector at his scrutiny, even the factory foreman on his rounds?

It is also perhaps fair to suggest that Staff Officers, unless by prior experience solidly grounded in regimental work in the line, might cocoon themselves within the idea that the Regimental Officer would have no idea of the burdensome and endlessly problematic nature of the Staff Officer's work and this perception would hold a measure of truth. There are, however, numerous counterbalancing snippets in letters and diaries from officers and men paying tribute to the organisational work behind the assemblage of so many facilities, so much materiel and so many men of different units engaged in separate but related tasks before the onset of some major endeavour.

Field Marshal Lord Harding, a subaltern in the First World War, told the author that a lesson he had learned from the Great War was to avoid the gulf between the Staff and the Line which he had experienced in 1915–18. The Field Marshal did not serve in France but much has been written in support of this point. It may be considered however that the gulf was there almost by definition both by reason of the particular nature of the First World War and perhaps by the structure of any army at war. In that event then the missing element was High Command concern to stress the inter-dependence of each and a wider understanding by each of the work of the other. Staff Officers with regimental experience had this, but otherwise ignorance prejudiced the view across the divide. Tackling this in war may not have seemed a high priority and would not have been easy to organise. We can see with hindsight that it would have been beneficial.

It remains to be said on this matter that while Haig's severest critics make no documented case against him of indifference to his men, the charge remains by implication. However, it simply cannot be substantiated; there is too much evidence to the contrary. From subaltern to general the man in command had men 'to use' in battle. For him to be unnerved by the full meaning of this, and for him to have given inadequate thought to the best employment of them to achieve the aims of the endeavour; these two factors together would show an unfitness for command. Perfection, freedom from error, and with tragic significance, freedom to operate outside the constraints of the warfare in which commander and men are engaged, this we cannot expect. Whether Haig were to have failed his men on the Somme will continue to be debated; the baser charge that he was indifferent to them, does not stand serious examination. As a liaison officer at GHQ, Charles Armitage, sharing responsibility for feeling the pulse of the men under Haig's command, was infuriated by what he termed such a 'wicked slander which has never been substantiated; the exact opposite is the truth'.[7] By character, personality and upbringing, Douglas Haig was inescapably a product of an age which determined that his paternalistic attitude to his men would give rise among later generations with their different values and social norms, to a range of judgemental reaction – certainly, regret, probably, some lack of comprehension and, in all likelihood, scorn. Could or should anything different have been expected? A hundred years on, the 'mateyness' which society seems to expect between leader and led in any walk of life, frequently looks shallow, artificial and unrealistic to a discerning observer. No, in 1916, Haig showed that he had not got the 'common touch'. In addition to the points already raised, he lacked an essential element in exhibiting it, verbal fluency. How extraordinary it would have been if he were to have had it. Perhaps he did develop something approaching it post-war with his work for the Royal British Legion, but that is another matter.

With German operations at Verdun diminishing rapidly as the Battle of the Somme maintained its momentum in July – on 11 July, Falkenhayn, the Commander-in-Chief, had ordered the suspension of offensive operations at Verdun – had not the Somme justified itself and hence could be halted during the latter part of that month? No, the offensive had been conceived as a huge co-ordinated Allied vision to wrest the war's initiative from the grasp of the Central Powers and there was the continued belief in the possibility of achieving a breakthrough – 1 July at Montauban and 14 July had both indicated that such a chance might be there. There was something else, previously referred to, but deserving re-emphasis, the advance by the Somme of High Command education in the nature of the war in which they were engaged. Attritional erosion of the capacity of an enemy to continue the fight was not new. It was not new when it was waged by the North in the American Civil War, though it was then on an unprecedented scale, and new in the sense that the North had the basis of industrial power to forge the weaponry for this form of destruction of its adversary, but even if it were fundamentally built-in to Allied strategy as agreed in December 1915, it was to be a new experience for Britain in the following year.

The war had become one in which populous, industrialised societies increasingly utilised every fibre of their national resources. However, regardless of this, the current stage of weapon technology gave every advantage to the defender, in this case the Germans, who had advanced into Belgium and France, been checked and, preserving their 1914 initiative, had dug in. To attack them to throw them out of their gains meant challenging the approach to positions commandingly defended by concealed machine-gun and rifle fire supported from the rear by well-sited artillery. There was no flank to turn except by the huge gamble of seaborne invasion of the occupied coast of Belgium and so a fundamentally frontal assault was decreed by definition though the configuration of the line in some sectors seemed to offer flanks for assault – again frontally. With the Entente committed to attack and the Germans advantaged in their defensive posture, the Western Front had become a battle of will and materiel. For Britain, the Somme was the first major test. Gallipoli had devalued strategic alternatives and French requirements focused concentration upon Picardy. Even when the higher aim of breakthrough dissolved in frustration after 15 September, there could be little question of calling off the battle. Furthermore, in the turning of the screw upon the enemy, valuable objectives had been won in the south which invited exploitation to attack, in the flank, positions which were still resisting frontal assault further north. That this is not simply a Headquarters view, nor a retrospective view, is illustrated in the letter sent home on 30 September by the Medical Officer of the 10th Battalion Northumberland Fusiliers, C. K. McKerrow: 'We still push ahead and kill many Huns. Our losses are smaller than at first and I really believe we are doing pretty well. It will be great if we can get Bapaume before the winter sets in.'[8]

The twin arguments of maintaining the pressure and securing further tactical advantage were used in the attempt to sustain a momentum of attack which German resistance and worsening weather were combining to halt. As GHQ and Fourth and Fifth Army HQs weighed judgements based on weather reports, ground conditions, progress on the map, Intelligence gained from aerial photography and written reports, interrogation of prisoners and other sources, further factors were being evaluated. British casualty statistics, ammunition resources, troops in reserve, morale, the needs of allies and an awareness of wavering support and even opposition in Westminster and Whitehall; all this was being considered as the battle was prolonged into exceptionally adverse campaigning conditions. Gough's keenness to attack has been mentioned and there is the possibility that Haig believed a success might refurbish his damaged reputation, even his command which he may have perceived as being under threat. Were Beaumont Hamel and Beaucourt worth their price in November? From the privileged position of hindsight the answer may be in the negative. At the end of September or at some stage in early October, even in the then recognised attritional nature of this battle, there was evidence available on ground conditions alone that there was no profit in its continuance. In a sense, the battle was evidently won, with the aerial photographs indicating German preparations for retirement; however, does the boxer show readiness to halt his assault with his opponent clearly wobbling?

In a denial of access to post-December 1916 developments in assessing the Somme, what can be said about its balance sheet? German casualties could only be estimated, hence British statistics, however gathered or interpreted, lack a point of comparison. Certainly the manpower resources of the British Empire were deeper than the resources of their adversary, and the losses, dreadful as they were, would in a numerical sense be more than made up by the trained readiness of conscripts in 1917.

British losses in killed, wounded and missing have been variously estimated from figures of just over 400,000 to 424,000, the French at around 202,000. German losses may have been as high as 680,000 but there is no consensus over these figures. Even in an understanding of the nature of war and of this war in particular, there can be no minimising of the scale of the blight upon the young manhood of the British nation, the Empire and the other Allies – and of those of their antagonists. However, war is waged within the constraint or with the opportunity of available weapons and technology and the requirement to attack or defend with their attendant disadvantage or advantage – the awful figures simply represent the consequence of the military collision of Great Powers at this particular time. To extend the enquiry into the ultimate areas of responsibility for the actual outbreak of this terrible struggle or still more provocatively but tenuously into the hypothesis that if Britain were to have been better prepared militarily then might war have been avoided, does not lie within the terms of reference of this book.

What is clear is that by joint endeavour France had been protected from the most serious threat both to her front and to the condition of her army since the disasters on the frontiers in 1914. German recognition that she could not maintain her existing position against sustained British pressure was recognised by the September 1916 commencement of the new defence line to which in February 1917 her troops began to retire. In this, Terraine saw an 'unquestionable Allied victory, mainly a British one' in that 'it was a settled German principle not to retire if this could possibly be helped; the decision to do so at the beginning of February 1917 was dictated by one consideration only – the imperative need to avoid another Somme'.[9] If, in view of what was known at the turn of the year, there were evidence for the High Command to claim, as Haig did in his Official Dispatch, that a full half of the German Army, the mainstay of the Central Powers, 'despite all the advantages of the defensive, supported by the strongest fortifications, suffered defeat on the Somme this year',[10] then few should dispute that it had been a victory, terrible in its price, but a victory.

Of the men themselves – how had they endured the circumstances and avoided any vestige of a collective breakdown in discipline? The Somme, for the soldier of the New Army and to a large extent for the Territorial who served there, stands in many ways representative of the whole war. We have seen from letters and diaries the evidence of attitude and opinions before initiation into the reality of war, at the enlightening of a man's ignorance and then during his prolonged exposure to the stress of battle. We have seen men being 'educated' by the Somme – tried and tested. The constituent elements which together determined their state of morale can be highlighted but before so doing we must remind ourselves that these elements would need different emphasis if we were to have the Regular soldier predominantly in our sights.

How were men, who were not by profession soldiers, motivated to accept privation and danger and then physically and mentally to exert themselves to do things which, before they had donned uniform, most would have considered totally alien – to fight and to kill? What factors gave a body of men a collective strength of will to strive to achieve a common purpose against opposition of whatever nature and what had to be in each individual, if not by nature then by implantation or constraint, to give the chain of collective will sufficient strength in each link?

If men were to be required readily to do things which did not come naturally to them and which involved their subjugation of every instinct to avoid danger and not think solely of self-preservation, then at the foundation there had to be a strong adherence to a cause which was consistently more inspirational than self. While a range of reasons impelled enlistment in 1914, for most men the bedrock of the decision to enlist was a belief in the case presented by poster and newspaper and from within, that King and Country had need of him. Unemployment, boring jobs, a desire for adventure, breaking away from current constraints, wanting to be with friends, fear of being left out, marginalised, yes, such factors were certainly there in varying measure for many in the queues at recruiting stations but that which drew everything together and for many men was itself the total almost tangible impulsion, was patriotism. It is not appropriate here to account for the springs of such an emotion, to look at education or the power of the press for example, but to recognise the beat of the nation's pulse, remaining aware, as Peter Simkins properly reminds us, that 'thousands simply appear to have succumbed to the heady atmosphere which enveloped them in the early months of the war, particularly as the national and local recruiting campaigns got into their stride'.[11] There is no doubt at all that to be out of step with this mood invited external and internal pressure.

Patriotism as a basic element in the morale of a soldier was not going to be sufficient in itself nor of course was there a monopoly of it: field grey as well as khaki was drawing on it for inspiration. In 1914, it was a concept which may have had the personifying face of the King and Kitchener but held within its adherent's perception, his hamlet, village, town, county, state within a Dominion, that Dominion itself, as well as the idea of Mother Country and of Empire which quite evidently influenced many who came from overseas in support of a call initially made from London. Symbolically it did not have to be London. A New Zealander on his way to war wrote: 'After the horrors of Hartlepool and Scarborough, I am proud that I will have the chance of getting a little back on them.'[12] George Bird, a Royal Marine Light Infantryman, spoke for many in trying to get his family to explain to his sister the obligation which impelled him. 'Poor Florrie, I was sorry to read of her crying about me. It is a matter of duty this war. I am out to save our home and you, the same as millions more are doing.'[13] Bird, a working-class lad, expressed his simple conviction powerfully; it matches nicely the more sophisticated analysis of a subaltern, O. W. Sichel, but we can scarcely deny the added significance of the latter's judgement in that it came from a man who had been serving with the 5th Royal Warwicks on the Somme in November 1916: 'After all this is a splendid cause, a magnificent race to be fighting for. Only he who comes out here can realise the greatness of England, the colossal strength of the Empire – the seemingly insurmountable obstacles that have been surmounted.'[14]

However much it may be natural in any conflict situation and whatever may be said about the educational ideals which gave rise to it, the assumption of a moral superiority over one's foe was a basic factor. It was rooted in the presentation to Britons of their history, raucously chorused in the Music Halls and now newly-proven by German beastliness to Belgians, the shooting of a nurse and a Merchant Navy captain and the sinking of a transatlantic liner. Such a sense of superiority was ample fuel for the engine of BEF morale. This is not to say that the patriotism of the citizen soldier was blazoned: it was felt. When superiority in materiel was added, as seemed the case in late June 1916, and perhaps in mid-September too, then confidence was further encouraged. If disaster were to strike, as it did on 1 July, if periods of protracted stress or misery were to erode that confidence in material superiority, there was still sufficient spiritual resilience. The cause in which they had their faith, retained its compulsion. The Somme of course soon shaved away from most men the expressions of patriotism still enunciated by Oliver Sichel but it left instead a resistant stubble of stoic acceptance of the need to do one's bit, something wholly different in character from the disillusionment which was the focus of much post-war fixation upon the battle and devalued the endurance of the men who were there.

An additional element in the maintenance of a collective resolve was the special pride and sense of something to prove which animated Canadian, Australian and New Zealand units. It was a powerful competitive stimulant and perhaps particularly in the case of the Australians held a degree of discriminatory judgement against the English, conceived, justifiably or not, on the Gallipoli Peninsula. A similar sense of distinctive difference fuelling resolve lay in the far more ancient pride of Welsh, Scottish and Irish regiments and in the new element of identity in the battalions of Pals from towns in the North and elsewhere.

Regimental pride itself is of course fundamental in all considerations upon morale. Whether of far distant or more recent origin, a regiment's past achievements raised high expectations of new honour and this was part of the unit's mystique. It seems that not merely superiority over one's foe is to be assumed, but over one's allies and the regiment to left and right. For all its cumulative human tragedy, the Somme played its part in fusing identity with one's unit. A subaltern, A. C. Slaughter, joining the 18th Battalion King's (Liverpool) Regiment on 3 July, wrote home: 'I feel proud of being posted to this Bn. after their work of the last 2 days. The only pity is that it is practically wiped out.'[15] Officer and man might express it differently but an undeniable pride in one's battalion, battery or field company is consistently a part of the testimony of men enduring the battle. No silly claim is being made that this was unique to this war or to the British as distinct from allies or enemy but it was certainly intrinsic in upholding the performance of the BEF.

Of unsung but major importance to men of the BEF on the Somme, was the Army's concern for the general welfare of its men in so far as circumstances permitted. Attempts were made to prevent units being exposed for too long a period in the line. There are numerous exceptions like that documented in William Strang's diary of the 4th Battalion Worcesters during ten days at the beginning of July and again in October but the need for adequate sleep and a hot meal was recognised. Tributes to the work of men with the Army field kitchens and those bringing meals into the line are frequently recorded. There were rest periods out of the line and, though some were sullied for the men by labouring duties and further training, they provided opportunity for relaxation from the stress of the line, for recreation and the varied pleasures of welfare huts, concert parties and estaminets. In between two fierce actions in the autumn, E. G. Bates, the cheerful Northumberland Fusilier, saw the 'Duds' concert party of three officers and seven men assisted by Engineers in the construction of their stage and the setting up of lighting. 'They had skits on all kinds of things including Chu Chin Chow. It was screamingly funny.'[16] Film shows, singsongs, band concerts, football and boxing matches were staged and billeting arrangements were at least better than sleeping arrangements in the line. Pay, more variety in food and optional extras, *oeufs* and *frites*, beer, *vin blanc* or *rouge*, letters and parcels to be received and letter-writing opportunities offered, baths, perhaps in the vats of a brewery, even some sightseeing, sexual release, just talking to women, all had their application towards a man's sense of well-being.

The production of trench news-sheets offered a legitimate vent for frustrations expressed as humour as did the popular songs which ridiculed aspects of army life and authority. In his book on troop morale and popular culture, J. G. Fuller informs us that the *R.M.R. Growler*, the trench journal of the 14th Battalion, Canadian Expeditionary Force, announced to its readers that 'our columns are open to every grouch in the Battalion, and a growl on any subject whether the grievance be either real or fancied, will be joyfully received and have immediate insertion'.[17]

For those men who welcomed or needed it, there was Communion, Christian Fellowship with others of like mind and for all men the opportunity to draw what sustenance they could from denominational services. It is clear that certain Padres, exceptional men in their own right, played a part in uplifting individual and perhaps even collective morale in particular units but it would be baseless to see religion as a potent factor in the maintenance of the morale of the BEF. Efficiency of administration was another matter.

If the administration of a unit were efficient then its effectiveness was strongly reinforced and the men's morale sustained. When inefficiency led to persistent unredressed grievance, the reverse was the case. In the same way as work to do and familiar responsibilities to perform took away some of the ground for fear or introspection in time of danger, being well-occupied out of the line vaccinated a unit from the disease of wider, co-ordinated grumbling. Given the nature of the battle, the organisational scale of providing rest and recreation for so many men and the relative inexperience of the Staffs of so many of the units concerned, the BEF record for this period is remarkably good and has to have a bearing on the total absence of evidence of there being a serious breakdown in the morale of any unit.

Training and discipline in the United Kingdom and then in overseas service had played their essential part in the development of military efficiency. They were a prerequisite of good morale and in this respect John Baynes, in his fine book *Morale*, made convincingly what some may consider a surprising point, that drill, when well-conducted, can be an inspiration and through efficient conformity can develop individual confidence.[18] There is satisfaction in doing something efficiently with others. It is a shrewd observation and it may be that not inconsiderable numbers of men in the New Army were getting such satisfaction for the first time in their lives. Such a view would find no echo in Fuller's book as this author scorns the 'bull' of the BEF as a congenital and distinctive defect. Never mind how distinctive by comparison with French and, within the BEF, Commonwealth practice, it may be that Fuller is deriding an integral element ensuring the resilient cohesion under stress which the British forces maintained.

It is of course reasonable to put forward against the evidence that good training produced good morale, the question of the consequence of musketry training being proved inadequate and tactical training inappropriate? It has to be recognised that the shock of the Somme, its initial crushing of confidence on 1 July, faced all who survived with the need for emotional adjustment. It required a harsh realignment of their expectations which did not at the same time diminish their resolve. There is abundant evidence that men coped with this adjustment. The nervously introspective William Strang, in an overstretched battalion, asserted in his diary concerning his own morale at a time of severe demands in October, that 'I shall be better in the morning. I shall stick it to the end.'[19] This extendable capacity to endure, a dogged tenacity, saw men through. When they did not cope it was as individuals and not as sections or platoons of men, still less as units of greater size. However, the fate of the poor man who did not cope could bring him into trouble, even Court Martial disciplinary procedures, the outcome of which might be the firing squad. It is this ultimate penalty and perhaps the humiliating indignity of Field Punishment Number One which retrospectively seems to dominate thinking about military discipline. Such a starting-point is ill-judged. Military discipline began on the very first training barracks square, and then later the defaulters on parade before the CO and the loss of pay and privileges for minor infringement. There may even have had to be a Court Martial for more serious transgression. As training progressed, fewer men were involved in the disciplinary procedures and they were usually the very same men. The proper perspective for looking at discipline in the Army is as part of the educational process by which men were conditioned to know what was required of them and held to it. To fall short was to fall into trouble and most men sought to avoid trouble. To this extent men were accustomed to military discipline before they crossed the Channel. Conformity avoided the rigour of military law and in France, with the newly-testing circumstances, the clean rifle, the feet protected from trench foot, the alertness of the sentry at his post in the trench, all were as recognisably essential as they were burdensome in their fulfilment. Of course circumstances could be demanding to a degree hitherto unimaginable and when all the factors already mentioned and others to be considered failed to steel the nerves of a man being tried beyond the limits of his control, then a failure to perform his duty could result. This might be in running away, acting in a cowering inability to obey an order or in a direct refusal to obey an order. Out of the line, one may presume, agonies of indecision could lead to desertion by men whose apprehensions offered no other recourse. Before an infantry assault, men were chosen temporarily from a battalion to act as Regimental Police under the command of an NCO of the Military Police Corps. They were stationed as stoppers against unwounded men straggling back and for the guidance of men who had lost their units. There is no fully substantiated evidence of such police summarily shooting men fleeing from the line and in an interesting article on Military Police, Gary Sheffield informs us that on 1 July 1916 'there were very few stragglers … The APM of 4th Division recorded only seven stragglers on 1st July and none at all during operations conducted on the 23rd of that month.'[20]

In Anthony Babington's book *For the Sake of Example,* and in Gloden Dallas and Douglas Gill's *The Unknown Army,* some of the tragic cases were more publicly exposed than had been the case before. From a succession of the contemporary General Routine Orders, names, units, the charge and the date of the carrying out of the execution are listed. 'The accused absented himself and remained absent for six months.' 'The accused absented himself from the fighting zone till apprehended, a week later, in the vicinity of a base port.' 'The accused from motives of cowardice, left the trenches during a gas attack.' 'Misbehaving before the enemy in such a way as to show cowardice.' 'On two occasions he absented himself after being warned for the trenches till apprehended at some distance from the firing line.'[21] Together with the personal disaster behind such phrases, a disaster compelling our sympathy, perhaps something stronger still, must be a twofold awareness. First the scale of the problem: for all British troops of the BEF during the period of the Somme, the figure for men executed after Court Martial for offences of the nature outlined above is in the region of forty-eight. To set against such a figure, one might relate the 19,000 killed on 1 July or the ten officers and 305 men of the 10th Battalion West Yorks who were killed or died of wounds received on that day. If one were then to put forward the figures of one estimate of the total British casualties of the battle, 420,000, and multiplied that by a factor of three for the numbers of men who are likely to have served there, then the scale for which we have been looking is evident.

The second point which has to be made is that there are arguments for the army of a nation at war to have an ultimate sanction. Anthony Babington, it may be presumed, carefully selected the title *For the Sake of Example* faithfully to reflect a viewpoint which saw no such usefulness in merciless punishment visited upon the heads of those whose cases he describes as being inadequately represented. He presents the mixture of misfortune and injustice in certain cases better than the poor men were represented in 1916. He may be right but, more objectively, it may be thought that, sympathy even shame, does not wholly efface the thought of 'awful necessity' in the context of the period.

The discipline which played its part in holding together the collective will of the BEF in 1916 was not out of keeping with the circumstances of the hour. It did not give rise at the time nor later to widespread outrage at its brutality and no one has painted a convincing picture to show thousands of men with sullen resentment nailed to their duty by fear of official retribution. Much is made of the disapproval of Australians at the strictness of discipline manifest in United Kingdom units, something which went quite naturally with their disrespect of the required formality of officer/man relationships in British regiments. Different societies, even kindred societies, do things differently and let there be no doubt about it, the ways of the Australians were not universally admired among men in the ranks of New Zealand units, never mind British.

Is there any evidence to show that the rewards the Army could offer, such as promotions in the field or decorations for gallantry, served as an inspiration to high morale? There is a need to be cautious in accepting the evidence of men openly disparaging awards when they might well privately have esteemed them. 'Awards coming up with the rations' is a phrase not infrequently met in letters and diaries and the dismissive implication is clear. Traditionally such awards and promotions were the practice and whether or not they were an inspiration to more than a small fraction of men as is evidenced in their personal documentation, the procedure must have been considered normal, necessary and of some stimulus. Writing to the father after the Military Medal had been awarded to his son, Sam Kelso, in July 1916, the soldier's Company Commander was 'sure all ranks of the Company share the honour as it was well deserved as a symbol of work done'.[22]

To see worth rewarded is good in the eyes of all but the small-minded and must be a proper procedure in the management of men. The soldier promoted in the field or whose brave action was officially recognised in some way, medal or certificate, was a good example, a figure worthy of emulation and this had a measure of relevance in looking at one basic ingredient in the fighting efficiency of a unit – the maintenance of a man's self-respect before his fellows. It was of importance to a man that his conduct was sufficient to hold him his place in their eyes and it was important in the close-knit fellowship of a group of men that none risked being weighed and found wanting. The social stigma of exclusion from what has been called 'mateship' was a burden none would contemplate lightly. Of course it embraced stealing for the good of all, quite happily, but it was a strict code nonetheless. Men bound inextricably together, to live and fight for each other, gave each man a greater strength than he on his own possessed. Their earlier kinship, perhaps as miners or railwaymen, or Royal Scots Fusiliers, or as Canadians, was forged by war into something still stronger. Private Hedges, in a locally recruited Gloucestershire Regiment, wrote from France to his local parson about the loss of a man known to both: 'Friendships out here seem to be so much more binding and sacred than at home … when we have our own chums and friends with us we can help each other and everything seems so much brighter.'[23]

Within groups of friends who would feel the obligation to fight for each other as well as for themselves, leaders would have emerged. If such a group were to have an NCO as leader, his authority would have a special character. In general terms, NCOs had earned their stripes by showing, not least, that they commanded respect among their fellows. There will have been a small percentage unworthy of its salt, perhaps bullies, perhaps corrupt in the exercise of their power, but the average NCO was sound, a figure on whom man and officer could rely. It was his worth and the worth of the regimental officer which do much to explain why the fabric of the Army held so effectively against disintegration during the Somme.

The quality of command exercised at its lowest commissioned level, the subaltern over his platoon, stood up to the sternest battle testing. It ought not to be presumed that this was exclusively the result of the sense of responsibility, the duty of leadership, inculcated in the Public Schools and in those schools which followed a similar ethic. The Army as such had played a significant role in codifying the duties of an officer in the exercise of his command and in giving professional training for the production of a new officer corps principally resourced from the phenomenon of the citizen in arms for the duration of the war. There is ample evidence to refute J. G. Fuller's repetition of a 1919 judgement that during the war new officers in training had been prepared by the Army for the exercise of command with a total lack of comprehension of the ordinary man's psychology.[24]

The notebook of Captain N. B. Chaffers at the Third Army Infantry School of Instruction, in February 1916, provides evidence to challenge Fuller strongly in his stricture and in some aspects just as strongly to contradict the charge of being distant from the reality of the test to be faced. It is in the area of human psychology and the importance of understanding it and acting upon it that there is something particularly impressive in Chaffers' notes. 'Men do not like their feelings wounded' by the inefficiency of their officer, it makes them 'ridiculous in the eyes of their fellows or other troops'. 'We are all parts of the machinery which maintain the Army as a going concern and provided each individual does his best and with the knowledge that right and justice are on our side and that materiel and personnel are equal, we must in the end prove victorious.'

The notes make it abundantly clear that good leadership can be developed as well as being naturally within some men. If a real effort were to be made to understand human nature, to set a correct example, to show intensity of purpose, to do all in one's power to help the men concerning adequacy of billeting arrangements, security in the line, putting the men's comfort before one's own, then the goodwill of the men will be earned and such an officer 'can always be assured of a ready response to any call he makes or any special effort he may demand'.

It is stressed that a soldier knows he is entitled to justice and where injustices occur then 'officers have not applied their minds to the study of human character and at times [have] treated their men as though they were machines'. Officers must be 'examples of endurance', courageous, cheerful, knowledgeable and keen. The men have a right to expect this. Foolhardy courage is to be avoided, it will lose the Army the services of a useful officer. What is enjoined is to 'be brave and courageous at all times when the necessity demands it'. On relationships with the men, a maxim of Lord Wolseley is particularly quoted: 'Study to be familiar without being vulgar and habit, if not intuition, will soon enable you to be gracious and intimate with your men without any loss of dignity.'[25]

Fuller's case, resting as it does in this area on published sources, that other ranks remained 'distant and unknowable' to their officers, is absurdly far from the truth. Unpublished letters and diaries consistently endorse the judgement that officer/man relationships and the exercise of command within a regiment emerge from the gloom of the Somme as a shining, virtually unsullied, aspect of the battle. Such few exceptions as there were, mar to no discernible degree this general picture. The leadership of the officers, their care for their men, the loyalty of the men, the awareness among both of their interdependence however much there may have been a gulf in social background, here we have a quality which is wholly admirable, a mutual respect which war, on occasion, could transmute into love. As an emotion between men in such circumstances, the word 'love' is to be neither exaggerated nor minimised, neither trivialised nor misunderstood, as by Paul Fussell, who races to the winning post of sexual connotation in the pruriently entitled chapter, 'Soldier Boys', of his book *The Great War and Modern Memory*.[26] The evidence is there to explain itself across an ocean of time separating us from men captured by a prolonged intensity of experience. While there would have been no readiness publicly to expatiate on such sensibility, inwardly many could have examined their feelings without the incubus of embarrassment but with a knowledge that outside the circle of those who had shared their experience, there could be little understanding. This is, in a sense, regrettable because their emotional response is not merely of sociological significance, it is of some importance in explaining the resilience of the hugely-expanded, predominantly amateur BEF, pitted against so formidable an adversary with its inbuilt level of professionalism to say no more about its advantage of standing in defence of a strategic initiative gained in the first weeks of the war.

Private Sam Woodhead wrote in July 1916 to the mother of his officer killed on the Somme. 'I have been servant to him for a long time and have been in three fights and never a better lad or soldier ever stepped on a field and what I say every word is true. Any lad in the Battalion would follow him and he was respected by all.'[27]

A stark recall of the evidence of an officer's identification with his battalion remained ineffaceably in the memory of Stanley Henderson, a bugler in the 16th Battalion Northumberland Fusiliers, standing beside his Colonel when the leading waves of the battalion were cut down – Colonel Ritson, shouting out in distress 'My men, my men, my God, my men', had to be forcibly restrained from clambering out after them.[28] Far more prosaic but pointing in the same direction is a paragraph in Lieutenant R. B. Marshall's October 1916 letter to his father: 'I wonder whether it will be possible to send out some chocolate or cigarettes now and then for the men. Not more than 1,000 mixture of Woodbines etc. I will send a cheque now and then if you will tell me the price, 100 or 200 bars of chocolate occasionally would be very nice and warming.'[29]

Care for the men is regularly interspersed with praise for the men in the letters of officers like D. G. Branson of the 4th Bn York and Lancasters. In letters during July he wrote: 'Thanking goodness we are now out and able to rest for a bit. The men are in wonderfully good spirits and have been most excellent throughout about the most trying week one could imagine. We have not had a single case of straggling which I think few other regiments can boast… When you think that we went in full hope of really getting to work in the open and in the end merely had to sit in a trench and be shelled to blazes you can see that they had a lot to put up with.'[30] Another officer in a Yorkshire Regiment, E. Bowly, confessing that the 'sights and smells make me feel awfully rotten', observed that his men 'are awfully good and don't mind a bit'.[31] It is patently obvious that his judgement here is subjective but at the same time he was both sufficiently interested in the response of his men and impressed by it to make this point of contrast to his own inner state of mind under the shelling to which they had been subjected.

No attempt is being made to show British morale as being superior to that of her ally or of her opponent – factors keeping the Germans tenaciously holding on to their positions have not been the focus of this book, though the recent verdict by the widely-respected William Philpott seems apposite here, that the battle had shown to British soldiers, to British people and to Britain's allies that the German army could be beaten. 'By instilling this belief in the Allied armies, and by gaining the initiative and advantage in the land war that up to that point had lain with Germany, the Somme was the decisive victory of the attritional war of which it was the centerpiece: a moral victory based on growing *materiel* predominance and improving tactical and operational ability.'[32]

What is being claimed in this book, is first, that in 1916–17 terms, a British victory was won on the Somme, not one to be greeted with bell-ringing and bunting, indeed one more appropriately honoured by the draperies of mourning, but a victory nevertheless. Second, that the resolve of the soldier of the British Expeditionary Force in France, had not been broken by the experience of the Somme. The significance of this in the context of the war overall should never be under-estimated. To do so, demeans the men in khaki who won the victory and, through the most challenging of circumstances, somehow retained the resilience to attempt what was required of them – no mean achievements. It is surely time for the 1916 Battle of the Somme to be reconsidered.

Notes

(Items suffixed thus * are unpublished sources in the Liddle Collection of the University of Leeds. Most of the published works cited are listed in the Bibliography, where full bibliographical details will be found.)

Introduction

1.* Lance-Corporal Elmer, letter (papers of J. Pocock).
2.* W. A. D. Goodwin, letter, 27 June 1916.
3.* E. Polack, 4th Bn Gloucestershire Regiment, letter, 30 June 1916.
4.* E. U. Green, undated letter, papers of Rev. M. S. Evers
5. A. E. Shewing, letter, 4 October 1916 (Blathwayt papers, Gloucestershire County Record Office).
6. Jerrold, 'The Lie about the War'.
7. Fussell, *The Great War and Modern Memory*.
8. Keegan, *The Face of Battle*, p. 281.
9.* Interviews with W. Towers, S. Pears, W. Watson, J. Hogg, H. Gaffron, H. Heath, H. Davies, J. Davies, and the papers of W. G. K. Boswell.
10. Hynes, *A War Imagined*, p. x.
11. Cecil, 'The Literary Legacy of the War'.
12. Simpson, *Dr. Dunn and Battle Stress*, p. 76.
13. Lehmann, *The English Poets of the First World War*.
14. Ibid., p. 39
15. J. M. Winter, *The Great War and the British People*, London, Macmillan, 1985, p. 304.
16. Slack, *Grandfather's Adventures in the Great War. Joffrey's War* is the memoir of Geoffrey Ratcliff Husbands, edited and introduced by J. M. Bourne and Bob Bushaway.
17. Sheffield and Inglis (eds.), *From Vimy Ridge to the Rhine*, p. 70.
18. Richardson (ed.), *A Manchester Pal on the Somme*.
19. Uys, *Delville Wood*.
20. Uys, *Longueval*.
21. Maddox, *Liverpool Pals*, p. 164.
22. Stewart and Shee, *Tyneside Scottish*.
23. Philpott, *Bloody Victory*, p. 6.

Chapter 1

1. Edmonds, *Military Operations, France and Belgium, 1916*, Vol. I, p. 12.
2. Terraine, *Douglas Haig, The Educated Soldier*; *White Heat: The New Warfare 1914–18*; 'Leadership in Coalition War'.
3. Travers, *The Killing Ground*.
4. Winter, *Haig's Command*.
5. Travers, *The Killing Ground*, p. 131.
6. Terraine, *Douglas Haig*, p. 201.
7. Sheffield, *The Chief*, p. 173.
8. Terraine, *Douglas Haig*, p. 201.
9. Philpott, *Bloody Victory*, p. 151.
10. Keegan, *The Face of Battle*, p. 236.
11. Marshall-Cornwall, *Haig as Military Commander*, p. 170.
12. Jones, *Official History, War in the Air*, Vol. II, pp. 197–8.
13. Boraston (ed.), *Sir Douglas Haig's Despatches*, p. 20.
14. Quoted in James Marshall-Cornwall, *Grant as Military Commander*, London, Batsford, 1970, p. 171.
15. Jones, *Official History, War in the Air*, Vol. I, pp. 206–7.
16. Three good books detail men, machines, exploits and the RFC organisation during the Battle of the Somme. They are: Shores, Franks and Guest, *Above the Trenches: A Complete Record of the Fighter Aces and Units of the British Empire Air Forces 1915-1920*; Bruce, *The Aeroplanes of the Royal Flying Corps (Military Wing)*; and Hart, *Somme Success: The*

Royal Flying Corps and the Battle of the Somme.

17. Edmonds, *Military Operations, France and Belgium, 1916*, Vol. I, p. 266.
18.* Rifleman C. M.Woods, 1st Bn London Regiment, contemporary account.
19.* Private T. Easton, 21st Bn Northumberland Fusiliers, manuscript recollections.
20.* Major R. C. Money, 15th Bn DLI, diary, June 1916.
21.* Lieutenant William Strang, diary, June 1916.
22.* Corporal H. G. R. Williams, 5th Bn City of London Regiment, typescript recollections.
23.* George Norrie, letter, 29 June 1916.
24. Farndale, *History of the Royal Regiment of Artillery, The Western Front*, p. 142.
25.* Lieutenant T. L. W. Stallibrass, No 3 Squadron RFC, log-book.
26.* Second Lieutenant I. R. H. Probert, RFA, diary, 30 June 1916.
27.* Lieutenant A. Laporte Paine, contemporary official papers.
28.* Lieutenant William Strang, diary, June 1916.
29. Edmonds, *Military Operations, France and Belgium, 1916*, Vol. I, p. 308.
30.* Copy in the Liddle Collection.

Chapter 2
1. National Archives WO/95 2463 X/K 1098.
2. Edmonds, *Military Operations, France and Belgium, 1916*, Vol. I, p. 314.
3.* E. Polack, letter, 30 June 1916.
4. Foulkes, *Gas! The Story of the Special Brigade*, p. 163.
5.* Letter in *Two Brothers*, a private publication (1918) about Eric and Arnold Miall-Smith, both killed in action in 1917 and 1916 respectively.
6.* Lieutenant D. J. Capper, 8th Bn Royal Sussex, manuscript recollections
7.* E. W.Willmer, typescript recollections.
8.* Captain G. D. Fairley, diary, July 1916.
9. Atkinson, *The Devonshire Regiment 1914-18*, p. 147.
10.* Second Lieutenant J. D. Upcott, 9th Devons, diary.
11.* Lance-Corporal Elmer, letter, 9 July 1916 (Pocock papers).

12. Middlebrook, *The First Day on the Somme*, pp. 129–30, 144–5, 177, 202, 205–7.
13. Edmonds, op.cit, p. 364. In a journal article, 'The Mystery of Major Kent' (see Bibliography) pp. 18, 19 and 27, John Sly attempts to cast more light on the premature advance of A Company, 7th Bn Green Howards.
14. War diary, 7th Bn East Yorkshire Regiment, Regimental Museum, York.
15.* R. C. Money, diary, 1 July 1916.
16.* R. Archer-Houblon, typescript recollections.
17.* Lieutenant T. L. W. Stallibrass, RFC log.
18. Stewart and Sheen, *Tyneside Scottish*, pp. 136–8.
19. Second Lieutenant W. A. D. Goodwin (killed in action 1 July) 1916 papers.
20.* T. Easton, manuscript recollections.
21. National Archives WO/95 2398 X/K 1098.
22.* Lance-Corporal T.Quinn, manuscript recollections.
23.* E. J. Brownlee, manuscript recollections.
24.* D. G. Branson, letter, 10 July 1916.
25.* F. Moakler, typescript recollections.
26.* Sergeant A. T. Fraser, manuscript recollections.
27.* Captain W. Carden Roe, typescript recollections.
28.* Corporal R. N. Bell, typescript recollections.
29.* D. Duxbury, letter in the papers of Robert H. Tolson.
30.* Corporal W. G. Martin, manuscript recollections and contemporary papers.
31.* Rifleman C. M. Woods, diary, 1 July 1916.
32.* Rifleman E. A. Cannon, diary.
33.* Lance-Corporal H. G. R. Williams, typescript and tape-recorded recollections.
34.* Private H. Barber, manuscript recollections.
35.* Major A. W. French, diary, 1 July 1916.
36. Staffordshire Regimental Museum, Lichfield.
37. Anon, *War History of the 6th Bn South Staffordshire Regiment*, p. 137.
38. *The 6th Battalion, The Sherwood Foresters*, pp. 42–3

Chapter 3

1. Croft, 'The Somme, 14 July 1916', *Army Quarterly*.
2.* Lieutenant T. L. W. Stallibrass, RFC log, 14 July 1916.
3.* Lance-Corporal V. C. Crask, diary, 14 July 1916.
4. Croft, 'The Somme, 14 July 1916'.
5. Uys, *Delville Wood*.
6. Ibid, p. 115.
7. Ibid, p. 120.
8.* Sir Hugh Boustead, South African Scottish, typescript recollections.
9. Jones, *War in the Air*, Vol. I, p. 153.
10. Charlton, *Pozières 1916*.
11.* Gunner R. J. Brownell, diary, July 1916.
12.* B. Champion, typescript recollections.
13.* Sergeant J. F. Edey, typescript recollections.
14.* E. W. Moorhead, typescript recollections
15. A remarkably detailed study of the work of the DH 2 by Barrington J. Gray and members of the DH 2 Research Group has been published in *Cross and Cockade International*. See Volume 22, No 1 and No 4, 1991 for the part of this study which relates to June, July and August 1916 'in the Field'.
16. Cole (ed.), *Royal Flying Corps Communiques*, p. 258.
17.* Major L. G. Hawker VC, letters, July/October 1916.
18.* Log-book of 8th AA Battery, August 1916 (Captain J. J .A. Foster).
19.* Hugh Chance, No 27 Squadron, RFC, log-book.
20.* Lieutenant I. R. H. Probert, diary, August 1916.
21.* Captain R. Macleod, letters, July 1916.
22. Liddle, *The Soldier's War*, pp. 89–92.
23.* Sister Alice Slythe, diary, August/September 1916.

Chapter 4

1. Denis Winter, in *Haig's Command* (p. 64), offers an unattributed hindsight reference to the lack of proper consideration of how Guillemont might have been taken earlier.
2.* Lt-Colonel E. Vaux, papers.
3. Prior and Wilson, '15 September 1916: The Dawn of the Tank', pp. 61–5.
4.* R. Tate, tape-recorded recollections.
5.* J. Baker, letter, 19 September 1916.

6.* Lieutenant G. B. de Courcy Ireland, KRR, letter, 18 September 1916.
7.* V. Huffam, recollections (papers of J. W. Staddon).
8.* J. W. Staddon, recollections.
9. Liddell Hart, *The Tanks*, p. 74.
10. From research papers (National Archives and Liddell Hart Centre for Military Archives), collected by Sergeant Edward's son John, and in an article by J. R. Sherratt, 'Following in Father's Tank Tracks'.
11.* Sergeant W. Rumming, diary, 15 September 1916.
12.* R. C. Bingham, diary, September 1916.
13.* W. A. F. L. Fox Pitt, letter, September 1916.
14.* H. Macmillan, tape-recorded recollections.
15. Byrne, *History of the Otago Regiment*, p. 119.
16.* Sergeant J. Campbell, letter, September 1916.
17.* Private F. B. Hirsch, letter 23 September 1916 and typescript recollections.
18.* Edward Ramsden, 5th Royal Irish Lancers, letter, 24 September 1916.
19.* Private M. M. Hood, typescript recollections. The British Official History describes the work of this tank as subsequent to the capture of the factory.
20.* H. R. Hammond, letters, September 1916.
21. Williams, *Byng of Vimy*.
22.* Sergeant P. Heptinstall, typescript recollections.
23.* Sergeant R. Dawson, diary, 2/3 September 1916.
24.* R. C. Bingham, diary, 27 September 1916.
25.* Private V. C. Crask, diary, 25 September 1916.
26.* E. G. Bates, letters, September/October 1916.
27. Winter, *Haig's Command*, p. 155.
28. Nicholls, *The 18th Division in the Great War*, p. 107.

Chapter 5

1.* H. A. Eiloart, papers.
2.* William Strang, diary and official papers, October 1916.

3.* Philpott, *Bloody Victory*, p. 403.
4.* Lieutenant D. P. Hirsch, letters. Hirsch was to be posthumously awarded the Victoria Cross following an action at Wancourt in April of the following year.
5. V. F. S. Hawkins, Lieutenant, 2nd Bn. Lancashire Fusiliers, typescript recollections, Museum of the Fusiliers, Bury, Lancashire.
6. Miles, *Military Operations, France and Belgium, 1916,* Vol. II, p. 468.
7. National Archives WO 95/3115 042191: research material made available by A. F. F. Froom.
8.* Sub-Lieutenant J. H. Bentham, typescript recollections.
9. See note 7 above.
10.* F. W. Davy, RND Engineers, letter, 21 November 1916.
11.* Second Lieutenant A. Cheyne, diary, 13 November 1916.
12.* Captain G. Stewart, letter, 16 November 1916.
13.* Lieutenant E. G. Bates, letter, 26 November 1916.
14.* G. Chapman, diary, 16 November 1916.
15. Crookenden, *History of the Cheshire Regiment*, p. 97.
16. Nicholls, *The 18th Division in the Great War*, p. 133.

Chapter 6
1. Philpott, *Bloody Victory*, p. 597.
2. Ibid, p. 603.
3. Terraine, *Douglas Haig*, p. 181.
4. Sixsmith, *British Generalship*, p. 90.
5. Bond (ed.), *Staff Officer: The Diaries of Lord Moyne.*
6. Marshall Cornwall, *Haig as Military Commander*, p. 22.
7. Brian and Cave, *Haig: A Reappraisal 70 Years On*, p. 216.
8.* C. K. L. McKerrow, letter, 30 September 1916.

9. Terraine, *Douglas Haig,* pp. 230–1.
10. Boraston (ed.), *Sir Douglas Haig's Despatches*, pp. 58–9.
11. Simkins, *Kitchener's Army*, p. 172.
12.* E. H. Honnor, letter, 1 January 1915.
13.* G. Bird, letter, February 1915.
14.* O. W. Sichel, letter, November 1916.
15.* A. C. Slaughter, letter, 3 July 1916.
16.* E. G. Bates, letter, 29 September 1916.
17. Fuller, *Troop Morale.*
18. Baynes, *Morale: A Study of Men and Courage.*
19.* William Strang, diary, 4 October 1916.
20. Sheffield, 'British Military Police', p. 37.
21. Babington, *For the Sake of Example*, and Gill and Dallas, *The Unknown Army.*
22.* Liddle Collection, see General Aspects section, Military Medals.
23. Private J. Hedges, letter, 15 September 1916; Blathwayt papers, Gloucestershire County Record Office.
24. Fuller, *Troop Morale*, p. 47.
25* Captain N. B. Chaffers, 6th Bn Duke of Wellington's Regiment, Instruction Notebook, February 1916.
26. Fussell, *The Great War and Modern Memory.*
27.* Pte Sam Woodhead letter in papers of Second Lieutenant J. W. B. Russell, 9th Bn Duke of Wellington's Regiment.
28.* Bugler Stanley Henderson, manuscript recollections.
29.* Lieutenant R. B. Marshall, 7th Bn East Surrey Regiment, letter, 20 October 1916.
30.* Captain D. G. Branson, letters, 9/10 July 1916.
31.* Second Lieutenant E. Bowly, 6th Bn East Yorks, letter 5 September 1916.
32. Philpott, *Bloody Victory*, pp. 624–5.

Bibliography

(Books listed include both those which are quoted in the text and others to which particular attention is drawn.)

1. Official Histories

Edmonds, Brigadier-General Sir James E., *Military Operations, France and Belgium, 1916*, Vol. I, London, Macmillan, 1932.

Miles, Captain Wilfred, *Military Operations, France and Belgium, 1916*, Vol. II, London, Macmillan, 1938.

2. Monographs, Biographies and other works related to political and military High Command

Bond, Brian, and Cave, Nigel, *Haig: A Reappraisal 70 Years On*, Barnsley, Pen and Sword, 1999.

Boraston, J. H. (ed.), *Sir Douglas Haig's Despatches*, London, J. M. Dent, 1920.

Marshall-Cornwall, Sir James, *Haig as Military Commander*, London, Batsford, 1973.

Neillands, Robin, *Attrition: The Great War on the Western Front-1916*, London, Robson Books, 2001.

Pegler, Martin, *Attack on the Somme: Haig's Offensive 1916*, Barnsley, Pen and Sword, 2005.

Philpott, William, *Bloody Victory: The Sacrifice on the Somme and the Making of the Twentieth Century*, London, Little, Brown, 2009.

Prior, Robin and Wilson, Trevor, *Command on the Western Front: The Military Career of Sir Henry Rawlinson, 1914-18*, Barnsley, Pen and Sword, 2004.

Sheffield, Gary, *Forgotten Victory: The First World War, Myths and Realities*, London, Headline, 2001.

——, *The Chief: Douglas Haig and the British Army*, London, Aurum Press, 2011.

——, *Command and Morale: The British Army on the Western Front 1914-1918*, Barnsley, Pen and Sword, 2014.

Sixsmith, E. K. G., *British Generalship in the Twentieth Century*, London, Arms & Armour Press, 1970.

Terraine, John, *Douglas Haig, The Educated Soldier*, London, Hutchinson, 1963.

——, *White Heat: The New Warfare 1914-18*, London, Sidgwick & Jackson, 1983.

Travers, T. H. E., *The Killing Ground: The British Army, The Western Front and the Emergence of Modern Warfare*, London, Unwin Hyman, 1987.

Williams, Jeffery, *Byng of Vimy: General and Governor General*, Barnsley, Pen and Sword, 1992.

Winter, Denis, *Haig's Command: a reassessment*, London, Viking, 1991.

3. Other Monographs

Babington, Anthony, *For the Sake of Example: Capital Courts-Martial 1914-1920*, London, Leo Cooper, 1993.

Baynes, J., *Morale: A Study of Men and Courage*, London, Cassell, 1967.

Charlton, Peter, *Pozières 1916*, London, Leo Cooper, 1986.

Fuller, J. G., *Troop Morale and Popular Culture in the British and Dominion Armies*, Oxford, Clarendon Press, 1991.

Gill, Douglas, and Dallas, Gloden, *The Unknown Army*, London, Verso, 1985.

Horsfall, Jack, and Cave, Nigel, *Serre: Somme*, Barnsley, Pen and Sword, 2003.
Keegan, John, *The Face of Battle*, London, Allen Lane, 1971.
Langford, William, *Somme Intelligence: Fourth Army HQ 1916*, Barnsley, Pen and Sword, 2013.
Liddle, Peter H., *The Soldier's War, 1914-1918*, London, Blandford Press, 1988.
Maddocks, Graham, *Montauban: Somme*, Barnsley, Pen and Sword, 1999.
Middlebrook, Martin, *The First Day on the Somme*, London, Allen Lane, 1971.
Renshaw, Michael, *Mametz Wood,* Barnsley, Pen and Sword, 2011.
Simkins, Peter, *Kitchener's Army,* Manchester University Press, 1988.
Stedman, Michael, *La Boisselle: Somme*, Barnsley, Pen and Sword, 1997.
Uys, Ian, *Delville Wood,* Rensburg, South Africa, Uys, 1983.
——, *Longueval,* Rensburg, South Africa, Uys, 1983.

4. Memoirs, Published Letters and Diaries
Bond, Brian (ed.), *Staff Officer: The Diaries of Lord Moyne 1914-18*, London, Leo Cooper, 1987.
Bourne, J. M., and Bushaway, Bob (eds.). *Joffrey's War: A Sherwood Forester in the Great War, Geoffrey Ratcliff Husbands*, Nottingham, Salient Books, 2011.
Dunn, Captain J. C., *The War the Infantry Knew, 1914-1919*, London, Jane's, 1987.
Richardson, S., *Orders are Orders: A Manchester Pal on the Somme*, Swinton, Richardson, 1987.
Sheffield, G. D., and Inglis, G. I. (eds.), *From Vimy Ridge to the Rhine: The Great War Letters of Christopher Stone DSO MC,* Marlborough, Crowood Press, 1989.
Slack, Cecil, *Grandfather's Adventures in the Great War*, Illfracombe, Stockwell, 1977.

5. Books related to the Air Battle of the Somme
(a) Official History
Jones, H. A., *War in the Air,* Vol. II, Oxford University Press, 1928.
(b) Others (see also Journal articles)
Bruce, J. M., *The Aeroplanes of the Royal Flying Corps (Military Wing)*, London, Putnam, 1992.
Cole, C. (ed.), *Royal Flying Corps Communiques 1915-16,* London, Tom Donovan, 1990.
Hart, Peter, *Somme Success: The Royal Flying Corps and the Battle of the Somme 1916*, Barnsley, Pen and Sword, 2001.
Shores, C., Franks, N., and Guest, R., *Above the Trenches: A Complete Record of the Fighter Aces and Units of the British Empire Air Forces 1915-20,* London, Grub Street, 1990.

6. Regimental, Battalion, Brigade, Divisional and Corps Histories
Anon (a committee of officers), *The War History of the Sixth Battalion, The South Staffordshire Regiment (T.F.)* , London, Heinemann, 1924.
Anon, *The 6th Battalion, The Sherwood Foresters*, Chesterfield, private publication, 1958.
Atkinson, C. T., *The Devonshire Regiment 1914-18,* Exeter, Eland Brothers, 1926.
Byrne, A. E., *History of the Otago Regiment in the Great War 1914-18,* Dunedin (NZ), J. Wilkie, n.d.
Cooksey, Jon, *Pals: The 13th and 14th (Service) Battalions (Barnsley) The York and Lancaster Regiment,* Barnsley, Wharncliffe, 1986.
Crookenden, A., *The History of the Cheshire Regiment in the Great War,* Chester, W. H. Evans, 1939.
Farndale, General Sir Martin, *History of the Royal Regiment of Artillery: The Western Front 1914-18,* Woolwich, Royal Artillery Institution, 1986.
Foulkes, Major-General C. H., *'Gas!'* – *The Story of the Special Brigade,* Edinburgh, William Blackwood, 1934.
Gibson, R. and Oldfield, P., *City: The 12th (Service) Battalion (Sheffield) The York and Lancaster Regiment,* Barnsley, Wharncliffe, 1988.
Liddell Hart, Sir Basil, *The Tanks*, London, Cassell, 1959.
Maddocks, Graham, *Liverpool Pals: The 17th, 18th, 19th and 20th (Service) Battalions The King's (Liverpool Regiment),* London, Leo Cooper, 1991.
Nicholls, G. H. F., *The 18th Division in the Great War,* Edinburgh, William Blackwood, 1922.

Stewart, Graham and Sheen, John, *Tyneside Scottish, 20th, 21st, 22nd and 23rd (Service) Battalions Northumberland Fusiliers*, Barnsley, Pen and Sword, 2014.

Turner, William, *Pals: The 11th (Service) Battalion (Accrington) The East Lancashire Regiment*, Barnsley, Wharncliffe, 1987.

Wood, Stephen, *The Leeds Pals*, Stroud, Amberley Publishing, 2014.

7. Literary Works

Blunden, Edmund (ed.), *The Poems of Wilfred Owen*, London, Chatto and Windus, 1965.

Cecil, Hugh, 'The Literary Legacy of the War' in Liddle, Peter H. (ed.), *Home Fires and Foreign Fields*, London, Brasseys, 1985.

Fussell, Paul, *The Great War and Modern Memory*, Oxford University Press, 1975.

Hynes, S., *A War Imagined: English Culture and the First World War*, London, The Bodley Head, 1990.

Jerrold, Douglas, 'The Lie about the War', *Criterion Miscellany* No. 9, London, Faber and Faber, 1930.

Lehmann, John, *The English Poets of the First World War*, London, Thames and Hudson, 1981.

Silkin, Jon (ed.), *The Penguin Book of First World War Poetry*, London, Penguin, 1979.

Winter, J. M., 'The Legacy of the Great War (Part III)' in *The Great War and the British People*, London, Macmillan, 1985.

8. Journal Articles

Croft, Major The Reverend J., 'The Somme 14 July 1916 – A Great Opportunity Missed', *Army Quarterly* (July 1986).

Gray, B. J., and others, 'The DH2 in the Field', *Cross and Cockade International*, Vol. 22, No. 1 and No. 4 (1991).

Liddle, Peter H., 'The British Soldier on the Somme 1916', *Strategic and Combat Studies Institute* No. 23 (1996).

Prior, R. and Wilson, T., '15 September 1916: The Dawn of the Tank', *Journal of the Royal United Services Institution* (Autumn 1991).

Sheffield, G. D., 'British Military Police and their Battlefield Role 1914-20', *Sandhurst Journal of Military Studies*, 1 (1990).

Sherratt, J.R., 'Following in Father's Tank Tracks', *Stand To!: The Journal of the Western Front Association*, No. 29 (Summer 1990).

Simpson, Keith, 'Dr Dunn and Battle Stress', *The Great War: The Illustrated Journal of First World War History*, Vol. 3, No. 3, 1991.

Sly, John S., 'The Mystery of Major Kent', *Stand To!: The Journal of the Western Front Association* No. 32 (Summer 1991).

Terraine, John, 'Leadership in Coalition War', *Journal of the Royal United Services Institution* (December 1982).

9. Official Unpublished Sources

The War Diary of the 7th Battalion East Yorkshire Regiment, The Regimental Museum, York

The War Diary of the Hood Battalion Royal Naval Division, National Archives WO/95 3115 042191.

The War Diary of the 16th Battalion Northumberland Fusiliers, National Archives WO/95 2398 XK 1098.

The War Diary of the 23rd Battalion Northumberland Fusiliers, National Archives WO/95 2463 XK 1098.

The War Diary of the 6th Battalion North Staffordshire Regiment, The Regimental Museum, Lichfield.

Personal Experience Documentation

Unless stated otherwise the papers listed below are held in the Liddle Collection, Brotherton Library, The University of Leeds. The men are named and given their rank and unit as in 1916. No subsequent distinction is shown.

ARCHER HOUBLON, R.	Lt	RFA
BAKER, J.	Gnr	RGA
BARBER, H.	Pte	5th Bn London Regiment
BATES, E. G.	Lt	9th Bn Northumberland Fusiliers
BELL, R. N.	Cpl	15th Bn West Yorks
BENTHAM, J. H.	Sub-Lt	Hood Bn Royal Naval Division
BINGHAM, R.C.	Lt	3rd Bn Coldstream Guards and 1st Guards Brigade Machine Gun Coy
BIRD, G.	Pte	RMLI, killed in action 1915
BOOTH	Cpl	8th Bn York and Lancasters
BOUSTEAD, H.	Pte	South African Scottish
BOWLY, E.	2/Lt	6th Bn East Yorks
BRANSON, D. G.	Maj	4th Bn York and Lancasters
BROWNELL, R. J.	Gnr	Australian Field Artillery
BROWNLEE, E. J.	Pte	Machine Gun Corps
CAMPBELL, J.	Sgt	6th Bn Cameron Highlanders (Machine Gun Section)
CANNON, E. A.	Rfn	3rd Bn London Regt
CAPPER, D.J.	Lt	8th Bn Royal Sussex
CASSON, V.	Pte	1st Bn South African Brigade, from Ian Uys, *Delville Wood*
CHAFFERS, N. B.	Capt	6th Bn Duke of Wellington's Regt
CHAMPION, B.	Pte	5th Bn Australian Imperial Force
CHANCE, H.	Lt	No 27 Squadron RFC
CHAPMAN, G.	2/Lt	13th Bn Royal Fusiliers
CHEYNE, A.	2/Lt	5th Bn Gordon Highlanders
COULSON, J. R.	Cpl	RMLI
CRASK, V. C.	L/Cpl	8th Bn Suffolk Regt
DAVEY, F. W.	Spr	Royal Naval Divison Engineers
DAWSON, G. A.	Cpl	5th Bn Royal Leicestershire Regt
DAWSON, R.	Sgt	RE ('F' Company) Special Brigade
DUXBURY, D.	Pte	15th Bn West Yorkshire Regt (with R. H. Tolson papers)
EASTON, T.	Pte	21st Bn Northumberland Fusiliers
EDEY, J. F.	Sgt	5th Bn Australian Imperial Force
EILOART, H. A.	Capt	1st Bn London Regt
ELMER	L/Cpl	9th Bn Devons
FAIRLEY, G. D.	Capt	RAMC attached to 2nd Bn Royal Scots Fusiliers
FOSTER, J. J. A.	Capt	8th Anti-Aircraft Battery Royal Artillery

FRASER, A. T.	Sgt	1st Bn Border Regt
FRENCH, A. W.	Maj	RAMC (London Field Ambulance)
GOODWIN, W. A. D.	2/Lt	8th Bn York and Lancasters
HAMMOND, H. R.	2/Lt	Canadian Field Artillery
HAWKER, L. G. VC	Maj	CO No 24 Squadron RFC
HAWKINS, V. F. S.	Lt	2nd Bn Lancashire Fusiliers (Museum of the Fusiliers, Bury, Lancashire)
HEDGES, J.	Pte	In an infantry regt (Blathwayt Papers, Gloucestershire County Record Office)
HENDERSON, S.	Pte	16th Bn Northumberland Fusiliers
HEPTINSTALL, R.	Sgt	RE
HIGSON, G. I.	Cpl	RE 106 Company Special Brigade
HILL, A. H. G.	Sgt	1st Bn HAC
HIRSCH, D. P.	2/Lt	4th Bn Yorkshire Regiment (Posthumous VC, 1917)
HIRSCH, F. B.	Pte	6th Bn Cameron Highlanders
HONNOR, E. H.	Capt	1st Bn Wellington Regt New Zealand Expeditionary Force
HOOD, M. M.	Pte	24th Bn Canadian Expeditionary Force
HOUSTON, A. G.	Pte	17th Bn Highland Light Infantry
HUFFAM, V.	Lt	Heavy Branch Motor Machine Gun Corps
IRELAND, G. B. de Courcy	Capt	9th Bn King's Royal Rifles
JACKSON, T.	Pte	8th Bn East Lancashire Regt
KELSO, S.	Pte	Highland Light Infantry
KING, V.	Pte	1st Bn Royal Welsh Fusiliers
MACLEOD, R.	Capt	RFA
McKERROW, C. K.	Capt	RAMC, attached to 10th Bn Northumberland Fusiliers
MACMILLAN, H.	Lt	4th Bn Grenadier Guards
MARSHALL, R. B.	Lt	7th Bn East Surreys
MARTIN, W. G.	Cpl	Machine Gun Corps
MASON, K. S.	2 Lt	Machine Gun Corps
MATTHEWS, T. F. V.	Lt	4th Bn Worcesters
MIALL-SMITH, E.	2 Lt	8th Bn Norfolks
MILBURN, C. H.	Capt	RAMC
MOAKLER, F.	Pte	1st Bn Newfoundland Regt
MONEY, R. C.	Maj	15th Bn Durham Light Infantry
MONTAGU, L.	Maj	Hood Bn Royal Naval Division (National Archives source: see Hood Bn War Diary reference)
MOORHEAD, E. W.	Pte	5th Bn Australian Imperial Force
NORRIE, G.	2/Lt	Attached 6th Bn Queen's Royal West Kent Regt
PAGE, E. K.	2/Lt	RFA
PAINE, A. Laporte	Lt	RFA
PALK, W. J.	2/Lt	10th Bn East Surreys
PAUL, C. A.	2/Lt	1st Bn Hertfordshire Regt
PEARSON, A. V.	Pte	15th Bn West Yorks
POLACK, E.	2/Lt	4th Bn Gloucesters
PROBERT, I. R. H.	2/Lt	RFA
QUINN, T.	L/Cpl	10th Royal Irish Rifles
RAMSDEN, E.	Lt	5th Royal Irish Lancers
ROE, W. Carden	Capt	1st Bn Royal Irish Fusiliers
ROTHWELL, W.	Pte	Casualty in Warloy-Baillon Field Hospital
ROUND, W. H.	Capt	7th Bn Sherwood Foresters
RUMMING, W.	Sgt	2nd Bn Coldstream Guards

RUSSELL, J. W. B.	2/Lt	9th Bn Duke of Wellington's Regt
SELLICK, S. S.	Capt	Heavy Branch Motor Machine Gun Corps
SHEWING, A. E.	Pte	20th Trench Mortar Battery
SICHEL, O. W.	2/Lt	5th Bn Royal Warwicks
SLAUGHTER, A. C.	2/Lt	18th Bn The King's (Liverpool Regt)
SLYTHE, A.	Sister	Territorial Force Nursing Service (Field Hospital, Warloy-Baillon)
STADDON, J. W.	Lt	12th Bn East Surreys
STALLIBRASS, T. L. W.	Lt	No 3 Squadron RFC
STEWART, G.	Capt.	6th Bn Seaforth Highlanders
STRANG, W.	2/Lt	4th Bn Worcesters
SUTHERLAND, T. N.	Gnr	New Zealand Field Artillery
TATE, R.	Dvr	Heavy Branch Motor Machine Gun Corps
TOLSON, R. H.	2/Lt	15th Bn West Yorkshire Regt
UPCOTT, J. D.	2/Lt	9th Bn Devons
VAUX, E.	Lt-Col	7th Bn Durham Light Infantry
VLOK, N.	Pte	2nd Bn South African Brigade, from Ian Uys, *Delville Wood*
WILLIAMS, H. G. R.	L/Cpl	5th London Regt
WILLIAMS, W. W.	Pte	42nd The Royal Highlanders (Black Watch), Canadian Expeditionary Force
WILLIS, G. A. A.	2/Lt	RE (209 Field Company)
WILLMER, E. W.	Lt	17th Bn The King's (Liverpool Regt)
WILSON, A.	Gnr	New Zealand Field Artillery
WOODHEAD, S.	Pte	9th Bn Duke of Wellington's Regt
WOODS, C. M.	Rfn	1st Bn London Regt

Official Nomenclature for the Battle of the Somme and its Subsidiary Actions

(from *Report of the Battles Nomenclature Committee as approved by the Army Council*, Cmnd 1138, London, HMSO, 1922)

	Battle				Limits	
Operations	Name	Tactical Incidents Included	Actions, &C.	Miscellaneous Incidents	Chronological	Geographical
Operations on the Somme (1 July–18 November, 1916)	THE BATTLES OF THE SOMME, 1916	"	"	"	1 July–18 November	
	(i) BATTLE OF ALBERT, 1916	Capture of Montauban, Capture of Mametz, Capture of Fricourt, Capture of Contalmaison, Capture of la Boisselle	"	"	1–13 July	The Combles valley to Hardecourt: thence the road to Maricourt–Suzanne–Bray–Albert–Bouzincourt– Hédauville–Forceville– Bertrancourt–Sailly-au-Bois (*exclusive*)–Hébuterne–Puisieux-au-Mont.
			–with subsidiary Attack on the Gommecourt Salient	"	1 July	Road Puisieux-au-Mont–Hébuterne– Sailly-au-Bois–Bayencourt– Road Hardecourt– Souastre–Humbercamps–Pommier– Berles-au-Bois–Monchy-au-Bois.
	(ii) BATTLE OF BAZENTIN RIDGE	Capture of Longueval, Capture of Trônes Wood, Capture of Ovillers	"	"	14–17 July	Road Hardecourt–Maricourt–Fricourt–Bécourt–Albert (*exclusive*)–la Boutillerie– Bas Maisnil.
			–with subsidiary Attack at Fromelles*	"	19 July	Road Aubers–Fauquissart–Laventie–Rouge de Bout–Fleurbaix (*exclusive*)–la Boutillerie– Bas Maisnil.
			–and subsidiary Attacks on High Wood	"	20–25 July	Road Flers–Longueval–Bazentin-le-Grand–Bazentin-le-Petit–Martinpuich.
	(iii) BATTLE OF DELVILLE WOOD	"	"	"	15 July–3 September	Delville Wood.
	(iv) BATTLE OF POZIÈRES RIDGE	Fighting for Mouquet Farm	"	"	23 July–3 September	Road Bazentin-le-Petit–Contalmaison–Fricourt–Bécourt–Albert (*exclusive*): thence the river Ancre.

(v) BATTLE OF GUILLEMONT	"	"	3–6 September	The Combles valley to Hardecourt: thence road to Maricourt–Montauban–Longueval.
(vi) BATTLE OF GINCHY	"	"	9 September	"
(vii) BATTLE OF FLERS-COURCELETTE	Capture of Martinpuich	"	15–22 September	The Combles valley to Hardecourt: thence road to Maricourt–Fricourt–Bécourt–Albert (*exclusive*): thence the river Ancre.
(viii) BATTLE OF MORVAL	Capture of Combles Capture of Lesboeufs Capture of Gueudecourt	"	25–28 September	The Combles valley to Hardecourt: thence road to Maricourt–Fricourt–Becourt–la Boisselle–Bapaume.
(ix) BATTLE OF THIEPVAL RIDGE	"	"	26–28 September	The Bapaume road to Albert (*exclusive*): thence road to Martinsart–Englebelmer–Auchonvillers–Serre.
(x) BATTLE OF THE TRANSLOY RIDGES	Capture of Eaucourt l'Abbaye Capture of le Sars Attacks on the Butte de Warlencourt	"	1–18 October	The valley from Sailly-Saillisel to Combles: thence road to Ginchy–Longueval–Martinpuich–Courcelette: thence the valley to Warlencourt.
(xi) BATTLE OF THE ANCRE HEIGHTS	Capture of Schwaben and Stuff Redoubts and Regina Trench	"	1 October–11 November	Road Pys–le Sars–
(xii) BATTLE OF THE ANCRE, 1916	Capture of Beaumont Hamel	"	13–18 November	The Bapaume road to La Boisselle: thence road to Aveluy–Martinsart–Englebelmer–Mailly–Maillet–Colincamps–Hébuterne–Puisieux-au-Mont.

* On the Aubers Ridge.

Army, Corps and Divisional Unit Involvement in the Battle of the Somme, 1 July–18 November 1916

(from James, Captain E. A., *Battles and Engagements of the British Armies in France and Flanders 1914-1918*, Aldershot, Gale and Polden, 1924)

Armies: Third, Fourth and Fifth.[1]

Corps. II, III, V, VII, VIII, X, XIII, XIV, XV, Canadian and I Anzac.

Divisions: 1st Cavalry (1), 2nd Indian Cavalry (2), Guards (2), 1st (5), 2nd (2), 3rd (4), 4th (2), 5th (4), 6th (3), 7th (5), 8th (1), 9th (4), 11th (2), 12th (3), 14th(2), 15th (3), 16th(2), 17th (1), 18th (6), 19th (5), 20th (5), 21st (5), 23rd (6), 24th (2), 25th (4), 29th (2), 30th (2), 31st (2), 32nd (3), 33rd (3), 34th (4), 35th (1), 36th (1), 37th (4), 38th (1), 39th (3), 40th (1), 41st (2), 46th (1), 47th (2), 48th (4), 49th (4), 50th (3), 51st (2), 55th (4), 56th (5), 63rd (1), 1st Canadian (4), 2nd Canadian (4), 3rd Canadian (4), 4th Canadian (3), 1st Australian (1), 2nd Australian (1), 4th Australian (1), and New Zealand (3).

The 5th Australian Division went into line within the limits of the battles but did not participate in any specified battle. Total number of divisions engaged: fifty-four infantry and two cavalry.

(i) BATTLE OF ALBERT, 1916, 1–13 JULY

Fourth Army.

III Corps: 1st, 8th, 12th, 19th, 23rd and 34th Divisions.

VIII Corps: 4th, 29th, 31st and 48th Divisions.

X Corps: 12th, 25th, 32nd, 36th and 49th Divisions.

XIII Corps: 3rd, 9th, 18th, 30th and 35th Divisions.

XV Corps: 7th, 17th, 21st, 33rd and 38th Divisions.

Reserve Army.

This Army took over the VIII and X Corps from the Fourth Army on 4th July, 1916.

Tactical Incidents:

Capture of Montauban: 30th Division.

Capture of Mametz: 7th Division.

Capture of Fricourt: 17th Division.

Capture of Contalmaison: 23rd Division.

Capture of La Boisselle: 19th Division.

With subsidiary–

Attack on the Gommecourt Salient, 1 July.

Third Army.

VII Corps: 37th, 46th and 56th Divisions.

---

1 The Fourth Army was formed on 5 February 1916, and the Reserve Army on 23 May 1916. On 4 July 1916, during the Battle of Albert, the latter took over the VIII and X Corps from the Fourth Army. On and after 30 October the Reserve Army was designated the Fifth Army.

(ii) BATTLE OF BAZENTIN, 14–17 JULY.

Fourth Army.

2nd Indian Cavalry Division.
II Corps: 1st, 23rd and 34th[2] Divisions.
XIII Corps: 3rd, 9th and 18th Divisions.
XV Corps: 7th, 21st and 33rd Divisions.

Reserve Army.

X Corps: 25th, 32nd, 48th and 49th Divisions.

Tactical Incidents:
Capture of Longueval: 3rd and 9th Divisions. Capture of Trones Wood: 18th Division. Capture of Ovillers: 48th Division.

With subsidiary–

Attack at Fromelles (on the Aubers Ridge), 19 July.

First Army.

XI Corps: 61st and 5th Australian Divisions.

And subsequent–

Attacks on High Wood,[3] 20–25 July.

Fourth Army.

III Corps: 19th Division.
XV Corps: 5th, 7th, 33rd and 51st Divisions.

(iii) BATTLE OF DELVILLE WOOD, 15th JULY–3rd SEPTEMBER.

Fourth Army.

XIII Corps: 2nd, 3rd, 9th and 24th Divisions and 53rd Infantry Brigade of 18th Division.
XIV Corps:[4] 20th and 24th Divisions.
XV Corps: 7th and 14th Divisions.

(iv) BATTLE OF POZIÈRES, 23 JULY–3 SEPTEMBER.

Fourth Army.

Ill Corps: 1st, 15th, 19th, 23rd and 34th Divisions.

Reserve Army.

II Corps:[5] 12th, 25th, 48th and 49th Divisions.
X Corps: 12th, 48th and 49th Divisions.
I Anzac Corps: 1st Australian, 2nd Australian, and 4th Australian Divisions.

---

2 The 102nd and 103rd Infantry Brigades of the 34th Division had suffered very heavy losses in the Battle of Albert. These two Brigades changed places with the 111th and 112th Infantry Brigades of the 37th Division and and went into line with the 37th Division, IV Corps, First Army, on Vimy Ridge, while the two Brigades of the 37th Division, mentioned above, fought in the Battle of Albert, Battle of Bazentin and Battle of Pozières under the 34th Division.
3 High Wood was finally captured by the 47th Division, III Corps, on 15 September 1916.
4 The XIV Corps relieved the XIII Corps at midnight 16–17 August 1916.
5 The II Corps took over the front and divisions in line of the X Corps on 24 July 1916.

Tactical Incidents:
Fighting for Mouquet Farm,[6] 12th, 25th, 48th, 1st Australian, 2nd Australian and 4th Australian Divisions.

(v) BATTLE OF GUILLEMONT, 3–6 SEPTEMBER.

Fourth Army.
XIV Corps: 5th, 16th and 20th Divisions.
XV Corps: 7th, 24th and 55th Divisions.

(vi) BATTLE OF GINCHY, 9 SEPTEMBER.

Fourth Army.
XIV Corps: 16th and 56th Divisions.
XV Corps: 55th Division.

(vii) BATTLE OF FLERS–COURCELETTE,[7] 15–22 SEPTEMBER.

Fourth Army.
1st Cavalry and 2nd Indian Cavalry Divisions.
III Corps: 1st, 15th, 23rd, 47th and 50th Divisions and 103rd Infantry Brigade of 34th Division.
XIV Corps: Guards, 5th, 6th, 20th and 56th Divisions.
XV Corps: 14th, 21st, 41st, 55th and New Zealand Divisions.
Reserve Army.
II Corps: 11th and 49th Divisions.
Canadian Corps: 1st Canadian, 2nd Canadian and 3rd Canadian Divisions.

Tactical Incidents:
Capture of Martinpuich: 15th Division.

(viii) BATTLE OF MORVAL, 25–28 SEPTEMBER.

Fourth Army.
III Corps: 1st, 23rd and 50th Divisions.
XIV Corps: Guards, 5th, 6th, 20th and 56th Divisions.
XV Corps: 21st, 55th and New Zealand Divisions.

Tactical Incidents:
Capture of Combles: 56th Division.
Capture of Lesboeufs: Guards and 6th Division.
Capture of Gueudecourt: 21st Division.

(ix) BATTLE OF THIEPVAL, 26–28 SEPTEMBER.

Reserve Army.
II Corps: 11th and 18th Divisions.
V Corps: 39th Division.
Canadian Corps: 1st Canadian, 2nd Canadian and 3rd Canadian Divisions.

---

6 Part of Mouquet Farm was captured by the 3rd Canadian Division on 16 September 1916, and the Farm was finally captured by the 11th Division on 26 September 1916.

7 This battle is particularly noteworthy for two reasons. It was the first occasion on which tanks went into action and was the first day on which British artillery fired a creeping or, as it was then called, rolling barrage.

(x) BATTLE OF LE TRANSLOY, 1–18 OCTOBER

Fourth Army.

Ill Corps: 9th, 15th, 23rd 47th and 50th Divisions.
XIV Corps: 4th, 6th, 20th and 56th Divisions.
XV Corps: 12th, 21st, 30th, 41st and New Zealand Divisions and 88th Infantry Brigade of 29th Division.

Reserve Army.

Canadian Corps: 1st Canadian, 2nd Canadian, 3rd Canadian and 4th Canadian Divisions.

Tactical Incidents:
Capture of Eaucourt l'Abbaye: 47th Division.
Capture of Le Sars: 23rd Division.
Attacks on the Butte de Warlencourt:[8] 9th, 15th, 23rd and 47th Divisions.

(xi) BATTLE OF THE ANCRE HEIGHTS, 1 OCTOBER–11 NOVEMBER.

Reserve Army.

II Corps: 18th, 19th, 25th, 39th[9] and 4th Canadian[10] Divisions.
V Corps: 39th Division.

Canadian Corps: 1st Canadian, 2nd Canadian, 3rd Canadian and 4th Canadian Divisions.

Tactical Incidents:
Capture of Schwaben Redoubt: 18th and 39th Divisions.
Capture of Stuff Redoubt:[11] 25th Division.
Capture of Regina Trench: 18th, 25th, 39th and 4th Canadian Divisions.

(xii) BATTLE OF THE ANCRE, 1916, 13–18 NOVEMBER.

Fourth Army.

Ill Corps: 48th Division.

Fifth Army.

II Corps: 18th, 19th, 39th and 4th Canadian Divisions.
V Corps: 2nd, 3rd, 32nd, 37th, 51st and 63rd Divisions.
XIII Corps: 31st Division and 120th Infantry Brigade of 40th Division.

Tactical Incidents:
Capture of Beaumont Hamel: 51st Division.

---

8   The 48th and 50th Divisions came in after the end of the Battle of Le Transloy and carried out attacks on the Butte de Warlencourt.
9   The 39th Division was transferred from the V Corps to the II Corps on 4 October 1916.
10   The 4th Canadian Division was transferred from the Canadian Corps to the II Corps on 17 October 1916, when the Canadian Corps was withdrawn from the battle front.
11   The 11th Division had gained a footing in the Stuff Redoubt in the fighting at the end of September.

Order of Battle, 1 July 1916

Abbreviations: NA – New Army; TF – Territorial Force; R – Regular Army

Division	Brigade	Battalion	Designation	(and origin for NA)	A 'general' indication of the divisional objectives
46th	137th	1/5th South Staffs	TF		**N. Gommecourt**
		1/6th South Staffs	TF		
		1/5th North Staffs	TF		
		1/6th North Staffs	TF		
	138th	1/4th Lincolns	TF		
		1/5th Lincolns	TF		
		1/4th Leicesters	TF		
		1/5th Leicesters	TF		
	139th	1/5th Sherwood Foresters	TF		
		1/6th Sherwood Foresters	TF		
		1/7th Sherwood Foresters	TF		
		1/8th Sherwood Foresters	TF		
	Pioneers	1/1st Monmouths	TF		
56th	167th	1/1st London	TF		**S. Gommecourt**
		1/3rd London	TF		
		1/7th Middlesex	TF		
		1/8th Middlesex	TF		
	168th	1/4th London	TF		
		1/12th London	TF		
		1/13th London	TF		
		1/14th London	TF		
	169th	1/2nd London	TF		
		1/5th London	TF		
		1/9th London	TF		
		1/16th London	TF		
	Pioneers	1/5th Cheshires	TF		
48th	143rd	1/5th Royal Warwicks	TF		**No attack 1 July 1916. Two battalions holding Sector south of Gommecourt to north of Serre**
		1/6th Royal Warwicks	TF		
		1/7th Royal Warwicks	TF		
		1/8th Royal Warwicks	TF		
	144th	1/4th Gloucesters	TF		
		1/6th Gloucesters	TF		
		1/7th Worcesters	TF		
		1/8th Worcesters	TF		
	145th	1/5th Gloucesters	TF		
		1/4th Oxford & Bucks Light Infantry	TF		
		1st Bucks	TF		
		1/4th Royal Berks	TF		
	Pioneers	1/5th Royal Sussex	TF		
31st	92nd	10th East Yorks	NA	1st Hull Commercials	**Serre**

Division	Brigade	Battalion	Designation	(and origin for NA)	A 'general' indication of the divisional objectives
		11th East Yorks	NA	2nd Hull Tradesmen	
		12th East Yorks	NA	3rd Hull Sportsmen	
		13th East Yorks	NA	4th Hull 't'others'	
	93rd	15th West Yorks	NA	Leeds 'Pals'	
		16th West Yorks	NA	Bradford 1st 'Pals'	
		18th West Yorks	NA	Bradford 2nd 'Pals'	
		18th Durham Light Infantry	NA	Co. Durham 'Pals'	
	94th	11th East Lancs	NA	Accrington 'Pals'	
		12th York & Lancs	NA	Sheffield 'City Bn'	
		13th York & Lancs	NA	Barnsley 1st 'Pals'	
		14th York & Lancs	NA	Barnsley 2nd 'Pals'	
	Pioneers	12th KOYLI	NA	Leeds, Dewsbury and Featherstone area miners	
4th	10th	1st Royal Irish Fusiliers	R		**South of Serre to north of Beaumont Hamel**
		2nd Royal Dublin Fusiliers	R		
		2nd Seaforth Highlanders	R		
		1st Royal Warwicks	R		
	11th	1st Somerset Light Infantry	R		
		1st East Lancs	R		
		1st Hampshires	R		
		1st Rifle Brigade	R		
	12th	1st King's Own	R		
		2nd Lancs Fusiliers	R		
		2nd Duke of Wellington's	R		
		2nd Essex	R		
	Pioneers	21st West Yorks	NA	Leeds 'Wool Textile' Pioneers	
29th	86th	2nd Royal Fusiliers	R		**Beaumont Hamel**
		1st Lancs Fusiliers	R		
		16th Middlesex	NA	London 'Public Schools'	
	87th	1st Royal Dublin Fusiliers	R		
		2nd South Wales Borderers	R		
		1st King's Own Scottish Borderers	R		
		1st Royal Inniskilling Fusiliers	R		
		1st Border	R		
	88th	1st Essex	R		
		1st Newfoundland (Volunteers)			
		4th Worcesters	R		
		2nd Hampshires	R		
	Pioneers	1/2nd Monmouths	TF		

Division	Brigade	Battalion	Designation	*(and origin for NA)*	A 'general' indication of the divisional objectives
36th	107th	8th Royal Irish Rifles	NA	East Belfast – Belfast Volunteers	**Either side of the Ancre and N. Thiepval**
		9th Royal Irish Rifles	NA	West Belfast – do	
		10th Royal Irish Rifles	NA	South Belfast – do	
		15th Royal Irish Rifles	NA	North Belfast – do	
	108th	11th Royal Irish Rifles	NA	South Antrim – Antrim Volunteers	
		12th Royal Irish Rifles	NA	Central Antrim – do	
		13th Royal Irish Rifles	NA	1st County Down – County Down Volunteers	
		9th Royal Irish Fusiliers	NA	County Armagh – Armagh, Cavan and Monaghan Volunteers	
	109th	9th Royal Inniskilling Fusiliers	NA	County Tyrone – Tyrone Volunteers	
		10th Royal Inniskilling Fusiliers	NA	Derry – Derry Volunteers	
		11th Royal Inniskilling Fusiliers	NA	Donegal – Fermanagh Volunteers	
		14th Royal Irish Fusiliers	NA	Belfast 'Young Citizens'	
	Pioneers	16th Royal Irish Rifles	NA	2nd County Down – County Down Volunteers	
32nd	14th	19th Lancs Fusiliers	NA	Salford 3rd 'Pals'	**Thiepval and associated strongpoints**
		1st Dorsets	R		
		2nd Manchesters	R		
		15th Highland Light Infantry	NA	1st Glasgow 'Tramways'	
	96th	16th Northumberland Fusiliers	NA	Newcastle 'Commercials'	
		2nd Royal Inniskilling Fusiliers	R		
		15th Lancs Fusiliers	NA	Salford 1st 'Pals'	
		16th Lancs Fusiliers	NA	Salford 2nd 'Pals'	
	97th	11th Border	NA	Cumberland & Westmorland 'Lonsdales'	
		2nd KOYLI	R		
		16th Highland Light Infantry	NA	2nd Glasgow 'Boys Brigade'	

Division	Brigade	Battalion	Designation	(and origin for NA)	A 'general' indication of the divisional objectives
		17th Highland Light Infantry	NA	3rd Glasgow 'Commercials'	
	Pioneers	17th Northumberland Fusiliers	NA	Newcastle 'Railway Pals'	
8th	23rd	2nd Devons	R		**Ovillers La**
		2nd West Yorks	R		**Boisselle**
		2nd Middlesex	R		
		2nd Scottish Rifles	R		
	25th	2nd Lincolns	R		
		2nd Royal Berks	R		
		1st Royal Irish Rifles	R		
		2nd Rifle Brigade	R		
	70th	11th Sherwood Foresters	NA	Derby	
		8th KOYLI	NA	Pontefract	
		8th York & Lancasters	NA	Pontefract	
		9th York & Lancasters	NA	Pontefract	
	Pioneers	22nd Durham Light Infantry	NA	County Durham	
34th	101st	15th Royal Scots	NA	Edinburgh 1st 'City'	**La Boisselle**
		16th Royal Scots	NA	Edinburgh 2nd 'City'	
		10th Lincolns	NA	Grimsby 'Chums'	
		11th Suffolks	NA	Cambridge 'Cambridgeshire'	
	102nd	20th Northumberland Fusiliers	NA	Tyneside 1st Scottish'	
		21st Northumberland Fusiliers	NA	Tyneside 2nd 'Scottish'	
		22nd Northumberland Fusiliers	NA	Tyneside 3rd 'Scottish'	
		23rd Northumberland Fusiliers	NA	Tyneside 4th 'Scottish'	
	103rd	24th Northumberland Fusiliers	NA	Tyneside 1st 'Irish'	
		25th Northumberland Fusiliers	NA	Tyneside 2nd 'Irish'	
		26th Northumberland Fusiliers	NA	Tyneside 3rd 'Irish'	
		27th Northumberland Fusiliers	NA	Tyneside 4th 'Irish'	
	Pioneers	18th Northumberland Fusiliers	NA	Tyneside 'Pioneers'	
21st	62nd	12th Northumberland Fusiliers	NA	Newcastle	**North of Fricourt**
		13th Northumberland Fusiliers	NA	Newcastle	
		1st Lincolns	RA		
		10th Green Howards	NA	Richmond, N. Yorks	
	63rd	8th Lincolns	NA	Lincoln	
		8th Somerset Light Infantry	NA	Taunton	
		4th Middlesex	R		
		10th York & Lancs	NA	Pontefract	
	64th	9th KOYLI	NA	Pontefract	
		10th KOYLI	NA	Pontefract	

Division	Brigade	Battalion	Designation	(and origin for NA)	A 'general' indication of the divisional objectives
		1st East Yorks	R		
		15th Durham Light Infantry	NA	Newcastle	
	Pioneers	14th Northumberland Fusiliers	NA	Newcastle	
17th	50th	10th West Yorks	NA	York	**Fricourt**
		7th East Yorks	NA	Beverley	
		7th Green Howards	NA	Richmond, N. Yorks	
		6th Dorsets	NA	Dorchester	
7th	20th	8th Devons	NA	Exeter	**Mametz**
		9th Devons	NA	Exeter	
		2nd Border	R		
		2nd Gordon Highlanders	R		
	22nd	2nd Royal Warwicks	R		
		20th Manchesters	NA	Manchester 5th 'Pals'	
		1st Royal Welsh Fusiliers	R		
		2nd Royal Irish	R		
	91st	2nd Queen's	R		
		1st South Staffs	R		
		21st Manchester	NA	Manchester 6th 'Pals'	
		22nd Manchester	NA	Manchester 7th 'Pals'	
	Pioneers	24th Manchesters	NA	Oldham 'Pals'	
18th	53rd	8th Norfolks	NA	Norwich	**West of Montauban**
		6th Royal Berks	NA	Reading	
		10th Essex	NA	Warley	
		8th Suffolks	NA	Bury St Edmunds	
	54th	11th Royal Fusiliers	NA	Hounslow	
		7th Bedfords	NA	Bedford	
		6th Northamptons	NA	Northampton	
		12th Middlesex	NA	Middlesex	
	55th	7th Queen's	NA	Guildford	
		7th Buffs	NA	Canterbury	
		8th East Surreys	NA	Kingston-upon-Thames	
		7th Royal West Kents	NA	Maidstone	
	Pioneers	8th Royal Sussex	NA	Chichester	
30th	21st	18th King's	NA	Liverpool 2nd 'Pals'	**Montauban**
		19th Manchester	NA	Manchester 4th 'Pals'	
		2nd Wilts	R		
		2nd Green Howards	R		
	89th	17th King's	NA	Liverpool 1st 'Pals'	
		19th King's	NA	Liverpool 3rd 'Pals'	
		20th King's	NA	Liverpool 4th 'Pals'	
		2nd Bedfords	R		
	90th	2nd Royal Scots Fusiliers	R		
		16th Manchester	NA	Manchester 1st 'Pals'	

Division	Brigade	Battalion	Designation	(and origin for NA)	A 'general' indication of the divisional objectives
		17th Manchesters	NA	Manchester 2nd 'Pals'	
		18th Manchesters	NA	Manchester 3rd 'Pals'	
	Pioneers	11th South Lancs	NA	St Helen's 'Pioneers'	
In Reserve					
17th	51st	7th Lincolns	NA	Lincoln	**South of Albert**
		7th King's Own Scottish Borderers	NA	Berwick-on-Tweed	
		8th South Staffs	NA	Lichfield	
		10th Sherwood Foresters	NA	Derby	
	52nd	9th Northumberland Fusiliers	NA	Newcastle	
		10th Lancs Fusiliers	NA	Bury	
		9th Duke of Wellington's	NA	Halifax	
		12th Manchester	NA	Ashton-under-Lyne	
	Pioneers	7th York and Lancs (Pioneers)	NA	Pontefract	
19th	56th	7th King's Own	NA	Lancaster	**Behind Albert**
		7th East Lancs	NA	Preston	
		7th South Lancs	NA	Warrington	
		7th Loyal North Lancs	NA	Preston	
	57th	10th Royal Warwicks	NA	Warwick	
		8th Gloucesters	NA	Bristol	
		10th Worcesters	NA	Worcester	
		8th North Staffs	NA	Lichfield	
	58th	9th Cheshires	NA	Chester	
		9th Royal Welsh Fusiliers	NA	Wrexham	
		9th Welsh Regiment	NA	Cardiff	
		6th Wilts	NA	Devizes	
	Pioneers	6th South Wales Borderers	NA	Brecon	
37th	110th	6th Leicesters	NA	Leicester	**In the line, north of Gommecourt**
		7th Leicesters	NA	Leicester	
		8th Leicesters	NA	Leicester	
		9th Leicesters	NA	Leicester	
	111th	10th Royal Fusiliers	NA	Lord Mayor & The City of London	
		13th Royal Fusiliers	NA	Hounslow	
		13th King's Royal Rifles	NA	Winchester	
		13th Rifle Brigade	NA	Winchester	
	112th	11th Royal Warwicks	NA	Warwick	
		6th Bedfords	NA	Bedford	
		8th East Lancs	NA	Preston	
		10th Loyal North Lancs	NA	Preston	
	Pioneers	9th North Staffs (Pioneers)	NA	Lichfield	

Index